M

SILVER AGE

THE SECOND GENERATION OF COMIC BOOK ARTISTS

BY DANIEL HERMAN

HERMES
PRESS
Neshannock, Pennsylvania

Published by Hermes Press
2100 Wilmington Road
Neshannock, Pennsylvania 16105
(724) 652-0511
www.HermesPress.com

Cover design by Daniel Herman
Book design by Daniel Herman

First printing, October, 2004

Library of Congress Control Number: 2004100129
Hardcover limited edition ISBN 1-932563-72-5
Hardcover edition ISBN 1-932563-65-2
Trade paperback ISBN 1-932563-64-4

Proof reading by Louise Herman, Sabrina Herman, Lori Geramita, Francesca Occhibone, Elaine DeVivo, Richard Sprow, and Carmelita E. Veloro.

Cover image: Gil Kane, pencils, Sid Greene, inks, original panel artwork from *Green Lantern* #61, ©1968 DC Comics. Back cover image: Joe Kubert, pencils and inks, original panel artwork from *The Brave and the Bold* #21, ©1959 DC Comics.

Image scanning by H + G Media

Printed in China

ACKNOWLEDGMENTS

A book of this nature cannot be written without the help of many people. First and foremost, many of the artists and writers whose careers and work are chronicled by this book graciously consented to be interviewed to assist me in better understanding what really happened during the Silver Age. This book would not be possible without their candid insights and help. Many thanks to Gil and Elaine Kane, Julie Schwartz, John Romita, Marie Severin, Al Feldstein, Alex Toth, Joe Giella, Ramona Fradon, Will Eisner, Ray Bradbury, Roy Thomas, and Mark Evanier.

As this book deals with the history and images of the Silver Age, it was extremely important to secure artwork which illustrates exactly why the work of the many artists described in this book is really so noteworthy. A number of collectors pitched in with artwork from their collections which is featured in this book. A tip of the ole hat to George Hagenauer, Ethan Roberts, Scott Dunbier, Jim D'Amico, Ray Cuthbert, Terrance Doyle, Frank Giella, Mike Burkey, and Glen Brunswick. Special thanks to Mitch Itkowitz of Graphic Collectibles, who, as always, came through with some of the images on display in this book and who served as a valuable sounding board for me to toss around ideas and then, after further thought, chew on them some more.

This book was completed over a period of several years, and during that time many of the artists, writers, and editors whose work is discussed and featured in this tome passed away. Hopefully, the publication of this book will give readers unfamiliar with this subject insight into these unsung heroes of the funny books.

Many of the illustrations appearing in this book were reproduced from the originals and accordingly are referred to as "original artwork."

For L and S

TABLE OF CONTENTS

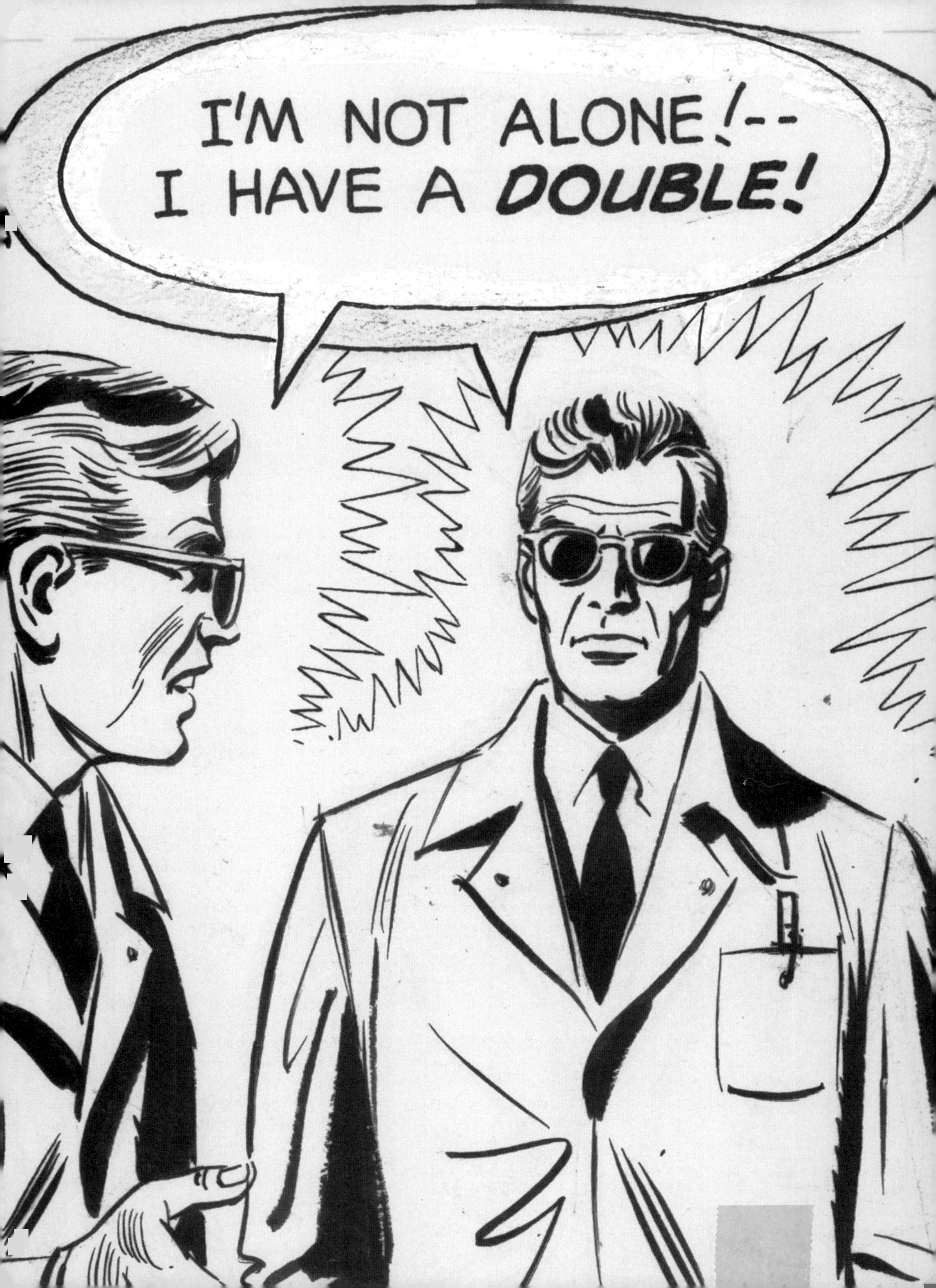
I'M NOT ALONE!-- I HAVE A DOUBLE!

INTRODUCTION

Why a book about comic book artists? Well, now that the likes of the X-Men, Daredevil, Hulk, and Spider-Man, not to mention Superman and Batman, are household names with movies, dvds, books, and mass-media attention as figures of symbolism and pop culture, there seems to be a great deal of confusion and downright misinformation as to who was responsible for creating the images and storytelling devices that have made comic books worthy, or not, of such consideration. In the publicity surrounding the recent spate of movies, the real people behind the great comic books have become obscured by the publicity machines promoting these most recent mass market endeavors.

In fact, history is being rewritten and the artists who toiled with pencil, pen, and brush are being forgotten and supplanted by more media savvy figureheads who now claim credit for everything. This book therefore comes at a time when the record needs to be set straight as memories fade and are reworked in a manner quite at home with the surreal tone of many of the great comic book stories. The focus of this book is to look at the evolution of the American comic book through the artists who created and developed the medium and to focus on the art of comic book storytelling.

Every age has its myths and fairy tales. Adult and children's literature, whether clothed in fanciful images, sugar coated, or presented in the form of a scary story, recycle archetypal concepts and ideas, over and over again. The Greek and Norse myths have been used as subject material in just about every form imaginable. The Arthurian legend has served as the basis for books and movies aimed at adults and children. It should come as no surprise that comic books have used myths as the basis for their stories and have created new myths infused and nourished by the originals. The comic book, however, presents the reader with words and pictures, and as a medium, requires artists who can effectively and entertainingly tell stories with pictures. The comic book is a unique American creation which was born during the Great Depression and grew to its maturity in the 1960s, but more about that later.

The words "comic book" conjure up images of adventure, suspense, mystery, romance, and most importantly, fun. This is what comic books from the 1950s through the end of the 1960s were all about: a multitude of amusements and entertainments contained in a colorful, attractive, cheaply printed package. In order for comic books to hit the newsstands and drug store racks, it was necessary for a small group of artists and artisans to work together to produce, on never ending deadlines, a stream of illustrated short stories aimed at kids. For the publishers of comic books, they were a product, nothing more. The life and death of a comic book title was based on sales figures. Although the comic book publishers may have looked at their wares cynically, many of the artists who came into the field were naïvely enthusiastic about their craft. The sheer fun some of the artists had, drawing and writing these stories, was not lost on the millions of kids who were their audience. For anybody growing up in the 1950s and 1960s, comic books were a regular part of being a kid in the United States. Indeed, the entertainment options open to 6 to 13-year-olds were severely limited. Kids of the 1950s and 1960s had their entertainment options limited to only a small number of movies and television, and, for older kids, science fiction and fantasy books. Comic books were an entertainment mainstay for kids growing up in the United States during this time. It was not uncommon for popular comic book titles to sell over 500,000 copies of a single issue, unlike

today, when a comic book is considered successful if it sells 75,000 copies.

This book will not focus on the comic books themselves but on the artists, who as graphic storytellers, crafted the thousands of comic book stories produced yearly during the post World War II period until the end of the 1960s. Fans of comic books, who are notoriously fussy about minutia (that is part of the fun of reading comic books), have classified a portion of the era that this book deals with as the "Silver Age," which runs roughly from 1956 to 1968. Unfortunately fans have yet to

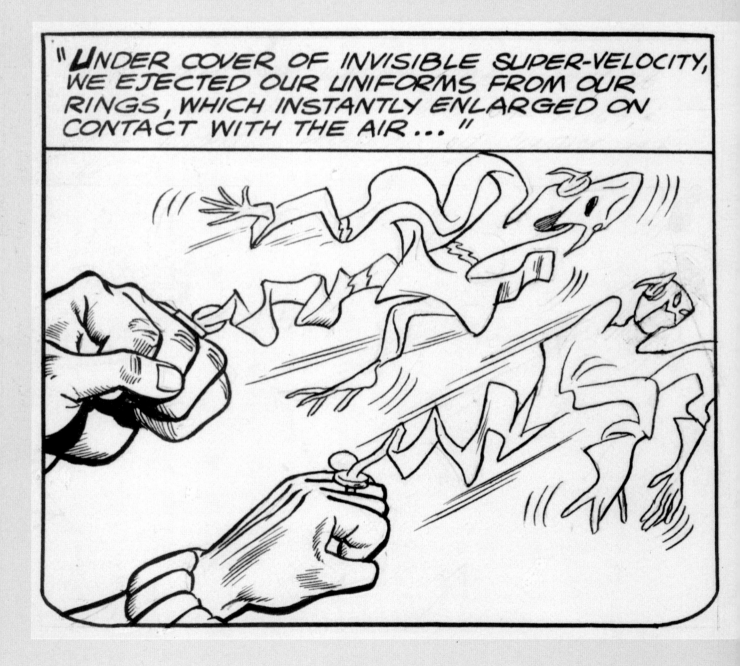

come up with a name for the period after the war and up to 1956, but for this book, the "Silver Age" is the period that encompasses the comic book storytellers who reached their artistic maturity, as did the medium itself, after 1945.[1]

Comic books, as with any entertainment medium, reflect the times in which they were created. As social attitudes and mores changed, the graphic storytellers who drew and staged comic books adapted their stories to keep pace with the times. The best artists of the second generation used this freedom to move comic books farther away from being pedestrian craft.[2] This, however, was not true of the entire industry. Only a few talented and driven artists took what they were doing seriously enough to see comic book storytelling as a distinctly American art form.

In illustrating how the art of graphic storytelling matured during the Silver Age, this book primarily relies on the original artwork created by the artists. This artwork, which comprised the cover illustrations and interior pages for comic books, was rendered in pen-and-ink on bristol board and was produced in

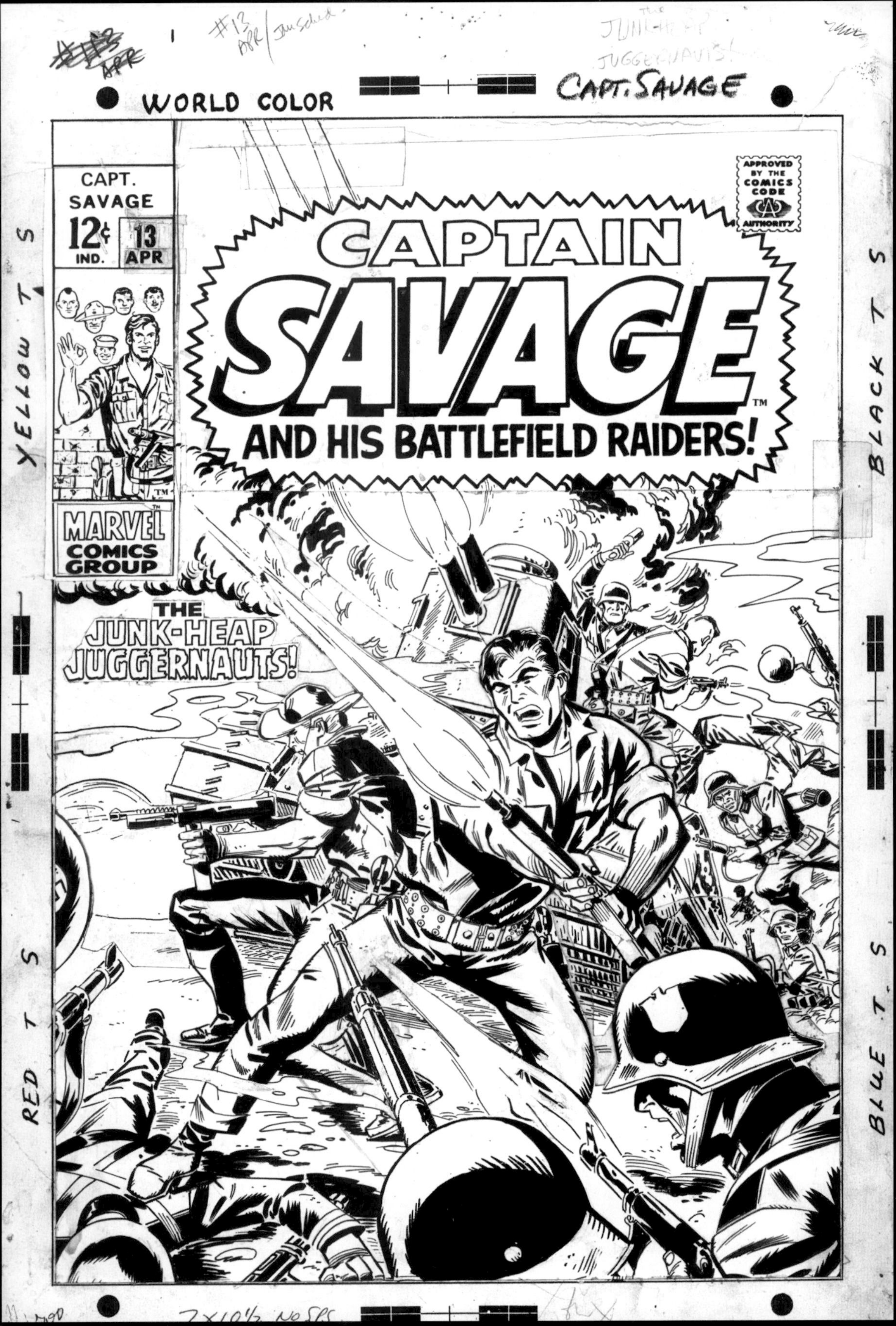
WORLD COLOR
CAPT. SAVAGE
CAPT. SAVAGE
12¢
IND.
13
APR
MARVEL COMICS GROUP
APPROVED BY THE COMICS CODE AUTHORITY
CAPTAIN SAVAGE
AND HIS BATTLEFIELD RAIDERS!
THE JUNK-HEAP JUGGERNAUTS!
YELLOW T S
RED T S
BLACK T S
BLUE T S

Opposite page: Don Heck, pencils, Frank Giacoia, inks, original cover artwork, *Captain Savage* #13, April, 1969, ©1969 Marvel Characters, Inc. Below: Russ Heath, pencils and inks, original panel artwork from an interior page, *Sea Devils* #9, February, 1963, ©1963 DC Comics.

roughly an 18 inch by 12 inch size. As this artwork was sometimes reduced more than fifty percent to fit into a comic book and then poorly reproduced, this book will allow the artwork to be seen in its original form for the first time. It should also be noted that as this art was created for the purpose of producing a comic book, it was not uncommon for these pen-and-ink drawings to have corrections that were whited-out and then redrawn, leaving a telltale blotch of white stuff underneath the redrawn area. Also, the artwork frequently had smudges from handling and blue-pencilled notations, instructions, and comments from the artists, writers, and editors who worked on the story. All of these characteristics will be apparent with the artwork on display in this book.[3]

Comic books were once the object of derision, characterized as nothing more than "kitsch." The images, plots, and characters of the best comic books have become firmly implanted in the American psyche, putting to rest, once and for all, the question of the relevance and saliency of the medium. Merit is usually assessed in retrospect, and it is now quite apparent that the attraction of many of the myths and tales espoused by 20th century comic books have proven very compelling to a number of artists toiling writing books and screenplays, and directing and producing films. This is not to say that mass market appeal validates the art of the comics; rather it is merely indicative of their lasting influence and pervasive impact on popular culture. However, this book will not seek to dryly and academically look at the

Gil Kane, pencils, Murphy Anderson, inks, original interior page
artwork, *The Atom* #5, February/March, 1963, ©1963 DC Comics.

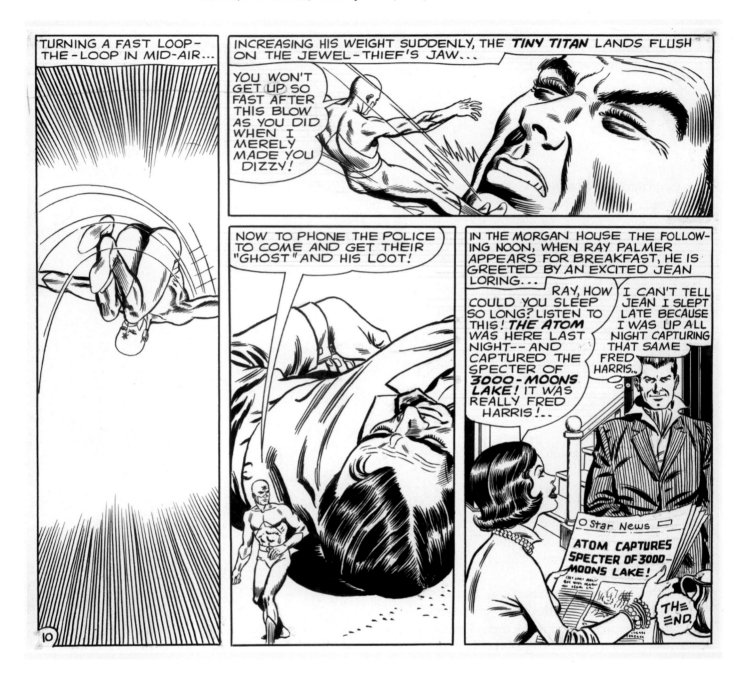

artists of comic book stories. The graphic storytellers who created so much wonder and whimsy would be done a disservice by a commentary on their work devoid of the fun they worked so hard to put into their art. In looking at and considering the art of comic books, it is important to remember that storytelling with words and pictures requires the integration of choreographed images with dialogue which creates a fusion of art and text. The end product, when successful, is neither illustration nor literature.

In order to fully appreciate the evolution of the art of comic book storytelling and action/adventure storytelling, it is necessary to focus on the precursors of the comic books: the great newspaper cartoon strips. This is, accordingly, our next stop. As we shall see, although the creators of the first comic books using original material and later the second generation of artists relied upon numerous sources, the strips were always of paramount importance as a source of reference and inspiration.

NOTES

[1] The first "Age" denoted by comic book fandom is the "Golden Age," which began with the creation of Superman and his first appearance in *Action Comics* #1 in 1938 and continued until the end of World War II. However, many comic book historians point to the creation, in 1933, of the first comic book, as the beginning of the Golden Age. There is no date for the beginning of this era which is set in stone. There is also dispute and confusion as to how to characterize the period after World War II. Some comic book fans have taken to calling the period from the end of World War II to 1956 the "Atomic Age." This denotation is neither descriptive nor widely used or accepted.

[2] The first generation of comic book artists worked in the industry at its birth, after publishers started to use original material instead of strip reprints. Chronologically the first generation began to ply their craft beginning in the late 1930s until the end of World War II, as is detailed in Chapter Two of this book.

[3] Blue-pencil was used as it does not show up when photographed; therefore, it is "invisible" for the purpose of reproduction. When most of the artwork illustrating this book was originally created, no thought was ever given to its survival, let alone how the materials used in its production would stand the test of time. It was just a comic book story, which would usually be discarded after it was photographed. Over the years, the glue used to hold many of the title "stats" secure, and word balloons in place, has dried up or become so brittle that these parts of the production artwork have fallen off. Some of the artwork presented in this book have portions that are missing, but this rarely detracts from its impact or appeal. The original pen-and-ink artwork illustrating this book were but one step in the creation of a comic book. The final stage in creating a funny book, after the black-and-white pages have been photographed, is the preparation of a color guide. A color guide, as the name implies, shows the printer how the pages are to be colored, and how they will finally appear after the comic book is printed. After the colors for the comic book are established, it is sent to the printer.

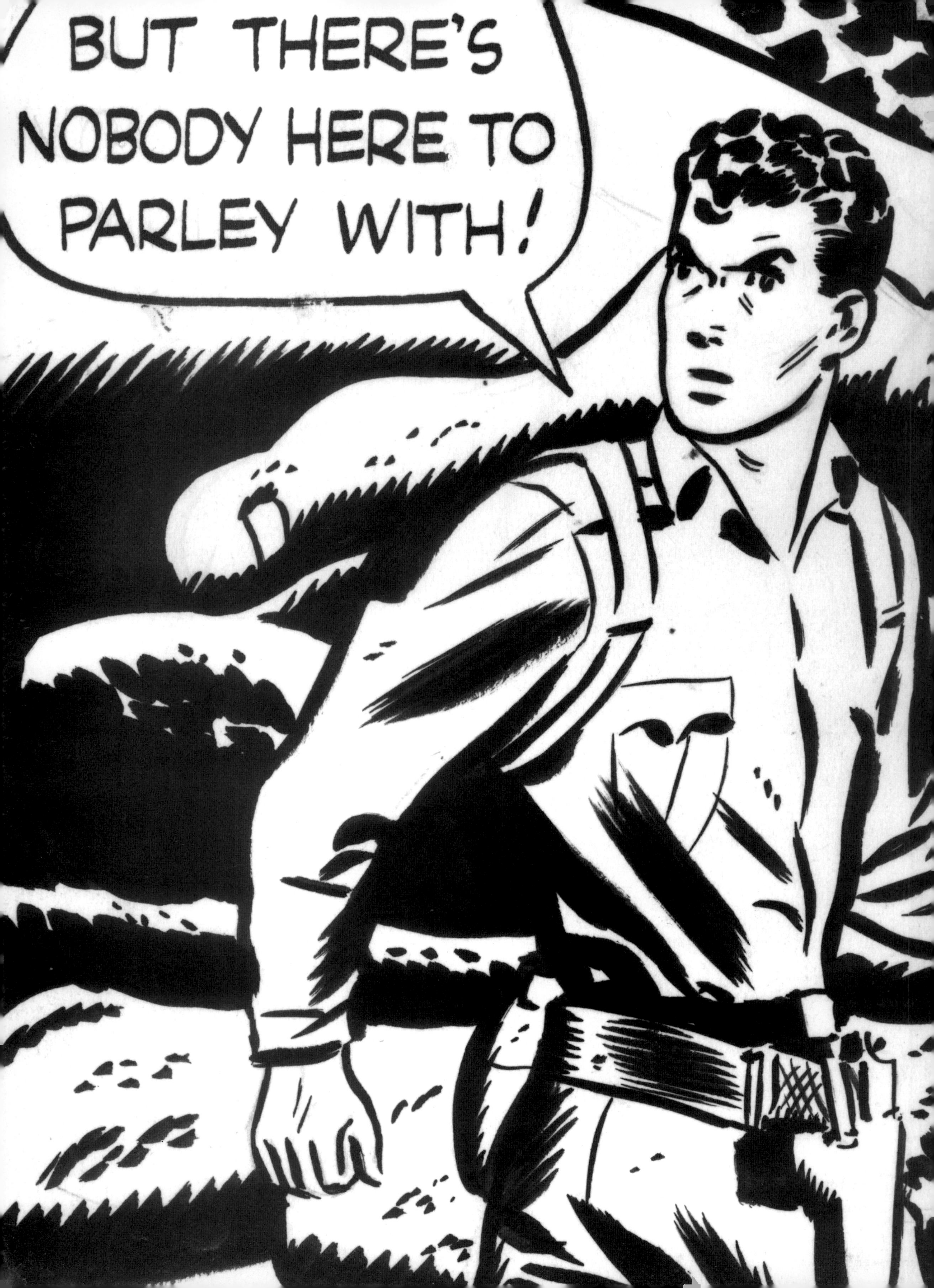
BUT THERE'S NOBODY HERE TO PARLEY WITH!

1 THE STRIPS; THE PRECURSORS OF THE COMIC BOOK

Before the advent of the comic book that is familiar today, stories using cartoons and illustrations were primarily found in daily installments in newspapers and were commonly called "funnies" or "strips." These terms, however, apply to any comic story continuity, including comic books. The American newspaper strip was developed in the mid-1890s, and the first popular strip generally cited by comics historians is Richard E. Outcault's *Yellow Kid*, which was introduced in the *New York World* on May 5, 1895.[1]

As the strip medium began to mature in the early 20th century, several strips began presenting themes that not only were entertaining, but which also had a subtext which appealed to a broad audience.

Of the many strips produced during this time, the work of two artists stands out: George Herriman and Winsor McCay.

Herriman is best known for the creation of *Krazy Kat*. The *Krazy Kat* strip remains interesting almost ninety years after its creation.[2] It has slapstick elements but, at the same time, has subtle overtones and, in some respects, anticipated or even influenced the best Warner Brothers animation of the late 1940s-1950s. Herriman's strip was admired by artists and newspaper readers alike and was inspirational to European abstract artists. It remains relevant even today.

Winsor McCay also created two strips that presented images and ideas that have weathered the years and still remain fresh: *Little Nemo in Slumberland* and *Dream of the Rarebit Fiend*. McCay created surreal and sometimes bizarre vistas, which also makes his work enjoyable to kids and their parents.

Although these strips were artistically noteworthy for creating visions that are unique and which tread the thin line between art and commercial craft, they did not influence, in any tangible way, the artists who would begin to create the action/adventure genre of strips a decade later. The artists of the strips that laid the groundwork for comic book storytelling matured during a ten year period beginning in 1924. These strips told stories of soldiers of fortune, detectives, adventurers, and heroes in the future fighting unearthly villains.

By far the most important strip artist in the action/adventure genre was Roy Crane. Indeed, many aspects of Crane's early life read like an adventure strip and no doubt form at least part of the basis for his pioneering efforts. Crane was born on November 22, 1901. By the age of 14, he was taking the Charles N. Landon cartooning correspondence course. In 1918, he enrolled in college at Hardin-Simmons University in his hometown of Abilene, Texas. Within a year, he had transferred to the University of Texas at Austin and then went on to the Chicago Academy of Fine Arts.

It was in Chicago that he met Leslie Turner, who would later serve as his assistant on his second strip as well as on Crane's subsequent efforts. After six months in Chicago, Crane quit school and hopped freight trains throughout the southwestern United States.

Over the next two years, the ever restless Crane worked for newspapers and again at-

Frank Robbins, pencils and inks, original panel artwork from the *Scorchy Smith* daily strip which appeared on August 7, 1941, ©1941 World Wide Features.

tempted a return to college. In 1922, he shipped out on a freighter bound for Europe and, upon returning to the United States, tried his hand at newspaper work again. Crane's first try at a strip, a single panel called *Music to the Ear*, syndicated by United Feature Syndicate, did not fare well and ran for only a few installments. As a result of this first effort, however, came his big break. On the suggestion of an editor at United, Crane sent the Newspaper Enterprise Association (NEA), which was located in Cleveland, *Music to the Ear*. Crane did not hear anything for several months and figured there was no interest; then he received a call from someone named Landon from NEA who wanted to see him. Landon had come to New York from Cleveland and wanted to interview Crane about ideas for a strip. Landon was the same Charles N. Landon whose course Crane had taken nine

years before. During the meeting Landon perused Crane's samples; he also found out that Crane was an alumnus of the Landon Correspondence Course. Landon immediately offered Crane a strip; thus *Washington Tubbs II* was born. The strip was named for its lead character and is always affectionately referred to as *Wash Tubbs*.[3]

On April 21, 1924, *Washington Tubbs II* made an inauspicious debut as a gag strip. The strip would not stay that way for long, as Crane soon began to transform *Wash Tubbs* into an adventure strip. He introduced exotic locales and a good, bad guy; the strip was progressing but needed something to fire readers up. On May 26, 1929, Crane introduced a character that defined the strip and which was influential on all adventure strips afterward, in the person of Captain Easy. Captain Easy, who had no first name, was a ruggedly handsome

soldier of fortune, who had done a little bit of everything, much like his creator. By teaming Easy with Wash Tubbs, Crane was able to play the two characters off each other and develop a lively and entertaining chemistry. Captain Easy became so important and popular that in 1933 the Sunday strip was retitled *Captain Easy – Soldier of Fortune*. The strip was also moving forward artistically as Crane struggled to better convey his action-packed episodes in a more realistic tone by advancing his storytelling style.

ters, drawn in a cartoony style; elegant background work, which gave the appearance of being semi-photographic; slam/bang action; and humor all in one package.

Wash Tubbs was not the only strip at the end of the 1920s which turned heads and fueled the imaginations of daily strip readers, artists, and kids just looking at the funnies, though. Nineteen twenty-nine, the year that witnessed the Great Depression, also saw the introduction of two highly influential strips that developed storytelling conventions and

The strip was still a cartoon, but now with a very important difference. Crane experimented with grease pencil, which gave the strip an aggressive tone and volume. He used craftint doubletone paper, a composition paper with an invisible diagonal line or cross hatch pattern, which when exposed to a chemical wash creates shading and tonal depth. So, with a combination of increasing skill, exciting story lines, and experimentation with different materials and techniques, Crane distinguished *Wash Tubbs* as the premier adventure strip of the early 1930s, a model to which other action/adventure strip artists would look. *Wash Tubbs* successfully combined cartoon charac-

advanced ideas and images which are still highly regarded, albeit for different reasons, even today: *Tarzan* and *Buck Rogers*. These strips are so memorable, that, just looking at their titles brings a cascade of images and story lines to mind.

The *Buck Rogers* strip actually started out as a pulp sci-fi short story entitled *Armageddon 2419 A.D.*, presented in the August, 1928 issue of the magazine *Amazing Stories* written by Philip Nowlan. Turning the story into a strip was the idea of the President of the National Newspaper Syndicate of America, John F. Dille. When Dille read the story, he knew the concept could be translated into an

Dick Calkins, pencils and inks, two *Buck Rogers*
dailies from 1931, ©1931 John F. Dille Co.

engaging daily feature. Dille convinced Nowlan to adapt his story and brought cartoonist Dick Calkins on board to provide artwork. The strip premiered on January 7, 1929, and introduced the American public to pulp science fiction.[4] The strip hit its mark and popularized many sci-fi conventions, mesmerizing kids and adults alike. *Buck Rogers* presented the story of a man, the namesake of the strip, who while investigating a mysterious gas in a deep mine is put into suspended animation and awakens in a future earth torn by war. Buck quickly joins a resistance movement of freedom fighters; finds an attractive girlfriend, Wilma Deering; and then settles down to the work of fighting earthbound bad guys, the Mongols, as well as alien invaders from Mars, the Tiger Men. The strip is distinguished by its ideas, characters, and gadgets, not by the crude artwork of Calkins. *Buck Rogers* inspired many kids of the Depression to aspire to write and draw science fiction, including many of the first and second generation artists of comic books. The strip became a national craze and its characters, their space ships, and ray guns became part of the American lexicon.

January 7, 1929 witnessed, not only the birth of *Buck Rogers*, but also saw the premiere of another feature that had its roots as a magazine story by Edgar Rice Burroughs: *Tarzan*. *Tarzan* did not really start out as a strip but as a daily illustration with text beneath the artwork. Harold "Hal" Foster was picked for the duty of bringing the lord of the apes to the comic pages, after J. Allen St. John, the artist who painted many of the covers and provided interior illustrations for the *Tarzan* books, turned down the assignment. Foster, who was an illustrator and advertising artist, had been formally trained at the Art Institute of Chicago, the National Academy of Design, and the Chicago Academy of Fine Arts. The strip had a limited run from January 7 to March 16, 1929. The strip proved popular and *Tarzan* returned to the funnies under artist Rex Maxon. Edgar Rice Burroughs was unhappy with Maxon's work, and by September 27, 1931, he was gone and Foster again provided artwork, this time for the Sunday version of the strip.

Foster's subsequent work on the Sunday *Tarzan* strip created a continuity which to this day still looks strong. Foster's use of the full Sunday page, coupled with his skill as an illustrator, allowed him to utilize many differ-ent methods to tell his story, including the use of cinematic techniques. *Tarzan* reads as if it was "shot" like a movie. Foster uses long shots, cuts to a close-up, and then pulls back while panning the "camera," all the while giving the reader plenty of plot and visual detail to digest. What really stands out with Foster's *Tarzan* is the integration of the storytelling, supported by skillfully choreographed illustration, to create a world within the confines of a cartoon strip. Foster's vision of Tarzan was a powerful lure to kids, their parents, and to someone with the money and power to make Foster an offer he could not refuse: to create

Hal Foster, pencils and inks, original artwork, *Tarzan*, March 26, 1933, ©1933 Edgar Rice Burroughs, Inc.

any strip he wanted. Newspaper magnate William Randolph Hearst, who was the owner of the King Features Syndicate, was also a really big fan of the strip. Hearst, who was also an unabashed admirer of Herriman's *Krazy Kat*, was so intent on getting Foster to do a strip for him that he conceded the rights for the new strip to Foster, something that was unheard of at the time. Foster's memorable run on *Tarzan* accordingly came to an end.

After Foster's departure, Burne Hogarth was selected to replace him. Hogarth had been biding his time working on the staff at the King Features Syndicate. Initially he did not attempt to deviate from Foster's style, but inevitably he gave Tarzan a more athletic look. Hogarth emphasized the ape man's anatomy and created a world for Tarzan very different than that imagined by Foster. Hogarth left the strip in 1945 but returned two years later and continued until 1950.

On February 13, 1937, Foster's new strip, *Prince Valiant,* premiered in the Sunday funnies (it ran exclusively on Sundays). Foster developed a carefully structured world within the confines of the *Prince Valiant* strip and continued to tell his stories using a multitude of cinematic techniques which occupied him for the rest of his career.

Forces outside the world of commercial illustration would now intervene in the development of comic strips, which would shape

Opposite page: Burne Hogarth, pencils and inks, orginal artwork, *Tarzan*, July 17, 1949, ©1949 Edgar Rice Burroughs, Inc. Below: Hal Foster, pencils and inks, *Prince Valiant*, two panels from the original artwork from the Sunday strip which appeared on December 11, 1938, ©1938 King Features Syndicate. Bottom: Chester Gould, pencils and inks, original artwork, *Dick Tracy*, April 1, 1944, ©1944 Tribune Media Services.

"QUICK! MY SADDLE AND HORSES! THE SAXONS COME!"

"SUMMON ALL THE FENS' PEOPLE AND BID THEM HARRY THE ENEMY SCOUTS THAT THEY MAY GATHER NO INFORMATION, I RIDE TO CAMELOT!"

NEXT WEEK—HORSE-TRADING

the history of the adventure strip. The event which influenced the tone and content of the future of comic strips came, not from artists or the syndicates, but from the stock market, with the crash of October, 1929, which caused the Great Depression. In what seemed like an instant, the United States' economy collapsed. The unemployment rate rose to twenty-five percent. The American public looked for some means of escaping their daily problems, and pulp magazines, funnies, radio, books, and movies provided a welcome outlet. Today, over seventy years later, it is hard to comprehend the devastating effects the Great Depression had on the American routine and psyche. Pulp magazines, newspapers, newspaper cartoons, radio shows, and movies of this era, however, open a window to better understand this period. The artists who would write and draw comic books for the next half-a-century were all witnesses to this period of American history, which shaped and influenced their attitudes, perceptions, and ideals.

In the 1930s, the heroes of the day were adventurers like Charles Lindberg and Amelia Earhart; athletes like Babe Ruth, Lou Gehrig, Joe DiMaggio, and Jesse Owens; and entertainers and movie stars like Will Rogers, Clark

Gable, Shirley Temple, Greta Garbo, and W.C. Fields. This period is now thought of as the "Golden Age" of Hollywood. It is also thought of as the "Golden Age" of the American newspaper strip and of radio as well. The popular radio programs of the day, *The Shadow*, *The Lone Ranger*, and *The Green Hornet* were listened to by millions. Readers were gobbling up the novels and stories of Dashiell Hammett and Raymond Chandler.

This milieu had a big influence and impact on newspaper strip artists and the syndicates that sold their wares to the newspapers. A little over a year after the beginning of the Great Depression, on October 4, 1931, yet another groundbreaking strip, a strip which would be the benchmark for tough, hardboiled, detectives, had its premiere as both a daily and a Sunday: *Dick Tracy*. Conceived by cartoonist Chester Gould, who had unsuccessfully tried for the previous ten years to launch a nationally syndicated strip, *Dick Tracy* was Gould's reaction to the crime and criminals which held Chicago captive during the late 1920s and 1930s. Originally conceived as *Plainclothes Tracy*, under the guidance of the head of the Chicago Tribune Syndicate, Captain Joseph Medill Patterson, the strip and its main character were changed to *Dick Tracy*. Gould thought of Tracy as a modern day Sherlock

Holmes, set in crime-ridden contemporary Chicago. Tracy, not only would confront gangsters and hoodlums, but would also deal with an establishment inhabited by corrupt lawyers and judges. Murder, violence, and death, as with contemporary Chicago, were all parts of the strip.[5] With *Dick Tracy*, Gould created a tough and highly stylized world de-

SILVER AGE THE SECOND GENERATION OF COMIC BOOK ARTISTS

veloping characterizations and concepts which influenced comic book artists in the years to come. Gould flattened the look of his characters, inked with a bold line, and embraced the surreal possibilities of urban violence by creating characters and storylines that were as memorable as they were bizarre. Tracy had an unmistakable profile and fought villains who were models for a legion of comic book villains to follow. *Dick Tracy* embraced the fantastic and eccentric and made it popular to a wide audience. Sixty years after the creation of villains the like of Flattop, Pruneface, Big Boy, and Mumbles, these characters still resonate as influential archetypes. Gould depicted Tracy's Chicago as a dark, flattened,

menacing Gotham City, besieged by evil, a concept also frequently revisited by comic book artists.

The ten year period which witnessed the birth and development of the action/adventure strip, starting with the introduction of *Wash Tubbs*, was now coming into the home stretch. By 1934, the action/adventure strip, as a popular entertainment medium, was inspiring the syndicates, ever hungry for more newspapers to carry their products, to compete with already popular strips such as *Buck Rogers* and *Tarzan* and to continue to offer new material. This competitive environment, coupled with young ambitious artists vying to get their own strips, resulted in the creation of strip continuities that helped to further define the action/adventure newspaper strip.

For the action/adventure strip, 1934 is a magic year; readers of the funnies were introduced to *Flash Gordon, Mandrake the Magician, Terry and the Pirates,* and Noel Sickles officially took the helm as artist in *Scorchy Smith,* developing it into one of the most distinctive and influential comic strips ever.

The styles and techniques explored by the artists of *Scorchy Smith, Terry and the Pirates,* and *Flash Gordon* provided inspiration and served as examples of reference for other strip artists and for the kids reading these strips, who would inevitably become the second generation of comic book artists.

Of these strips, one, *Scorchy Smith,* set the tone and style for just about all action/adventure strips to follow. *Scorchy* provided the ingredients necessary for other strip artists to tell their tales, and its formula was frequently copied but rarely equaled. *Scorchy Smith* started out under its creator/artist, John Terry, on March 17, 1930. *Scorchy,* which was inspired by Charles Lindberg, ignited the imaginations of its readers by presenting the adventures of its "boy scout" aviator hero and became the Associated Press Syndicate's best selling strip. The strip, however, was not well rendered by Terry, and its popularity was due to its subject and not the quality of its artwork. In 1933, Terry became ill with tuberculosis and picked

SOON THE NIGHT IS FILLED WITH WAILING SIRENS AND THE SHOUTS OF AROUSED GUARDS. FLASH PULLS BACK THE COVER OF AN ABANDONED WELL—"DOWN HERE—QUICK!" HE WHISPERS.

AS THE GIRLS VANISH INTO THE WELL, BULON TURNS TO FLASH, GROWLING—"THOSE TUNNELS AREN'T BIG ENOUGH FOR BOTH OF US! RENA LOVED ME BEFORE YOU CAME ALONG! ONE OF US WILL REMAIN HERE AND IT WON'T BE ME!"

FLASH PICKS UP BULON AND CARRIES HIM DOWN THE WELL TUNNEL AND INTO THE LIGHTED POWER TUNNEL. THERE HE DROPS HIM AT RENA'S FEET, SAYING—"THIS BELONGS TO YOU, RENA. YOU AND DALE DRAG HIM TO SAFETY. I'M GOING BACK TO MAKE SURE WE HAVEN'T BEEN SEEN."

AS FLASH DODGES THROUGH THE BUSHES AROUND THE OLD WELL, HE HEARS A STEALTHY FOOTSTEP BEHIND HIM AND WHIRLS ABOUT—"DALE!" HE SAYS, "I THOUGHT I TOLD YOU TO STAY BEHIND!" "I'D RATHER BE WITH YOU," SAYS DALE.

NEXT WEEK:
PARTNERS IN PERIL

Noel Sickles, a staff artist with the AP, to act as his ghost for the strip while he recovered.

Sickles' first work on *Scorchy* appeared on December 4, 1933, under Terry's signature. In order not to disrupt the look of the strip, Sickles adopted Terry's style. Sickles observed that, "...I had to forget everything I learned about drawing – absolutely everything – because it was the worst drawing I had seen by anybody." Ultimately, with the death of Terry, the strip became Sickles' and in 1934 he began to sign the strip. Sickles wrote and drew the strip by working out the story on a day-to-day basis, rather than plotting out the continuity in advance. *Scorchy* was the perfect vehicle for Sickles to develop a method of newspaper strip storytelling, utilizing backgrounds which have a photographic look and feel without actual detail, and characters which are drawn and posed naturally with an emphasis on inking with a brush.

Sickles started his art education while in his teens by studying American and European cartooning in his hometown of Chillicothe, Ohio, at the public library. He also would "hitch rides up to Columbus" to get advice from newspaper cartoonists. It was on one of these trips that Sickles met Milton Caniff, then an up-and-coming cartoonist at the *Columbus Dispatch*. It was a meeting that would result

Opposite page: Austin Briggs, pencils and inks, *Flash Gordon*, April 15, 1945, ©
1945 King Features Syndicate. Below: Alex Raymond, pencils and inks, original
artwork, *Secret Agent X-9*, May 17, 1934, ©1934 King Features Syndicate. Bottom:
Frank Robbins, pencils and inks, original artwork, *Scorchy Smith*, August 7, 1941,
©1941 World Wide Features.

in the beginning of a long friendship and partnership. When Sickles graduated from high
school, he came to Columbus and started work
as a cartoonist for the *Columbus Citizen*.
Along the way, he took the Landon cartooning
correspondence course and added his name to
its distinguished list of alumni. After his stint
at the *Columbus Citizen*, he moved to Cleveland to work for the Landon Cartooning Correspondence Course critiquing students and
became aware of the work of Roy Crane.[6] His
friendship with fellow Ohioan Milton Caniff
continued and led Sickles to work in New York
City in the 1930s.

In fact, Caniff was already hard at work in
New York at the AP bullpen. Caniff precipitated Sickles' move to NYC by putting in a
good word for him with the big-wigs at the
AP. It is unfair to focus entirely on Sickles
because he and Caniff worked very closely together and in partnership. Caniff once observed in the introduction to the 1970 Nostalgia Press publication of a volume of *Terry and
the Pirates*, "It was not until Noel Sickles, then
drawing *Scorchy Smith*, and with whom I

shared a studio, worked out a means of deliv-
ering illustration quality pictures on a seven-
day basis was I able to buck some of the chains
of my working schedule while dramatically
improving the all-over value of *Terry*. I shall
always be grateful that Noel Sickles allowed
me to pick his brain those formative years."[7]

Caniff got his start in the newspaper business early, when he was hired at the age of 14
in the art department of the *Dayton Daily News*
as an office boy. Just as with Crane and Sickles, Caniff was also a graduate of the Landon
cartoon correspondence course. Caniff went
to Ohio State University in Columbus and
found work at the *Columbus Dispatch* as a
cartoonist. While at Ohio State, Caniff also
read and studied *Wash Tubbs*. Caniff, after
his graduation, together Sickles, opened a studio in Columbus to do commercial work.
Shortly, though, Caniff landed a job with the
AP in New York and he was off to the big city.
When Sickles came to New York, he shared a
studio with Caniff.

By 1933 Caniff had come up with a strip
idea which the AP put into production called

Dickie Dare, which premiered on July 31, 1933. Caniff's style in *Dickie* was unremarkable and gave no hint as to what would begin to develop shortly. Caniff was lured away by the Tribune-News Syndicate and the result was *Terry and the Pirates*, which premiered as a daily on October 22, 1934.

As Sickles and Caniff worked on their respective strips, the artwork began to quickly develop. Within one year, both strips underwent change after change, until what became known as the "Caniff style" began to emerge. The method of storytelling being pioneered, primarily by Sickles, was credited to Caniff because Sickles abandoned his work on *Scorchy* in late 1936, due to the AP's refusal to allow him to financially benefit from the strip's success. Sickles became a successful illustrator, never officially returning to the comics, except for uncredited work on *Terry* for Caniff and on a strip called the *Adventures of Patsy* for Charles Raab. Sickles' approach revolutionized cartooning by the use of a number of techniques. These techniques make the strip look bold and graphic, with characters who do not look posed, set against backgrounds which appear almost photographic, but which use clever inking rather than detail to create the illusion of complexity. Caniff used these techniques with great success in *Terry* in the late 1930s. Sickles commented that the details do not matter, "Reality comes from the feeling of the damn thing. If you understand the construction of the boat, and understand the man himself – who he is and what he looks like – you can get that over to a reader with a picture." Sickles did this with the use of line, shadow, and composition. Sickles also had an exceptional sense of design, which can be seen in the titles he created for Caniff for the *Terry and the Pirates* Sunday strip and later for the *Steve Canyon* Sunday strip. Sickles' style quickly spread to just about every strip and found its way into comic books with the first and second generation of comic book artists.

After Sickles departed *Scorchy*, a succession of other artists were brought in by the AP. By May 22, 1939, a 22-year-old kid named

Frank Robbins took over and after two years of hit-and-miss efforts, found his own voice on the strip, managing a variation on the Sickles style which was all his own. His lush inking emphasized shadows and his figures were fluid and handsome.

Nineteen thirty-four also witnessed Alex Raymond working on three strips almost simultaneously, one of which became a household word (or words): *Flash Gordon*. Raymond was born on October 9, 1909 into a middle-class family in New Rochelle, New York. Raymond's father died when he was twelve years old and while he did attend preparatory school, after graduating he was forced to look for work to support his family. He initially sought employment on Wall Street, but this was cut short by the Depression. In search of an income, Raymond consulted his former next-door neighbor, cartoonist Russ Westover, who suggested he try cartooning. Raymond, who had shown artistic aptitude since he was a child, took Westover's advice and, by 1930 with the elder artist's help, had secured a job as a staff artist at United Features. Raymond worked as an assistant to Westover on his *Tillie the Toiler* strip and as an assistant to Chic Young on *Blondie*. Raymond also ghosted the Sunday page for Lyman Young's *Tim Tyler's Luck* strip.[8] United Features' President, Joe Connolly, who was always looking for new strip ideas, had decided to challenge *Buck Rogers*. Connolly had also hired Dashiell Hammett to write a strip to be called *Secret Agent X-9* to compete with *Dick Tracy*, but he needed artists to bring these concepts to fruition. Raymond got both assignments and the added responsibility of turning out a third strip, *Jungle Jim*.[9] All three strips premiered in 1934.[10] At the ripe old age of 23, Raymond had his hands full. His work on all three strips, initially, was not especially impressive. After less than two years Raymond dropped his involvement with *Secret Agent X-9*.

Flash Gordon quickly pulled attention away from *Buck Rogers*, because the level of Raymond's illustration was far more attractive than the less inspired efforts supplied for

Buck Rogers. Raymond's ability to render the strip, while shaky at first, finally hit its stride by the mid-1930s. Looking at Raymond's work on the continuity in retrospect shows a clear progression until Raymond's mastery with a brush becomes undeniable. It is clear that Raymond grew as an artist, but another factor has also been attributed to the mastery of the strip during the late 1930s: the work of Raymond's assistant, Austin Briggs.[11] Many comic historians have attributed the lush dry brush inking of the late 1930s to Briggs, although Raymond fans hotly contest such assertions. The fact remains that from 1936 to 1944, *Flash Gordon* was one of the best rendered comic strips ever drawn. *Flash Gordon* did nothing to expand the art of comic storytelling, but the tableau created by Raymond, despite the soap operatic qualities of the strip, is still compelling to look at sixty years after its creation. It still retains a romantic majesty very rarely equaled. *Flash Gordon* also inspired its many young readers to draw for the comics and became a source of reference for many in the second generation of comic book artists.

Readers in 1934 were also introduced to *Mandrake the Magician* on June 11, 1934. Created by Lee Falk with art by Phil Davis, *Mandrake* gave its readers an entertaining dose of comic strip magic and occult in a daily and Sunday version. The strip was influential for its presentation of fantasy, magic, and mystery. Falk pitched his idea to the King Features Syndicate when he was only 19 and still a student at the University of Illinois, after having written and drawn several weeks of the strip himself. Falk acknowledged that he "thought of himself mainly as a writer" and accordingly called upon Davis to act as the artist for the strip. Two years later, Falk created what many view as an important precursor to the superheroes of the comic books: *The Phantom*. The daily version of *The Phantom* appeared on February 17, 1936, with art by Ray Moore, who had worked as Davis' assistant on *The Phantom*. Both *Mandrake* and *The Phantom* relied on Falk's fondness for mythology, which was reused and translated for a contemporary audience. *The Phantom* also offered readers a masked hero with a costume of sorts, epic adventure, and elements of the supernatural.[12]

Artist Fred Harmon was also helping define the look and conventions of western and cowboy strips, first with the strip *Bronc Peeler*, which appeared in newspapers sometime in late 1933 and ultimately with the strip *Red Ryder*, which made its first appearance in newspapers on November 6, 1938 (the strip appeared first as a Sunday).[13] *Red Ryder* was little more than a renamed version of *Bronc Peeler* but was sold through NEA all over the United States. *Red Ryder* combined pulp fiction and the Hollywood version of the old west but had a look and feel which impressed and influenced many of its young readers who would become influential comic artists. Indeed, many of the conventions for drawing the old west, albeit through the antiseptic haze of 1930s Hollywood, come from Harmon's *Red Ryder*.

By the end of the 1930s, the conventions which would be used as the initial basis for comic books were firmly in place; all that was needed was a catalyst to make the idea of an independent book of comic strips commercially and financially viable, but this was to come shortly, and, by 1938 with the creation of Superman, would become a big business requiring the talents of a legion of artists: the first generation of artists to toil in the medium.

NOTES

[1] The Yellow Kid appeared as an unnamed character in a strip called *At the Circus in Hogan's Alley*. The strip appeared as a single panel only but later was composed using several panels.

[2] Krazy Kat first poked his head into the funnies on June 20, 1910 in a strip called *The Dingbat Family* in *The New York Evening Journal*. The Kat officially appeared in his own strip on October 28, 1913.

[3] This is exactly how Crane related he got his foot in the door which led to *Wash Tubbs*. Jim Ivey interview with Roy Crane, May 5, 1971, *The Comics Journal* # 203, April, 1998.

[4] The genesis of the strip is reported in the preface of *The Collected Works of Buck Rogers in the 25th Century,* National Newspaper Syndicate of America, 1969. This book helped spur a re-evaluation of the strip and was prefaced with an introduction by Ray Bradbury. Bradbury reminded readers how exciting and influential *Buck Rogers* had been to him and other readers in the 1930s.

[5] The genesis of Gould's development as a cartoonist and the origin of *Dick Tracy* are recounted in *Dick Tracy: America's Most Famous Detective*, Carol Publishing Group, 1990.

[6] Gil Kane, Ron Goulart, and Dick Hodgins unpublished, unedited interview with Noel Sickles, September 6, 1973. An edited version of this interview was published in *The Comics Journal* # 242, April, 2002.

[7] Milton Caniff, "Terry, the Pirates and I," *The Golden Age of Comics, Terry and the Pirates*, #4, Nostalgia Press, 1970.

[8] Al Williamson, "Introduction," *Flash Gordon*, Nostalgia Press, 1967.

[9] *Jungle Jim* ran on top of *Flash Gordon* on the Sunday comics page and is referred to as the "topper."

[10] *Flash Gordon* and *Jungle Jim* both premiered on January 7, 1934. *Secret Agent X-9* premiered on January 22, 1934.

[11] Interview with Gil Kane. Also See: Alberto Becattini and Antonio Vianovi, *Alex Raymond: The Power and the Grace*, Glamour Associated, 2002.

[12] Lee Falk interview, *Cartoonist Profiles #27*, September, 1975.

[13] The exact date *Bronc Peeler* premiered is difficult to establish due to its sporadic distribution in different newspapers. The strip's problems with distribution also limited its popularity and success.

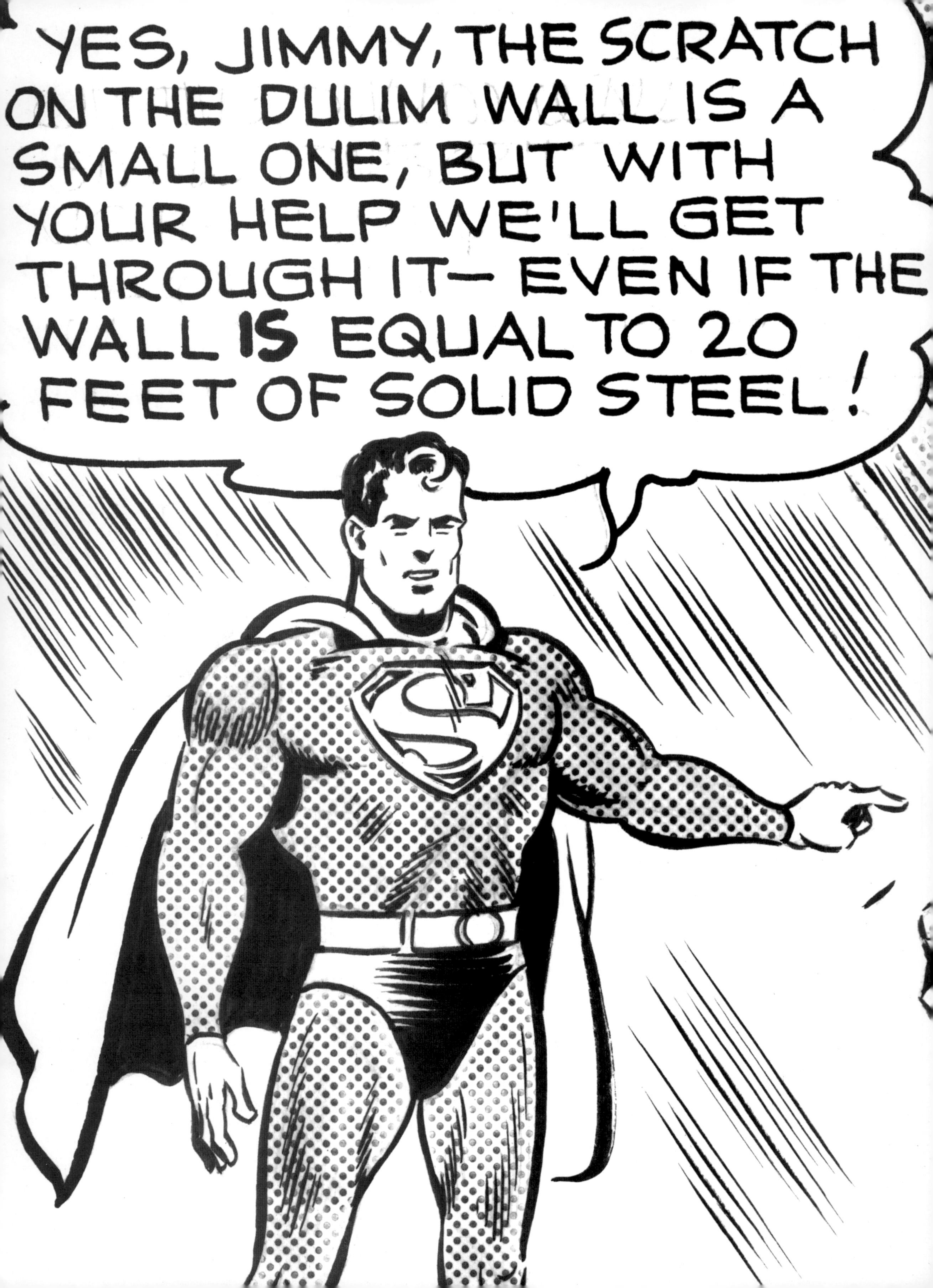
YES, JIMMY, THE SCRATCH ON THE DULIM WALL IS A SMALL ONE, BUT WITH YOUR HELP WE'LL GET THROUGH IT— EVEN IF THE WALL **IS** EQUAL TO 20 FEET OF SOLID STEEL!

2 THE FIRST COMIC BOOKS; THE MILIEU OF NEW YORK CITY; THE SHOPS; THE PUBLISHERS; THE FIRST GENERATION OF COMIC BOOK ARITSTS

Comic book historians generally refer to the period from 1935 to the end of the Second World War as the Golden Age.[1] There was nothing "golden," however, about this period for the artists and writers working for the shops, the packagers, and the publishers who helped give birth to the first comic books. The American comic book got its start inauspiciously enough, as a mere merchandizing ploy to keep printing presses running during the Great Depression.

There was no great design, nothing heroic or no artistic inspiration involved in the creation of the early comic books of the Golden Age, only the potential to perhaps make a modest profit for printers and publishers.

As the early comic books were purely a business proposition, many of the entrepreneurs involved in the creation of the first books of comics were hard-nosed, pragmatic businessmen.

The first comic books were created in 1933 as promotional give-aways.[2] The bright idea to repackage groupings of popular comic strips in one book which was given away as a promotional item, titled *Funnies on Parade*, distributed in the spring of 1933, is generally attributed to Harry Wildenberg, George Janosik, and salesman Max C. Gaines, all employees of Eastern Color Printing of Waterbury, Connecticut.[3] *Funnies on Parade* was printed for Proctor and Gamble and included reprints from *Mutt and Jeff*, *Joe Palooka*, and *Hairbreath Harry*. Advertising for such premiums began to pop up in newspapers all over, and by the

end of 1933, the Sunday, October 1, *Chicago Tribune* invited kids to clip and send in the coupon from a box of Wheatena cereal and get a comic book in return.

By 1934, Eastern was churning out comic book premiums, selling almost a half-million copies. Not content with just producing their current line of comic book premiums, Eastern pitched George Delacorte of Dell Publishing to foot the bill for printing another comic book premium which would again contain reprint material. Delacorte was no stranger to such an idea, in 1929 he had published a tabloid-sized comic strip reprint printed by Eastern, which proved unprofitable. Dell elected to take another chance with a comic strip promotional to be sold to department stores and placed an order with Eastern for printing. The result was *Famous Funnies*, Series 1, printed in early 1934. Delacorte was not encouraged by the response he received with *Famous Funnies* and relinquished Dell's rights to the title back to Eastern.

Eastern was not finished with the concept and repitched the idea of a book of comics for sale at newsstands and drug stores to the distributor American News (which had initially turned the idea of distribution down when Dell had the title). This time around American News assented to the proposal and ordered a quarter-of-a-million books, and in May, 1934 *Famous Funnies* #1 was released with a date of July, 1934, becoming the first newsstand released comic book.[4] To American News and Eastern, the most impressive thing about *Fa-*

mous Funnies was that it ultimately made money. The American newsstand comic book was now on its way as a marketable commodity.[5]

Within the next two years, comic books were appearing everywhere through the efforts of various publishers trying to test the waters of profitability. As the market expanded, new players entered the business who tried to distinguish their products. Among those scrambling for a piece of the market was Major Malcolm Wheeler-Nicholson, who could best be described, charitably, as a character. The Major was a jack-of-all-trades: a retired cavalry officer, pulp magazine writer, and comic book publisher. Wheeler-Nicholson had seen military service in Mexico, the Philippines, Russia, and Europe, and had left the army under less than good terms and ideal circumstances. He wore spats, sported a walking stick, and used a cigarette holder, which highlighted his brown teeth and was both charming and persuasive. He also had a habit of paying for work late or not at all. Wheeler-Nicholson was one of the first publishers who had the idea to sell something more than just reprints in comic books.

Wheeler-Nicholson went out and hired writers and artists to create books with original material as the distinguishing factor in his planned line of comic books.[6] His company, National Allied Periodicals, Inc., published its

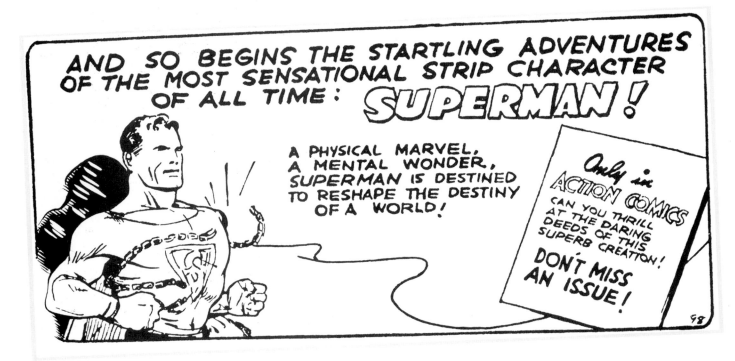

first comic book, *New Fun,* in a larger than usual format in early 1935. By the fall of 1935, Wheeler-Nicholson published *New Comics* #1, which was release dated December, 1935 and which contained original material. By its sixth issue *New Comics* had featured the work of three up-and-comers in the comic book field (who had wanted to break into strips but instead wound up working in comic books). Partners Jerry Siegel and Joe Shuster and Sheldon "Shelly" Mayer, would all shortly make indelible marks in the history of comic books.[7]

By 1936 there were five comic book publishers producing a half-dozen titles. Max C. Gaines, who had been a prime mover at Eastern, was now working for the McClure Newspaper Syndicate, using their presses to reprint strips packaged into comic books. For help, Gaines hired Sheldon Mayer who had been working producing original strip material for Wheeler-Nicholson. The comic book business was now a small community of artists, writers, and businessmen who continuously went back and forth, from company to company, looking for and getting work. There was no clear direction for comic books, no smash hit to draw in millions of readers. What comic books needed was a feature which had the lure of, say, *Buck Rogers* or *Flash Gordon.* The genesis for such a feature would come from the comic book lines being developed by Wheeler-Nicholson.

As it became obvious that comic books with reprinted strip material were selling, the syndicates originating the material decided to come out with their own products. Original material now became more important to keep the presses rolling and the comic book racks filled in newsstands and drug stores. Nineteen thirty-six also marked the beginning of comic book shops which, for the most part, collected many of the first artists of comic book stories together and gave them steady work. Artists were solicited through newspaper ads as well as word of mouth.[8]

There is no precise record of when the shops started, but the general perception is that Harry "A" Chesler (Chesler used the "A" as

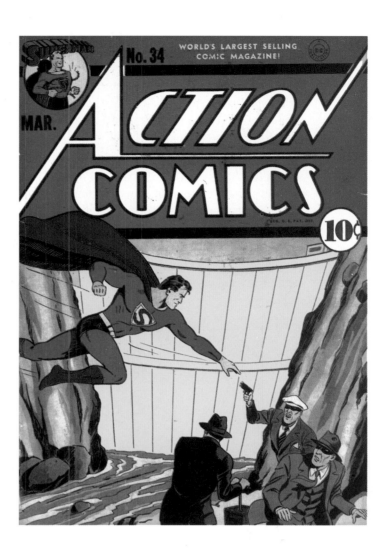

his middle name and not as an initial, hence it is always in quotation marks) set up the first one. A shop was a factory of artists, writers, an art director, and an editor or editors who supplied finished comic book material to packagers and publishers.[9] The artists and artisans attracted to the shops ranged from unemployed artists and illustrators, burned-out strip artists and up-and-coming strip artists, artists from advertising, and kids with artistic talent or potential (as well as kids without any potential, artistic or otherwise). Applicants could

just literally walk in with samples and pitch themselves for work. Chesler supplied stories to a host of different publishers, including Wheeler-Nicholson.

Chesler, who was in his mid-50s, had come to New York from Chicago. He was a rotund sort, who always seemed to have a big cigar in his mouth, and even though you would never know it by looking at him, was honest businessman. His shop consisted of a large room on the third or fourth floor of a tenement building at 276 Fifth Avenue. He had

eight to ten artists working, every day, at drawing tables churning out comic book stories. Among some of the alumni of his shop were Charles Biro, Jack Cole, Creig Flessel, Gill Fox, Irv Novick, Mac Raboy, Paul Gustavson, and Fred Guardineer. Additionally, a 12-year-old kid named Joe Kubert, another youngster who made his mark in the Silver Age, came around with an armful of samples and got his first work there as well.[10] After Chesler, shops started to pop up all over New York City.

Right on the heels of the Chesler shop, in late 1937/early 1938, was the partnership of Will Eisner and Jerry Iger, who opened the Eisner/Iger shop. Unlike many of the shops that followed, the Eisner/Iger shop paid its artists a weekly salary, and not for work by the page.[11] Iger was the salesman for the shop, but he also pitched in writing scripts and creating characters used in the stories turned out by the shop's artists.[12] Eisner was the driving force behind the style of the shop. Indeed, the Eisner/Iger shop was a good example of how careful control of the artwork could create discernible quality and consistency with the product produced. Eisner remembers, "I was really running the shop the way a player-manager runs a baseball team, sitting there working with artists; I wanted quality."[13] Eisner felt the only way to create comic stories which were fun to read and which had some visual flair was through close interaction and collaboration. Clearly, Eisner's efforts paid off.

The Eisner/Iger shop was literally started on a shoestring, and Eisner found rental space in a building that rented to bookies, for $10 a month, "No lease or anything, no questions asked."[14] The Eisner/Iger shop counted as its artists some who would go on to make significant contributions to the art of comic book storytelling. These artists included Lou Fine, Bob Powell, Mort Meskin, Chuck Mazoujian, Chuck Cuidera, Jack Kirby, Nick Viscardi (Cardy), Dick Briefer, Bob Kane, George Tuska, Klaus Nordling, and Reed Crandall. The Eisner/Iger shop supplied stories for several clients, including Everett "Busy" Arnold who assembled material from shops, as a packager, into comic books marketed under the Quality logo. Eisner/Iger also provided work for Fiction House and the Fox Features Syndicate.

Busy Arnold also directly hired artists and attracted some of the most creative talent of the first generation to provide work for his line of comic books. Lou Fine, Reed Crandall, and Jack Cole all directly worked for Arnold creating some of the most memorable comic books of the Golden Age. Arnold even paid generous bonuses to his artists when comic books proved to be successful.[15] Arnold was hardly a saint, however, and he was an assertive and stern taskmaster when it came to getting what he wanted, and on schedule.[16] He also precipitated the break-up of the Eisner/Iger shop and gave Eisner the chance to create and control his own comic book character.

The vehicle that would make comic books commercially profitable and would lead to

their rapid proliferation was on the horizon. By 1937, Wheeler-Nicholson's last comic book, *Detective Comics*, was being readied for its premiere, but as usual, Wheeler-Nicholson was in debt to just about everybody: artists, writers, and most importantly, printers. In order to get *Detective Comics*, off the launching pad, Wheeler-Nicholson was forced to make one of his creditors, Harry Donenfeld, a partner. Technically, Wheeler-Nicholson was listed as a partner with Jack Liebowitz, Donenfeld's accountant, who by many accounts was the brains behind Donenfeld's printing and distribution business.[17] Donenfeld published such gems as the risqué pulp magazines *Spicy Romance* and *Spicy Detective*. By 1938, before the next comic book title of Wheeler-Nicholson's company, now renamed Detective Comics, Inc., was introduced, he had been forced out of the company. The company's next comic book, called *Action*, introduced a strange visitor from another planet named Superman. The company and the staff Wheeler-Nicholson had created now moved on without him. After Donenfeld and Liebowitz took complete ownership of the company, it was generally referred to as DC Comics because of its logo, a circle with the letters "DC" in the middle.

Superman, the guy in the blue and red outfit, revolutionized the business and created a financial environment which would foster the development of comic book storytelling. Superman's creators, Jerry Siegel (who wrote the strip) and Joe Shuster (who drew it), were two kids from Cleveland who had been working in the business since 1935. They had unsuccessfully tried to pitch strips to syndicates and wound up reformatting these strips for comic books, selling their material to Wheeler-Nicholson. The idea of Superman had percolated and developed with Siegel and Shuster since 1933 and had been solicited to a number of publishers and printers, including Will Eisner, but had always been rejected.[18] Samples made their way to the McClure Syndicate where Max C. Gaines was now working. Gaines was now trying to keep McClure's presses running, and to assist him, he hired

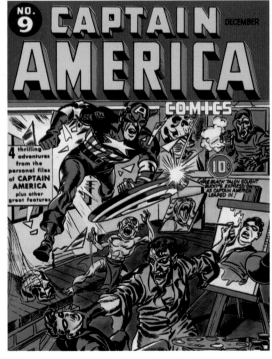

In their enthusiasm to have Superman published, Siegel and Shuster gave no thought to whether their character would ever have any value; they were, after all, being published. Business savvy DC Comics included language on the back of its checks that surrendered the rights for artists' creations to the company, so for the princely sum of $130 or $10 per page, Siegel and Shuster gave up their rights in Superman forever. It was, after all, just business, and the owners of DC Comics were no different from other publishers. Indeed, this would not change for the foreseeable future.

The enthusiasm that *Superman* garnered was due to its concept of a super man taken in the context of the American Depression. It was similar to other popular entertainments of the time; it was optimistic escapist fantasy aimed at kids. The popularity of the strip fortunately was not dependent on the quality of the artwork, which was crudely drawn, and badly paced. It was, however, a good starting point. *Superman* was an amalgam of numerous influences. Roy Crane's *Wash Tubbs* is clearly in evidence with the artwork coupled with the pulp heroes the Shadow and Doc Savage. In order to keep up with the demand for material, Siegel and Shuster set up a shop in Cleveland. With Shuster's eyesight worsening and the high demand for Superman stories, it was the obvious decision. Through newspaper ads and word of mouth, Siegel and Shuster assembled a group of artists, some of whom would stay with the strip for years. Their initial shop included Wayne Boring, Paul Cassidy and subsequently added were Dennis Neville, Leo Novak, and John Sikela. Eventually the shop moved to New York.[20] DC Comics brought newspaper cartoonist Jack Burnley on board, and he further tightened up *Superman's* drawing and storytelling as the strip gained in recognition everywhere with sales now flying through the roof.[21]

Less than a year later, DC Comics would release its second successful hero, this time a non-super one who relied on his wits rather than his non-earthly powers: Batman. Batman, the creation of artist Bob Kane and writer Bill Finger, further solidified DC Com-

cartoonist Sheldon Mayer. Siegel and Shuster's samples got the attention of Mayer, but the syndicate and Gaines were not interested. Mayer persisted, and finally Gaines gave the go-ahead to have the strip offered as a comic book feature where McClure would do the printing. Mayer showed samples of the strip to Vincent Sullivan at DC Comics, and after the strip was hastily cut and repasted into comic book form from its original strip format, it appeared in *Action* #1, which had a release date of June, 1938. DC Comics had a hit on its hands; they just did not know it. By the fourth issue of *Action*, the management at DC Comics got the message: kids loved Superman. The superhero boom was on.[19]

ics' line of superhero offerings. Batman premiered in *Detective* #27 with a release date of May, 1939. Kane started his own shop to turn out Batman stories using Jerry Robinson as his ghost. Soon he added George Roussos to handle the atmospheric backgrounds used in the strip, which helped define the character and ambience of the feature.[22] Ultimately, to protect its hold on Batman, DC Comics directly hired Robinson and Finger as it had with Superman's ghost artists. By 1942, DC Comics had its own bullpen of artists which varied but included Jack Kirby, Joe Simon, Fred Ray, Joe Shuster, Mort Meskin, Charlie Paris, George Roussos, Cliff Young, and Stan Kaye.[23]

By the end of 1938, with the demand for new superheroes and more material ever increasing, DC Comics entered into an agreement with Max C. Gaines to provide it with more product. The material would be produced by Gaines' new company, All American Publications, and marketed under the DC Comics logo. The line was overseen by Shelly Mayer as editor. Gaines, who never had any confidence in superheroes, was nevertheless inclined to listen to Mayer under whose guidance some of most enduring superhero characters were created. Inevitably, the popularity of characters the likes of Flash from *Flash Comics*, premiering with a release date of January, 1940; Green Lantern from *All-American Comics*, premiering with a release date of Fall, 1941; and Wonder Woman from *All Star Comics*, premiering with a release date of December/January, 1941-1942 (Wonder Woman got her own title in *Sensation Comics* premiering with a release date of January, 1942) won Gaines over.

Mayer was also influential as a mentor to new talent. He had a good instinct for young artists and worked to help them develop their skills as artists and storytellers.[24] It was under Mayer, in 1944, that Julius Schwartz was hired as an assistant editor at All American. Up until that time Schwartz had been the literary agent for an impressive stable of pulp science fiction writers. Schwartz and Mort Weisinger had been partners in the Solar Sales

NOW THAT WE HAVE MANAGED A LITTLE PRIVACY, JOE, WHAT CAN SUPERMAN'S SERVICE FOR SERVICEMEN DO FOR YOU?

IT CAN GO BACK TO MY HOME TOWN AND BEAT THE EARS OFF A SKUNK THAT'S TRYIN' T'BEAT MY TIME WITH MY GIRL FRIEND WHILE I AIN'T AROUND TO PROTECT MY INTERESTS!

THIS IS A BIT OUT OF MY LINE, JOE-- I CAN'T GUARANTEE TO KNOCK ANY EARS OFF, BUT I'LL DO WHAT I CAN TO--ER-- PROTECT YOUR INTERESTS.

THAT'S GOOD ENOUGH FOR ME, BUD--- GET GOING!

I BETTER TAKE TIME OUT TO MEND MY OWN FENCES WITH LOIS. AFTER ALL, I DID STAND HER UP ON A LUNCHEON DATE TO ANSWER JOE LYNN'S APPEAL.

WELL, THAT'S THAT--- GUESS I MIGHT AS WELL ATTEND TO THE TROUBLES OF MY SAILOR FRIEND.

STORE ROOM

FINE THING, TOO! I TOSS MONKEY WRENCHES INTO MY OWN ROMANCE JUST TO MEDDLE IN THE ROMANCE OF A COUPLE OF TOTAL STRANGERS! I GUESS IT'S THE PRICE I MUST PAY FOR BEING SUPERMAN!

U. S. AIRLINES

AND STRAIGHTENING OUT THAT OTHER ROMANCE IS NOT GOING TO BE SUCH A CINCH, EITHER...

Below: Jerry Robinson, pencils and inks, original cover artwork, *Detective* #62, April, 1942, ©1942 DC Comics. Opposite page: Jerry Robinson, pencils and inks, cover, *Batman* #13, October, 1942; Jerry Robinson, pencils and inks, cover, *Detective* #69, November, 1942; Jerry Robinson, pencils and inks, cover, *Batman* #14, December, 1942, ©1942 DC Comics.

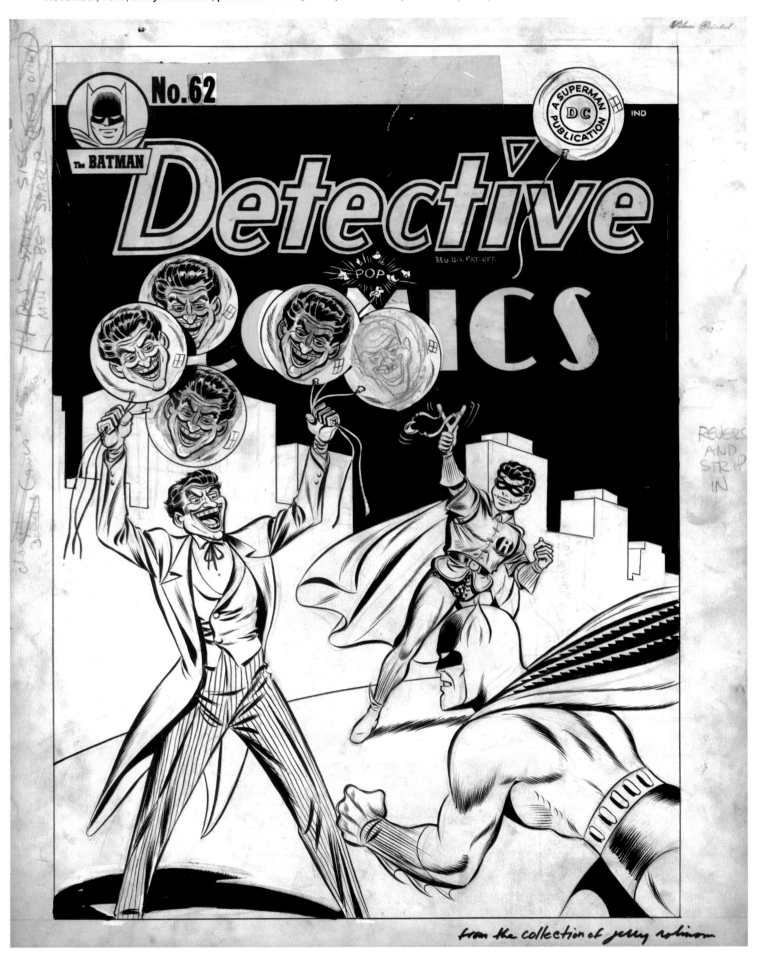

Service, which represented such notable pulp science fiction writers as Ray Bradbury, Alfred Bester, and Leigh Brackett. When Weisinger left the partnership in 1941 to work as an editor at DC Comics for *Superman*, Schwartz continued as an agent with a roster of clients including Ed Hamilton, Otto Binder, Robert Heinlein, and H.P. Lovecraft. The hiring of Schwartz was yet another example of how the comic book industry was raiding the talent of its precursors. Talent from the strips, illustration, and the pulps would all make contributions to shape what comic books were becoming.[25] Nineteen forty-four also marked the year Mayer hired a promising youngster already mentioned in these pages, Joe Kubert.[26]

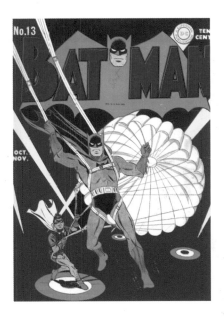

With all these developments, the comic book industry was quickly maturing as a competitive environment for businessmen and artists. The business created a symbiotic relationship, but the artistic half of the mix was expendable and easily replaceable. Artists and writers had no concept of their importance, and few had the inclination to do anything more than their assignment. The United States was, after all, still in the midst of a Depression, and it was good just to have work. Not to miss out on the profits from sales of comic books with superhero stars, publishers began looking to produce knock-offs of Superman and Batman. Some merely copied while others came up with clever variations which in several cases were more interesting than the originals. Shops were now being called upon to enter the fray.

Lloyd Jacquet, who had worked as an editor for Wheeler-Nicholson, opened a shop called Funnies, Inc. Jacquet set up a small office on 45th Street and had most of the work done off premises. Jacquet brought on board Bill Everett as an artist and art director. Funnies, Inc. attracted the talents of Carl Burgos, Bob Wood, George Mandel, Irwin Hasen, Paul Gustavson and Mike Roy. Basil Wolverton, remembered for his surreal and bizarre characters and sensibility, additionally provided work for the shop. Funnies, Inc. also boasted the writing talent of Mickey Spillane. Funnies, Inc. made its contribution in adding some

spark to the superhero boom with Everett's creation of the Sub-Mariner and Burgos' creation of the Human Torch. Initially, the Sub-Mariner appeared in a black-and-white comic book called *Motion Picture Funnies Weekly*. Later, when pulp publisher Martin Goodman wanted to make his own entry into the super-hero sweepstakes, Funnies, Inc. packaged Everett's already used story with Burgos' *Human Torch* story for *Marvel Comics* with a release date of October, 1939. [27]

On the heels of the success of Superman, newspapers were looking for a hot property to put in their Sunday newspaper editions to draw in more readers. Busy Arnold had been asked by a newspaper syndicate to provide a preprinted or "ready print" comic book which could be inserted into a Sunday newspaper for just such a purpose. In the summer of 1939, Arnold approached Eisner and asked him to create a comic book for newspapers. Eisner gave this proposal the thumbs up, but his agreement with Iger provided that, in the event of a break-up, one partner had the right to buy the other out. Iger exercised this provision with the understanding that Eisner would take only five staff members with him. After the dissolution of the shop, Eisner relocated in Tudor City, on the east side of New York. The artists Eisner brought with him included Lou Fine, Bob Powell, Chuck Mazoujian, and Chuck Cuidera.[28] Iger continued to turn out steady work, supplying artwork to comic book publisher Fiction House and for *Classics Illustrated*.

Shops were now proliferating all over the City, and Jack Binder, another Chesler alumni, tried his hand at the business as well. Binder, who had been Chesler's art director, found a loft on Fifth Avenue that was described as looking like an "internment camp." Binder had row upon row of drafting tables with artists busy at work churning out a nondescript hodge-podge. Binder's formula for producing comic art was to assign each part of a page—pencils on figures, pencils on backgrounds, inking on figures, inking on backgrounds—to different artists, and the result showed it. The Binder shop turned out a true

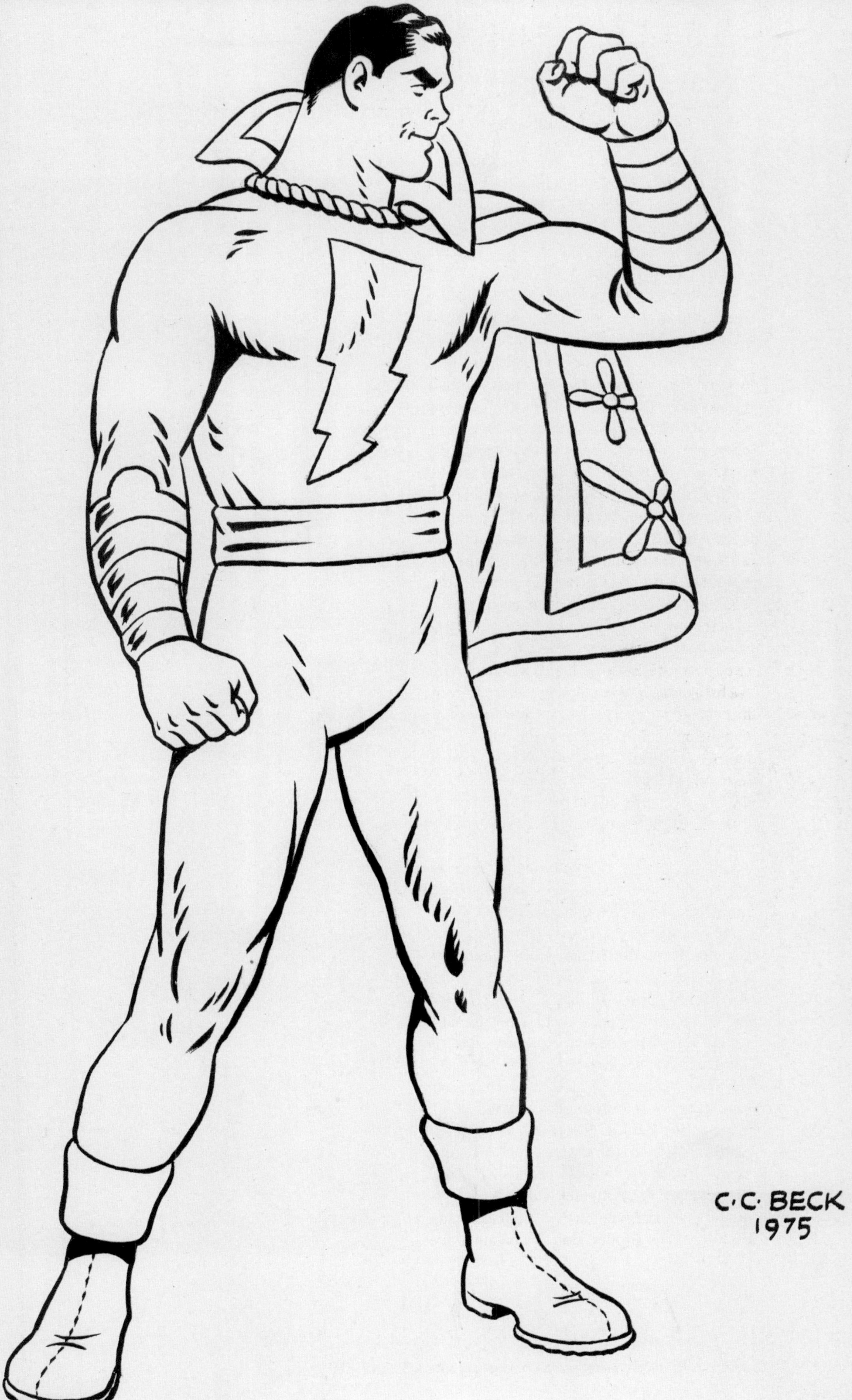
C.C. BECK
1975

assembly-line product which was not particularly distinguished. Later Binder moved his shop to a barn in Englewood, New Jersey. Binder supplied art to, among others, Fawcett.[29]

Some publishers, such as DC Comics, found it useful to control their own bullpens of artists. Other publishers which had artists working directly for them included MLJ Comics and Martin Goodman's Timely Comics. MLJ, which later became Archie Comics, were the first initials of the three partners in the company: Morris Coyne, Louis Silberkleit, and John Goldwater. MLJ attracted a number of artists to provide art for its comic books, including Irv Novick and Eisner/Iger alumni, Mort Meskin. Many artists passed through its doors looking for work, including 16-year-old Eli Katz (Gil Kane) who did his first comic book work there cleaning up pages by erasing pencil marks after the pages had been inked. Kane, as we will see, went on to learn significantly more after his first efforts with MLJ. Timely Comics boasted the talents of Joe Simon and Jack Kirby, who created one of the comic line's big stars, Captain America, but soon Simon and Kirby were working for DC Comics. It should be noted that Simon and Kirby also employed the use of numerous artists as ghosts at Timely as well as at DC Comics.

Fawcett, which owned the Captain Marvel line, along with other less well remembered titles, had the art for its comic books supervised by artist C.C. (Charles Clarence) Beck, who hired and carefully supervised the artists whose work was used in its products. Beck opened a shop in 1941, located at Broadway and 40th Street, to turn out enough material to supply the ever-growing popularity for the "big red cheese" (as Captain Marvel was affectionately called by his fans). During the long tenure of the shop, it employed, among others, Dave Berg, Al Fagley, Chic Stone, and Kurt Schaffenberger.[30] Beck split his duties as the chief of all things Captain Marvel with Pete Costanza. Beck and Costanza continued to add new accounts, including the advertising artwork for Tootsie Rolls, requiring the ad-

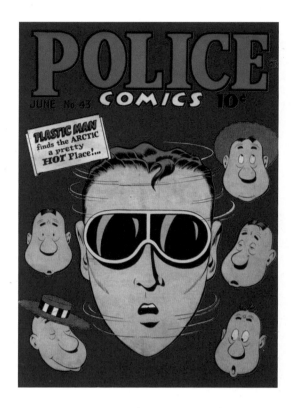

dition of another shop to handle the work, located in Englewood, New Jersey. The consistency and quality of much of the Captain Marvel line of comic books was clearly a result of Beck's and Costanza's hands.[31]

Shops continued to multiply during the 1940s, many lasting only for a short period. One of the last shops was set up by artists Bernard Bailey and Mac Raboy on West 43rd Street. Bailey and Raboy provided opportunities to more up-and-coming artists, including Carmine Infantino, Howie Post, Frank Frazetta, and the peripatetic Eli Katz.[32]

By 1940 *Action Comics* was grossing nearly $1,000,000 a year. By 1943 *Captain Marvel Adventures* was selling almost a million copies per issue. The comics were big business, which was further energized and fueled by the Second World War. The comics were also developing as a craft and as an art. The artists of comic book stories, many of whom started out in shops, were beginning to make their mark. A handful of these artists were creating, defining, and expanding the art of comic book storytelling.

First and foremost among those who helped define just what comic book storytelling was and could be during this period was Jack Kirby. Kirby was born Jacob Kurtzberg in 1917 on New York's lower east side. Kirby's was the same neighborhood that produced Edward G. Robinson and John Garfield, something that was not lost upon him. Kirby always liked to think of himself as a fair, hardworking, but tough guy. Kirby, like most boys growing up in the immigrant bastions of New York City during the 1920s and 1930s, was a child steeped in the movies, pulps, vaudeville, and comic strips of the time.

For kids of this era, these entertainments were their first exposure to art. As a kid, Kirby had been drawn to the funnies and the pulps. By the age of 14 he had enrolled at the Pratt Institute. His tenure there lasted only a week as he "didn't like places with rules."[33] Kirby continued his education on his own, relying on the study of anatomy, comic strips, and anything he could get his hands on. By 1935, he swung a job with Max Fleischer's animation studio, working as an "in-betweener" (drawing the images in between those drawn by other artists to give the effect of motion to a cartoon) on *Popeye*. He then moved on to newspaper strips for a small syndicate called Lincoln Newspaper Features. By 1938 he was working in the comics. Kirby did a stint at the Eisner/Iger shop, and by 1940, he had teamed up with Joe Simon. The two made an interesting counterpoint: Simon was six-foot-three, had attended Syracuse University, and was a natty dresser to boot, while Kirby was five-foot-six, dressed in a nondescript manner, and had graduated from the school of hard knocks. Simon would always be the deal-maker, idea man, and business manager; Kirby was the artist, although he frequently used assistants to get work done on schedule. Simon also pitched in, inking Kirby's work. The en-

ergy and excitement of the stories was all Kirby's. The team's first work was on *Blue Bolt*, then on to *Marvel Boy*. Kirby's breakthrough was with *Captain America*. *Captain America* came at the right place and at the right time, but Kirby's frenetic pacing and the sheer energy of his drawing got everybody looking, from little boys to other artists. Captain America, who wore a red-white-and-blue outfit, was a patriot super-guy, and was beating up German Nazi bad guys even before the United States entered the war. Kirby acknowledged that he had been a fan of Hal Foster, Milton Caniff and Chester Gould, but his work on *Captain America* was that of an artist who had finally found his own voice. The pages from *Captain America* #4, on pages 36-37, demonstrate how Kirby melds one panel into the next, pushing the story forward logically while keeping the pace speeding along. There is nothing unnecessary in his panels, and the draftsmanship is direct and straightforward. Kirby's was not an art of elegance; it was entertaining and had a subtext of pent-up anger that is there for all to see.

Kirby helped set the standard for action/adventure storytelling with *Captain America*. Due to financial disputes with Timely Comics' Martin Goodman, Simon and Kirby left *Captain America* after issue #10. They went on to DC Comics where they turned in topnotch work on the *Manhunter* strip in *Adventure Comics*, where they created the *Newsboy Legion* strip in *Star Spangled Comics*, and the *Boy Commandos* strip in *Detective*. Kirby's work in the business was put on hold when he was drafted, but he returned to become one of the seminal figures in comics.

Just as Kirby's work struck a note of primitive action, Lou Fine's comic book storytelling was the personification of idealized cartoon elegance. Fine understood the dynamics of anatomy and imbued his figures with a flair that has attracted comic artists to his work for the last sixty years. Perhaps one of the most stylish artists ever to work in the comics, Fine's work oozed both energy and finesse. Fine, who was born in 1915, contracted polio when he was a teenager, which forced him into a

--AN HOUR LATER, IN THE HEART OF THE CITY'S BUSIEST TRAFFIC ZONE---

FIVE MINUTES LATER, AND THE AMAZED MOTORISTS ARE WITNESS TO A MAJOR TRAFFIC JAM AS CARS CONVERSE FROM ALL CORNERS!

THE LIGHTS MUST BE STUCK OR SOMETHING! THEY'RE ALL **GREEN**!

NEARBY, THE HENCHMEN OF THE **RAINBOW MAN** EXIT FROM A JEWELRY STORE--

STOP... AAGGH!

RESISTANCE IS FUTILE, OLD MAN!

CUT THE GAB AND GET IN THAT MOTORCYCLE!

THE SMALL VEHICLE EXPERTLY WEAVES ITS WAY THRU THE TANGLED TRAFFIC!

A GREAT IDEA, THE BOSS'S FIXIN' IT SO THAT ALL THE LIGHTS STAY **GREEN**. NOBODY CAN FOLLOW US IN THIS JAM!

EXCEPT THAT MINION OF THE LAW YONDER, AND I AM ARRESTING HIS ACTIVITIES!

THE CRASHING SOUND OF GUNFIRE DRAWS GREG SANDERS, THE **PRAIRIE TROUBADOUR**, TO THE WINDOW OF HIS HOTEL ROOM---

BUSHWHACKERS! LOOKS LIKE A JOB FOR A FELLER I KNOW!

I COULD DO THIS BETTER ON A ROPE--

...AND I THINK I WILL!

POLICE

4

sedentary routine. He turned this limitation into an opportunity and devoted much of his time to reading and studying art and illustration. He studied art at the Grand Central Art School and briefly at the Pratt Institute. Fine was especially impressed by the artwork and illustration of J.C. Leyendecker, Harvey Dunn, Heinrich Kley, and John R. Neill, which was clearly reflected in his work.[34] In 1938, he started work for the Eisner/Iger shop. For the next eight years he worked in the comic book business, producing stories which personified what action/adventure material could be. Fine's forte was in exaggerating his presentation of figures and action, adding an enthusiastic liveliness and vigor to his stories and covers, which made them a blueprint for future comic book storytellers. In his interior pages, the pacing is flawless; the characters in Fine's pages glide through their panels effortlessly. Fine's cover for *Hit* #5 is indicative of how he could turn wrestling underwater with a shark into ballet on the cover of a comic book. Fine turned in many such covers for Fox's *Wonderworld Comics* and other titles for the line, including *Mystery Men* and *Hit*. By 1939 he was working for Busy Arnold at Quality, providing art for the *Black Condor, The Ray, Dollman*, and *Uncle Sam* strips. Fine created conventions for action which were swiped by other artists as the industry stan-

dard. In 1942 when Eisner was drafted, Fine took over duties on *The Spirit*. As can be seen from *The Spirit* page illustrated on page 53, while Fine did scale his style back so as to not conflict with what had already been established for the strip, classic Fine composition is still in evidence throughout the entire page. Another distinguishing feature in Fine's work was his inking of his own work, which for the time was almost unheard of.[35] Fine's use of a Japan brush gave his line a fluid quality which added to the vitality of his drawing. By 1946, Fine had gone on to a successful career in advertising, but his influence lasted well into the Silver Age.

While Kirby's artwork set the standard for frenetic action, and as Fine's draftsmanship espoused a fluid animated line, the artist who

translated the maniacal energy of animation into the pulp pages of comic books was a quiet and unassuming fellow named Jack Cole. Cole distinguished his stories with a surreal and wry sense of humor generally missing in comic books. His storytelling and sense of the bizarre still strikes a chord sixty years after his stories were first created.

Cole was born in New Castle, a small mill town nestled in Western Pennsylvania between Youngstown and Pittsburgh. When he was 15-years-old, like many up-and-coming artists already detailed in these pages, he took the Landon cartoon correspondence class. Not content with New Castle, by the age of 17, he had bicycled to California and back home again. By 1934 he was married and soliciting his cartoons while working at the American Can Factory. Borrowing $500 from relatives in 1937, Cole and his wife took a chance and relocated to New York where Cole took a stab at becoming a freelance cartoonist.[36]

After hearing about the Chesler shop through word of mouth, Cole went for an interview and, on the strength of his samples, landed a job for $20 a week.[37] Chesler's shop was a hotbed of up-and-coming talent and Cole clearly benefited from the experience and the environment. After a stint providing artwork for *Pep Comics* and *Silver Streak Comics*, he landed work with Quality in 1941. It was at Quality that Cole finally hit his stride, providing artwork for the pages of *Smash Comics*, working on a character he had created reminiscent of the Spirit called Midnight. Cole's take on the strip began to look more like a cartoon that had popped off the silver screen than a comic book story.

Cole is best remembered, however, for his creation of Plastic Man in *Police Comics* #1, release dated August, 1941, which came to typify archetypal Cole. Cole worked on other features, but Plas, as he was called in the stories, was his most inspired effort. Plas caught the eye of artists and publishers, including one named Hugh Hefner, who later hired Cole to work at *Playboy*. Cole brought a quirky inventiveness to his stories, which injected his odd take on the world into the fabric of the

stories. Cole's storytelling and pacing owed much to the cinematic cartoon shorts popular in the 1940s and 1950s, which made his work a bright light in the universe of the comic book. Cole would go on to other things, but it was with his stories with Plas that he ignited the imaginations of many of the future artists of the second generation.

The Golden Age produced other artists whose storytelling or artwork served to impress, instruct, and inspire artists working in the comics as well as comic book readers who were wannabe artists. Although Bob Kane and Bill Finger created the Batman (as he was called then), the young Jerry Robinson defined the look and tone of the strip as much as any artist.

Robinson got his start in the comic book business by sheer chance. The story goes that in the summer of 1939, Robinson, a then 17-year-old student, was at a resort waiting to play tennis, wearing a jacket with cartoons he had painted decorating the back. Kane was impressed with the artwork and, upon learning Robinson was the artist, offered him a job as his assistant on the then fledgling *Batman* strip. Robinson, who was an acknowledged fan of strip artists Hal Foster, Milton Caniff, and Chester Gould, over a two year period began to redesign the look and atmosphere of the strip.[38] By 1942, Robinson started to design a series of covers for *Batman* and *Detective,* which gave both titles' line work more depth and visual pizzazz, making the covers compelling advertisements for the strip. Robinson's covers and interior stories were not the result of a formulistic approach but rather were explorations into what could be done with comic book cover illustration and storytelling. The environment in which Robinson and his fellow DC Comics' artists worked was marked by a giddy enthusiasm which reflected a sense of pushing the limits of comic book storytelling coupled with an optimism that they could try just about anything. Robinson observed, "Our vision of Batman was not rooted in realism. Rather, we sought only to incorporate enough accuracy to make the fantasy believable. The stylized sets and distorted backgrounds were metaphors for danger."[39] While this may seem a bit pretentious, looking at the artwork sixty years hence validates Robinson's observations.

The studio where Robinson and other DC artists worked was a hang-out for artists and writers, and it was not unusual for him to work around-the-clock weekends completing work on a story where "beer and darts were the norm."[40] Also important was Robinson's relationship with writer Bill Finger, who became his cultural mentor, taking him to French and German expressionistic films. The atmosphere of these films was to a small extent interpolated into Robinson's storytelling. Robinson also was fascinated by Orson Welles' *Citizen Kane,* which was shot using unusual angles, rapid cutting, and montages, all of which further stimulated his imagination and found their way into *Batman* stories. Robinson would go on to work on other strips in comic books and newspapers, but his most influential work was

done on *Batman.* Robinson realized that comic book storytelling was not illustration and in fact was more effective when it embraced the surreal, and its images relied less on reality and more on imagination. Robinson went so far as to point out that, "We weren't after photographic reality…that sort of realism is re-

strictive, and loses some of the spirit and mystery and excitement."[41] Another important aspect of Robinson's growth was his relationship with Mort Meskin.

Today Meskin is primarily remembered as an artist who influenced other artists. His work after the late 1940s is problematic and usually

BY
E. LECTRON

uneven and uninspired. The work he produced during the early 1940s and with Robinson is another matter. Meskin, an Eisner/Iger alumnus, also worked for the Chesler shop, MLJ, and then DC Comics. While at MLJ, Meskin made Robinson's acquaintance. Robinson was so impressed with Meskin's work that he recommended him to DC Comics editor, Whit Ellsworth, who quickly hired him.[42] In 1941 he drew the premiere of the *Vigilante* strip in *Action* #42, released dated November, 1941. Meskin's pages were beautifully composed and relied on unusual shots and angles. He broke short scenes down into several panels, cutting back and forth to a character's face, coming closer in each panel, at a slightly different angle, to intensify the effect. His approach in cutting and shooting his stories was clearly an influence on Robinson and other artists. After he left DC Comics, he teamed up with Robinson for an inspired partnership which only lasted several years.

The Golden Age produced hundreds of artists who experimented with the comic book page as a compositional device. Despite the fact that it was more profitable and prestigious to work as a newspaper strip artist, comic book storytelling presented imaginative artists with far more possibilities than newspaper strips. For the most part, however, most of the work produced for comic books during this time was just plain bad. The conventions established during this time still present a blueprint for artists today. Two artists who helped further establish action storytelling devices during the Golden Age which were frequently swiped by other artists were Mac Raboy and Reed Crandall.

Emanuel "Mac" Raboy got his art training and did his first work for the Works Progress Administration during the Great Depression. By 1940, he was working for the Harry "A" Chesler shop. Within a year he was turning in simple and elegant work for Fawcett's *Whiz Comics*. Raboy worked on a number of Fawcett superheroes and finally firmly established himself with *Captain Marvel, Jr*. Raboy's drawing was precise and graceful. He also was excruciatingly slow and could never

Soon Crandall was working directly for Arnold at Quality on the *Blackhawk* strip in *Military Comics*. Crandall's *Blackhawk* stories would define his work for the rest of his career. His draftsmanship and ability to handle cinematic action with élan is what makes his work eye catching even today. During his time with Quality, Crandall imbued even less-than-inspired characters and stories with a vitality that has been rarely equaled. Crandall's mastery of how to handle human anatomy in action was not lost upon many youngsters who would become artists in Silver Age.

The range of material produced during the Golden Age was not limited to action and adventure. Humorous strips were also a mainstay, including a number of characters that crossed over from the movies to comic books. These comic books were often referred to as containing "funny animal" strips. Few were memorable from any standpoint, but there were several notable exceptions. Exceptions because the strips could be read on numerous levels by diverse age groups and still be enjoyed. The strips in question involved Donald Duck and his uncle, Scrooge McDuck, and the artist was Carl Barks. Bark's entry into the world of comic books was completely unintended. Barks, who as a kid was attracted to humor newspaper strips like *Happy Hooligan*, *Barney Google*, and *Old Doc Yak,* practiced drawing by copying strip characters. He tried a number of vocations and sold his first gag cartoon in 1929 at the age of 28 to a joke magazine located in Minnesota called *The Calgary Eye Opener.*

The Calgary Eye Opener, which was run on a shoestring, printing bawdy humor, offered Barks a job for $100 a month. Barks, who was living in his home state of Oregon, requested that they wire him the money, packed his bags and moved. In 1935, after answering a newspaper ad, he moved to California, finding work for Walt Disney as an in-betweener. After submitting a gag to Disney's story department, he found full time work there, where his job was to "think of stuff that was funny, and think of it fast!"[43] At Disney, Barks learned the art of pacing; "You don't waste

make his deadlines. To compensate, Raboy composed stock poses of Captain Marvel, Jr. which were photostated and used over and over again. These poses of the young Captain were so effective that they were frequently borrowed by other artists. Raboy's drawing of Captain Marvel, Jr. was also unusual in its depiction of the Captain as being curiously asexual. Raboy's figures often emphasized grace over substance. By 1946, Raboy's work was gone from the comic book pages and he occupied himself for the rest of his career with the *Flash Gordon* Sunday strip.

Reed Crandall, an Eisner/Iger alumnus turned in work while at the shop which was so slick that it caught the eye of Busy Arnold.

any footage in cartoons, you don't waste any pages in comics either…it's important to make the story tight and full of value from one panel to the next."[44]

Barks did his first comic book work on *Four Color* #9, a Donald Duck story, where he shared art chores with Jack Hannah. After quitting Disney for health reasons and deciding to raise chickens, Barks heard that Western Publishing was looking for artists to work on the comic book title *Walt Disney's Comics and Stories.* Barks got the job, and his second story appeared in April, 1943 in issue #31. During Barks' tenure with Donald and his three nephews, he gave the characters personalities and put them in stories (which he scripted) which were funny and satirical. In 1947 he created Uncle Scrooge. Barks deftly paced his stories, which were always immaculately drawn and timed. His work was so effective that it attracted artists who worked in the action/adventure genre. Barks continued to work on the strip for twenty-five years.

Even at this early point in the development of comic book storytelling, the industry had artists whose work was the basis for a shop's style or was swiped by artists throughout the industry. Two artists, who have already been mentioned as shop owners/businessmen and who also had an impact on comic book storytelling as artists, were C.C. Beck and Will Eisner

C.C. Beck ran the shop that supplied Fawcett with its art for the *Captain Marvel* strip, and it was his influence which dominated the strip, the best selling superhero title during the war, even outselling *Superman.* The popularity of the good Captain was due in no small part to Beck's simple, straightforward, cartoon style of storytelling. Beck, who received his art training at Chicago's Academy of Fine Art, handled a host of jobs until he landed employment with Fawcett Publications, which at the time was located in Minnesota, and supplied cartoons for the company's gag magazines. Fawcett moved to New York in 1939 with the idea of getting into comic books. Beck was given the nod to come up with a Superman knock-off, and

while Captain Marvel did have similarities with the man of steel, the tone of the strip and its storytelling were very different. Beck co-created the "big red cheese" with editor/scripter Bill Park, and the strip premiered in *Whiz Comics* #1 with a release date of February, 1940. Beck's storytelling in the early adventures of the Captain helped establish the look of the strip which was told in a crisp, handsome fashion. Beck, a professed admirer of strip artists Chester Gould and Harold Gray, followed their lead in keeping his stories free of excess.[45] As the popularity of Captain Marvel increased, Beck was forced to recruit a staff of artists to keep up with the demand for stories. Nevertheless, he continued to cre-

Will Eisner, pencils and inks, panel from *The Spirit* daily strip, 1941, ©1941 Will Eisner.

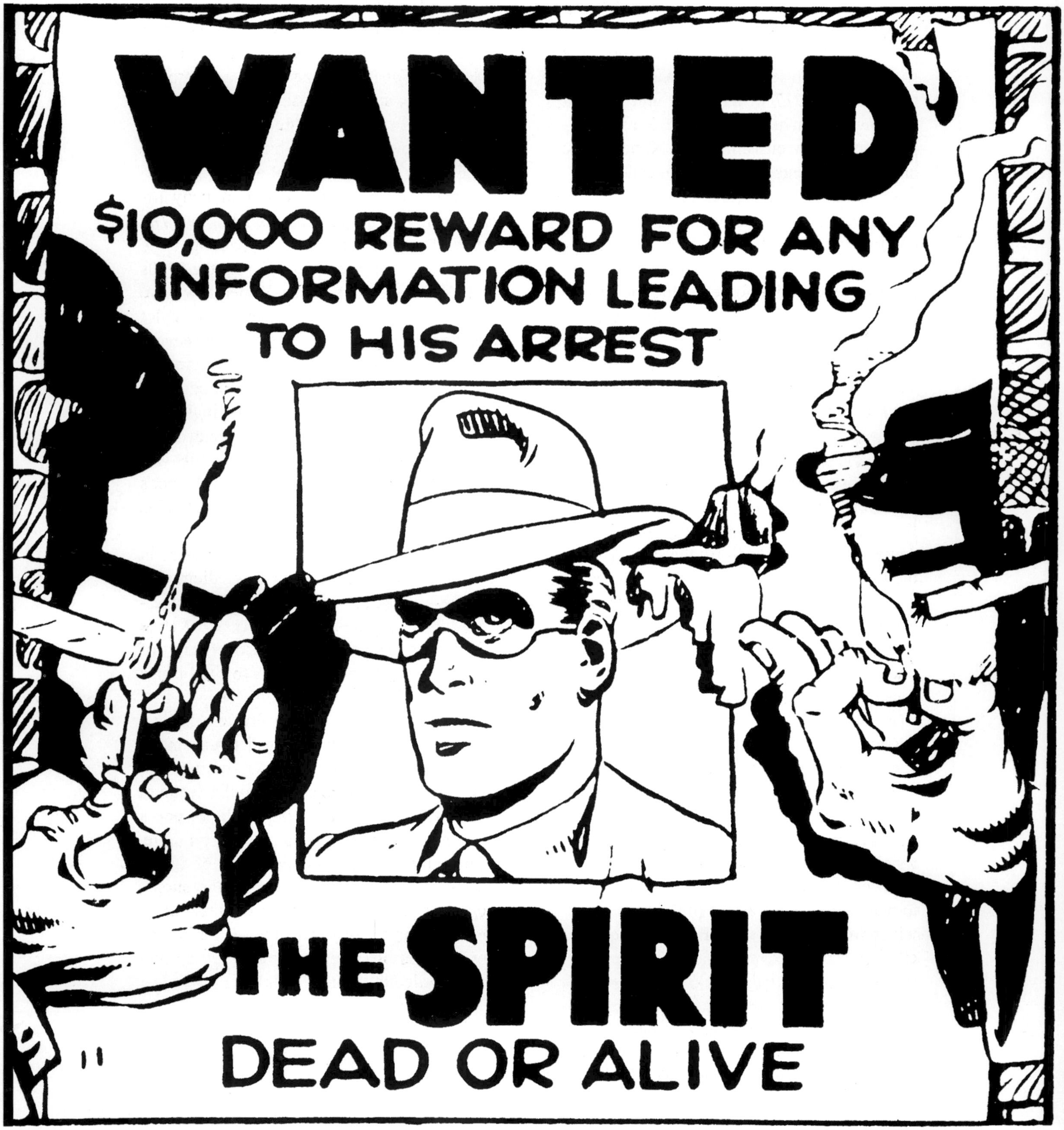
WANTED
$10,000 REWARD FOR ANY INFORMATION LEADING TO HIS ARREST
THE SPIRIT
DEAD OR ALIVE

ate the covers for most Captain Marvel titles, retaining the look of the strip and providing artwork which continued to snare readers.[46]

Will Eisner was another artist who ran a shop and continued to work as an artist. Eisner was born in 1917 in Brooklyn and was out hustling work in his teens. In 1936, after hearing from fellow classmate Bob Kane that he had sold drawings to a magazine called *Wow*, Eisner found their offices and after a little salesmanship got an assignment for his first comic book story. *Wow's* publisher was Jerry Iger, Eisner's future partner. Although Eisner's place as the creative force behind the Eisner/Iger shop is well known, his reputation as an artist lies with the strip he created for Busy Arnold, *The Spirit*. While Eisner did create the strip, he only drew it from its premiere in 1940 until he entered the service in 1942 (his last strip appearing on November 8, 1942), when Jack Cole and Lou Fine intermittently took over chores on the feature.[47] Eisner did return to the strip in December, 1945 after he finished his tour of duty, but he frequently used a number of ghosts to finish the strip. During the late 1940s and until *The Spirit* closed up shop in 1952, Eisner directed his energies toward his educational publication, *P.S. The Preventative Maintenance Monthly* created under contract for the Department of Defense.[48] In the twelve year life of the strip, Eisner took it from being rather ordinary to becoming a forum to try unusual logo designs, layout, and quirky plots. When the agreement was made for Eisner to come up with the strip, it was expected he would come up with a superhero, but Eisner was bored with such material, and when he designed the character, he only begrudgingly gave him a mask and gloves to placate the expectations of the newspapers which would run the strip. Eisner is frequently cited as a pioneer in the creative use of the splash or opening page of a comic book story, but this is only partially correct because his splash pages had to double as covers for the feature, as it was inserted into a newspaper and the splash was the cover. The first page had to grab the reader, and after Eisner's return from service in the Second World War,

many of his splashes became textbook examples of how to pull a reader into a story. Eisner's stubbornness in refusing to water down the strip contributed to his ability to develop *The Spirit*.[49] Eisner also again proved himself to be an astute businessman by seeing to it that when the strip stopped publication the rights reverted back to him.

Eisner's more thoughtful approach to design and content was not lost upon many artists in the second generations who read *The Spirit*. However, his overall impact upon the second generation, and later during the 1950s and 1960s, is problematic. Eisner may have created the strip and overseen many of its plot and design elements, but he did not leave a distinguishable imprint upon the comics, merely various suggestions of what could be done with storytelling. Eisner was singled out only in the 1970s, and later, as a contributor to the art of the comics. To many, this was revisionism which did not represent Eisner's influence at the time and immediately after his exit from comic books.[50]

The first generation of artists to work in comic books were thrust into the medium with no rules. These artists created stories and artwork which demonstrated a diversity of style which ranged from the aggressive energy of Kirby to the elegance of Fine to the bizarre slapstick of Basil Wolverton's strips. The shops, in an effort to quickly create a product to satisfy an ever increasing demand, made things up as they went along. As we have seen, the mature artists who came into the business had as their goal getting out of the business and on to better things as soon as possible. The many young kids enamored of funny books, who went on to work in the shops, populating the ranks of the second generation, would go on to further shape and define the conventions of comic book storytelling and have a little fun in the process.

NOTES

[1] Many comic book historians instead opt for the first appearance of Superman in *Action* #1 in 1938 as the beginning of the Golden Age.

[2] Historians of comic books love to argue about "firsts." What constitutes the first comic book is one of their favorites. For all practical intents and purposes, however, the forerunners to the American comic book which can be associated with the first comic books commercially available to American kids first appeared in 1933.

[3] Mike Benton, *The Comic Book in America*, Tyler Publishing Company, 1989.

[4] To give readers of this book a chronological perspective as to when various comic books hit the newsstands and were in the hot little hands of their audience, the "release date" of the titles noted are given. Keep in mind, though, that comic books traditionally had a release date which was usually several months after they were actually available. As a comic book with a release date of, say, October, may have been actually distributed in July, it also gave the comic book a longer "shelf life."

[5] Ibid. See also: Ron Goulart, *Ron Goulart's Great History of Comic Books,* Contemporary Books, 1986*; The Overstreet Comic Book Price Guide*, Thirty-third Edition, Random House, 2003.

[6] Ron Goulart, *Ron Goulart's Great History of Comic Books*.

[7] *Overstreet Comic Book Price Guide*, Thirty-third Edition.

[8] Interview with Gil Kane.

[9] A packager would put together a complete comic book for a publisher. The publisher would have the book printed and sold under its name.

[10] Gary Groth interview with Joe Kubert, *The Comics Journal* #172, November, 1994; Gary Groth interview with Creig Flessel, *The Comics Journal* #245, August, 2002; Interview with Gil Kane; Todd Severin interview with Fred Gaurdineer, *Comic Book Marketplace* #79, June, 2000.

[11] Interview with Will Eisner. Fred Gaurdineer pointed out, however, that artists working for the Eisner/Iger shop who freelanced were required to give a percentage of their fees to Eisner and Iger, Severin interview with Gaurdineer, *Comic Book Marketplace* #79.

[12] *Encyclopedia of American Comics*, Facts on File, 1990.

[13] Interview with Will Eisner.

[14] Ibid.

[15] Ron Goulart, *Focus on Jack Cole*, Fantagraphics, 1986.

[16] Cat Yronwode, "When Partners Collide," *Will Eisner Quarterly* #4, January, 1985.

[17] Interview with Gil Kane. See also: Ron Goulart, *Ron Goulart's Great History of Comic Books*.

[18] Mike Benton, *Superhero Comics of the Golden Age*, Tyler Publishing Company, 1992.

[19] Ron Goulart, *Ron Goulart's Great History of Comic Books*.

[20] Boring had already provided ghosting talent for Shuster when he pencilled and inked *Slam Bradley* and *Federal Men* for Wheeler-Nicholson's titles.

[21] Roy Thomas interview with Jack Burnley, *Alter Ego* #2, Autumn, 1999. Burnley also turned in work on Batman.

[22] Will Murray interview with Jerry Robinson, *Comic Book Marketplace* #70, August, 1999.

[23] Jerry Robinson, "Foreword," *Batman Archives* #3, DC Comics, 1994.

[24] Interview with Gil Kane. Gary Groth interview with Carmine Infantino, *The Comics Journal* #191, November, 1996. Correspondence with Alex Toth.

[25] Julius Schwartz with Brian M. Thomsen, *Man of Two Worlds*, Harper Entertainment, 2002. Interview with Julius Schwartz.

[26] In 1946 Gaines sold his interests in All American to DC Comics, which consolidated the products of both companies. DC Comics had marketed All American under its logo; now it owned both companies. Mayer continued to work for DC Comics, editing the All American line of comic books until he left to

work on his own strip.

[27] See: Roy Thomas, "The Torch that Lit the Way," *Reprint of Marvel Comics #1*, Marvel Comics, 1990; Ron Goulart, "Golden Age Sweatshops," *The Comics Journal #249*, December, 2002.

[28] Interview with Will Eisner. See also: Cat Yronwode interview with Will Eisner, *The Comics Journal #89*, March, 1984.

[29] Interview with Gil Kane. See also: John Coates interview with Kurt Schaffenberger, *Comic Book Marketplace #59*, May, 1998.

[30] Schaffenberger worked initially for the Binder shop, drawing Captain Marvel, Captain Marvel, Jr., Spy Smasher, and Ibis, to name a few. He was drafted in 1942, and after the war he returned to work for C.C. Beck's shop. The shop closed in 1952.

[31] James Steranko, *The Steranko History of Comics*, Vol. #2, Supergraphics, 1972.

[32] Interview with Gil Kane.

[33] Gary Groth interview with Jack Kirby, *The Comics Journal # 134*, February, 1990.

[34] "Eisner and Fox on Lou Fine," *Will Eisner's Quarterly #2*, Spring, 1984.

[35] Fine did not always ink his own work, however, and he was aided by many able and not so able collaborators.

[36] Press release, autobiographical summary issued by the Chicago Sun-Times Syndicate to promote Cole's newspaper strip, *Betsy and Me*.

[37] Ron Goulart, *Focus on Jack Cole*.

[38] Will Murray interview with Jerry Robinson, *Comic Book Marketplace #70*, August, 1999. See also: Jerry Robinson, "Foreword," *Batman Archives #3*.

[39] Ibid.

[40] Ibid.

[41] Ibid.

[42] Ibid.

[43] Michael Naiman interview with Carl Barks, *Oversteet's Golden Age Quarterly #2*, October/December, 1993. See also: John Stanley interview with Carl Barks, *The Comics Journal #250*, February, 2003.

[44] Ibid.

[45] Harold Gray was the creator of the *Little Orphan Annie* strip.

[46] See generally: C.C. Beck, "The Captain's Chief," *Alter Ego #2*, Autumn, 1999.

[47] The strip also ran as a daily from October 10, 1941-1944. The strip also ran in Quality Comics and in Fox Comics.

[48] Interview with Will Eisner.

[49] Cat Yronwode, "When Partners Collide," *Will Eisner's Quarterly #4*.

[50] Howard Chaykin, "Introduction," *The Complete Classic Adventures of Zorro*, 2nd Edition, Image, 2002.

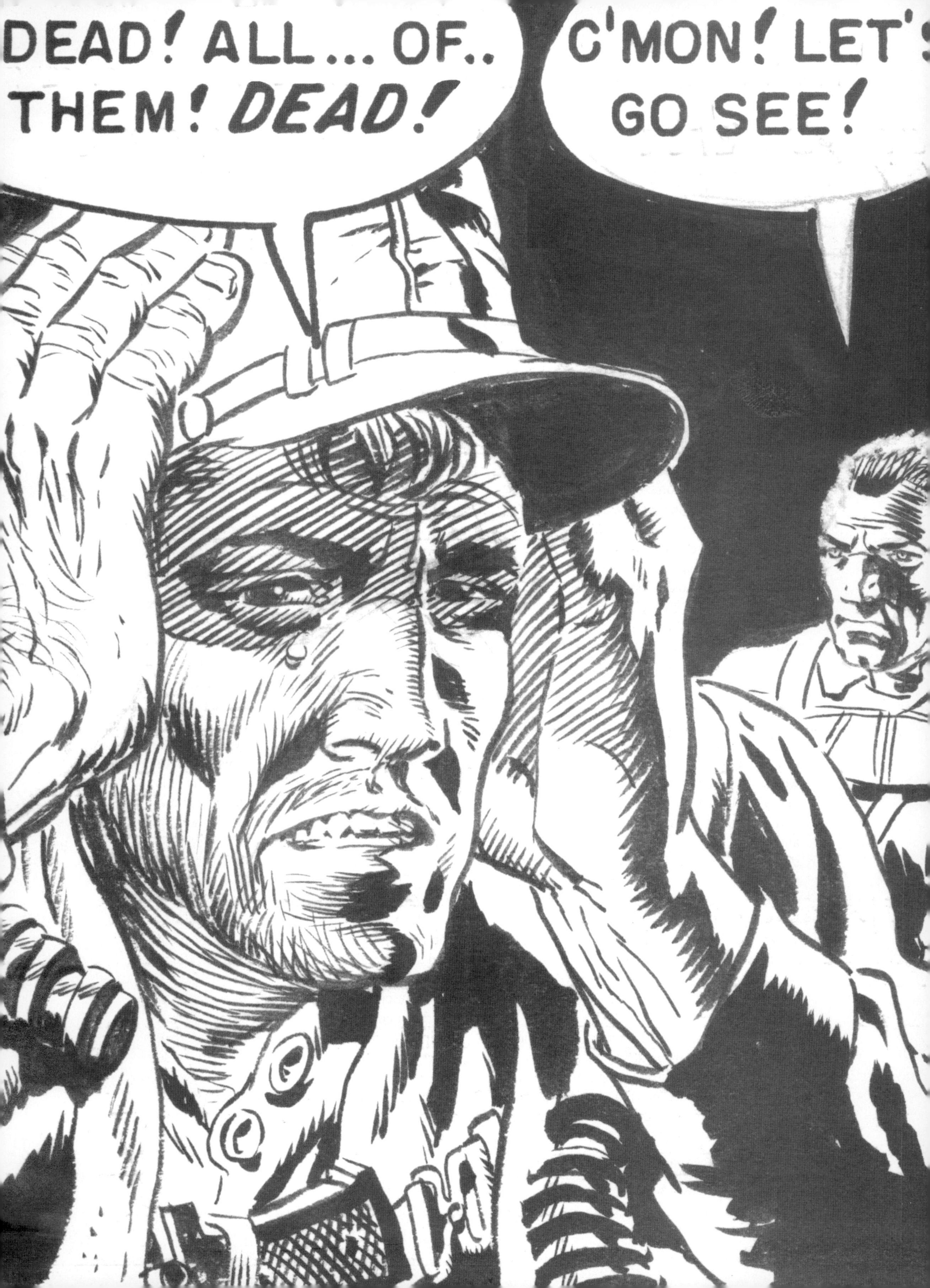
DEAD! ALL... OF.. THEM! DEAD!
C'MON! LET'S GO SEE!

3 THE WAR ENDS; TROUBLE FOR SUPERHEROES; THE SECOND GENERATION COMES OF AGE; THE EC REVOLUTION; CRISES FOR THE INDUSTRY; JACK KIRBY, ACT II

The Second World War was over, those artists who had survived the conflict were returning home but the welcome they had anticipated from the comic book industry, of finding quick, steady work, never materialized. After the war sales of superhero titles were beginning to drop, although Captain Marvel and Superman-related comic books were still doing well.[1] Comic books were still selling briskly, but publishers were searching for new genres. The atmosphere in the industry, however, at least as far as the artists were concerned, was chilly.[2]

Many of the artists who would drive the second generation and the development of comic book storytelling in the decade to follow were now demobilizing and looking for work. These artists included Murphy Anderson, Dan Barry, Gene Colan, Gil Kane, Bernard Krigstein, Harvey Kurtzman, Curt Swan, and Wally Wood. Other artists who stayed stateside during the war were also ready to fuel the art of comic books. Their ranks included Joe Kubert, Carmine Infantino, and Alex Toth. But things had radically changed. By the late 1940s the shops were going out of business. Artists were now applying directly to publishers who were paying better rates than the shops and already had staffs and little or no work available.

The emphasis in the industry would now be to produce humor strips in the vein of *Archie*, romance comics, good girl titles (scantily attired young women), and crime stories. The paper shortages of the war were over; pro-duction could now increase, but there was an air of caution in the industry. This atmosphere, however, did not limit the content of the books being produced.

The war had changed more than just the market. Many artists now had some concept of their importance to the industry, and an abortive attempt was made to unionize in 1946. A second attempt was started in late 1951 which led to the formation of the Society of Comic Book Illustrators, but it too failed to catch on and folded without gaining a foothold in the business. The widely held sentiment among many artists was that those associated with the union were frozen out of work.[3]

Despite all these things, the young artists who had started in the shops in their teens were still interested in returning to draw stories for the comics. Of the many artists to begin anew, two in particular led the direction for setting the standards to which many of the second generation of artists would look for inspiration. These two artists were Dan Barry and Alex Toth.

Born in 1923, Barry started in comics in the 1940s, first assisting artist George Mandel and then Mandel's brother, Alan. When Barry returned from service in the Air Force, he began a quick rise to the top, first providing artwork for comic books and later for the *Tarzan* strip and then for the *Flash Gordon* strip. Barry, as with many of his peers, had made the rounds among the shops showing his samples, trying to drum up work. Barry's work in the early 1940s was generally undistin-

This page and the next: Dan Barry, pencils and inks, original artwork from two interior pages and the splash page from a *Vigilante* story, *Action* #150, November, 1950, ©1950 DC Comics.

guished; his work during the late 1940s was another matter. Between 1946 and 1947 he drew stories for a number of different publishers, including Lev Gleason and DC Comics, where he focused on crime comics, western comics, and a few superheroes thrown in for good measure. What distinguished his storytelling was its clean, uncluttered look. Barry developed a style which allowed him to reduce his drawing to a series of shorthand effects, which gave the impression of detail and substance. Barry did not try to turn his cartoon stories into illustration. There was no pretense in his work, and the stories he created during this time were so attractive that many other artists and editors took notice of what he was offering.[4] DC Comics editors pointed to Barry as an example to be followed. Barry's brother Sy worked as an inker on his sibling's work, as well as with a host of other artists using the opportunity to impart similar effects to their artwork. His influence was felt well into the 1960s with what has been generally referred to as the DC Comics house style.[5] This style was not monolithic, however, as a diverse group of talent was being recruited by DC Comics which would set many standards for the industry.

Another artist, whose influence is still widely felt in comic books today, was one of several talented storytellers hired by Shelly Mayer to work at All American: Alex Toth. Mayer's instincts, and his eye for material and talent, were impeccable. Toth, who was born in New York City in 1928, is one of the great mavericks of the comic book business. He has his own way of doing things and is very opinionated about everything, especially his work. He went to the High School of Industrial Arts and began shopping his wares around in 1944. By the age of 15, he had started to find work in the business. In 1947 at the suggestion of Joe Kubert and Lee Elias, Toth went to see Mayer, and he was in. Toth's experiences with Mayer gave him a secure grounding in storytelling. Toth has characterized Mayer as his "mentor" who was "the first and only really creative and knowledgeable comics editor I've worked for in all these years in

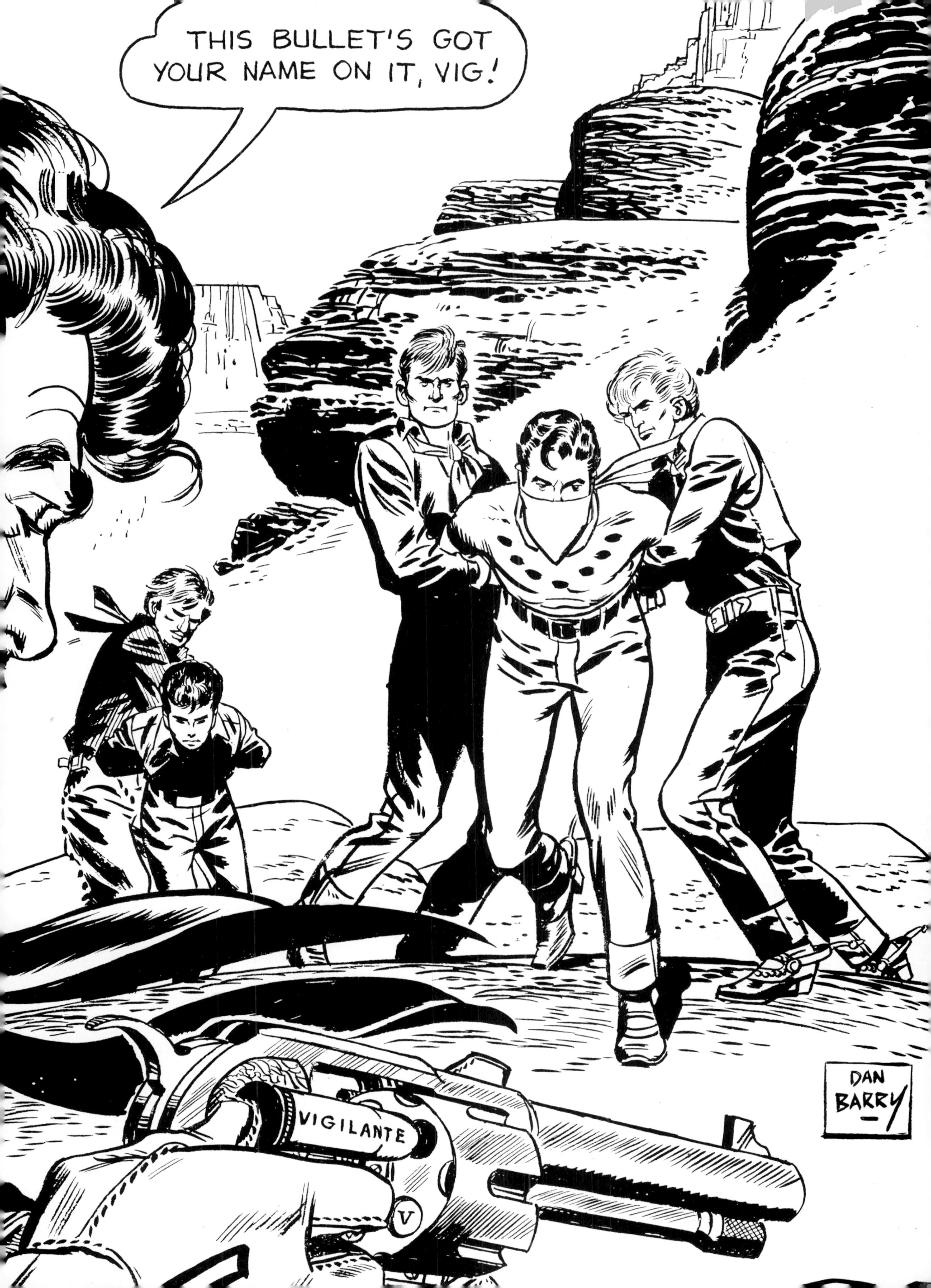
THIS BULLET'S GOT YOUR NAME ON IT, VIG!
DAN BARRY
VIGILANTE
V

the field."[6]   Toth's style of storytelling was a conscious analysis of a mélange of sources. He looked and thought about comic artists ranging from Irwin Hasen, Milton Caniff, Frank Robbins, Jerry Robinson, Fred Kida, Mort Meskin, and Dan Barry. He ruminated on illustrators the like of John McDermott, Peter Helck, Al Dorne, and Austin Briggs. Most importantly he studied Noel Sickles. Toth first discovered Sickles through reprints in the comic book *Famous Funnies*, which reprinted the strip, even though he could not make out the name of the artist. Later, after seeing Sickles' illustrations in *Life* magazine, Toth made the connection which fueled his career-long fascination with the artist. The lessons that Toth took from Sickles to make the drawing simple and direct, to make body language natural, and to use inking effects rather than detail to give the feeling of reality distinguished his storytelling and make it immedi-

ately recognizable. The four interior pages on this page and the next, all attest to Toth's direct, straightforward design and his very sophisticated method of storytelling.

Toth worked on a number of genres at All American, including mystery and crime, westerns, and superheroes. His approach and style while at All American was still developing. Toth matured quickly, and his work shifted to the non-superhero variety. By the end of 1947 superhero comic books were out; the trend was toward mystery and crime, westerns, and romance.[7] Toth went on to define how to tell a romance story for comic books while working for Standard (an imprint of Better Publications) in the 1950s. Toth also worked with war stories and crime material.   Forget about the plots, which are bad B-movie wannabes, and look at the storytelling. The page illustrated here (on the left side of page 63) from the story *The Crushed Gardenia* is a perfect

Below: Alex Toth, pencils and inks, interior page, *Who is Next* #5, January, 1953. Alex Toth, pencils, John Celardo, inks, interior page, *This is War* #9, May, 1953, ©1953 Standard.

example of Toth's approach. With a minimum of detail in a three panel sequence, he establishes the tone of what is to come. The fourth panel, showing the emotionally confused girl, only shows the tops of the hands of the character who will drive the story. The cropping of the hands is cinematic and adds an unexpected tension to the composition. Most artists would have shown the other character in the frame; Toth knew that all the reader had to see was the girl's expression juxtaposed against the hands to make his point. When the obviously unbalanced would-be boyfriend goes into an uncontrollable rage in the sixth panel, all we see again is his hand on the shoulder of his victim. Again, this is a framing technique used in cinematography and was not used in the comic books until Toth advocated the use of such thoughtful composition. The finishing panel is naturally composed, the antithesis of a superhero slugfest, and feels like

it is really happening; the body movements are natural and fluid. By 1954, Toth had been drafted to serve in the Korean war, but he would be back, and his influence would linger in the minds of every comic book artist who was seriously interested in the art of comic book storytelling.

While not nearly as influential as Barry and Toth, another artist, Lee Elias, also proved to be a prominent advocate of Milton Caniff's style of lighting and composition. Elias was born in 1920 in Great Britain. He was not only an artist but also a skilled violinist. Elias studied art at Cooper Union and the Art Students League and started in the business in 1943. His work at Harvey after the war, especially on the movie star, masked crime-fighter Black Cat, drew the attention of many of his peers. His control of blacks and solid inking ability was an eloquent argument for transplanting the Caniff style to comic books. He

Kubert, born in 1926 in Poland, emigrated to the United States with his parents when he was two months old. Kubert's father was a kosher butcher, and the family took up residence in Brooklyn. He has observed that as a kid, comic strips were his "world." Like most boys of the mid-1930s, he was especially fond of the work of Hal Foster, Alex Raymond, and Milton Caniff. In 1938 he swung his first unofficial job with MLJ by going to the publisher with an armful of samples wrapped in newspaper. Kubert picked up as much as he could from the artists working there, including Irv Novick. While at MLJ, Kubert also picked up a trick or two from Bob Montana, who a few years later created Archie Andrews, the teenager from Riverdale, who fueled the *Archie* line of comic books. Within two years he was working in the Harry "A" Chesler shop while also attending the High School of Music and Art.[8] During these early years he also inked the work of Jack Kirby and Lou Fine, which gave him experience working on the artwork of two of the best artists of the period and valuable insight into their penciling and composition methods. By 1944 Kubert was working on a

went on in 1952 to create, with science fiction writer Jack Williamson, the Sunday-only newspaper strip *Beyond Mars*. Although the strip only ran until 1955, it established Elias as an artist in his own right with his creation of an interesting variation on Caniff's style which could stand on its own. Unfortunately, after the demise of the strip, Elias' work was never able to recapture the sparkle or flair of his earlier efforts.

In addition to mentoring Toth, Mayer also brought Carmine Infantino on board to work at All American in 1946. In 1947 Mayer hired Gil Kane. As we have already seen, Mayer had hired Joe Kubert in 1944. More than any other artists from the second generation, Kane, Kubert, and Infantino would drive and define the look of action/adventure comic book storytelling in the 1960s.

Of these three artists, Kubert had started apprenticing in the business earliest at the age of 11 and was considered a child prodigy.

Left: Gil Kane, pencils and inks, original cover artwork, *All-American Western* #120, June/July, 1951. Below: Gil Kane, pencils, Bernie Sachs, inks, original interior page artwork, *All-Star Western* #59, June/July, 1951, ©1951 DC Comics.

sign), rubbing elbows with Gil Kane, Frank Giacoia, Mike Sekowsky and many others who aspired to become artists as well as comic book storytellers. As the school was on 42nd Street in Manhattan, Infantino took the subway everyday to go to this experimental vocational school. In his first year in high school, Infantino spent the summer apprenticing at the Harry "A" Chesler shop. Infantino put his experience at the Chesler shop to good use, and within a year he had swung a job working for Quality. At Quality he erased marks from pages and used white out to touch up artwork and, in the process, "saw the likes of Reed Crandall's *Blackhawks* come in...saw the...work of Eisner and Fine, and all sorts of wonderful artwork."[10] Infantino continued to make the rounds working for different publishers until he and Giacoia went to DC Comics where they were steered to All American and Shelly Mayer.[11] Mayer advised both aspiring artists that their work was competent enough to get them jobs but that six more months of study would do them "a world of

superhero called Hawkman. He turned in fairly sophisticated work which had interesting lighting effects, thoughtful staging, and solid storytelling. His work would quickly mature, and by the mid-1950s he had developed a distinct style which was supported by his skillful and fluent technique with a pen and a brush. Kubert never labored under any illusions about being an artist of comic book stories. He once commented that it was "a way to make money, that's all. Pure and simple. Nobody was proud of being a comic book artist. Matter of fact, it was a couple of steps below digging ditches..."[9] Despite these sentiments, which were held by many other comic book artists, Kubert's mature work was the product of a consummate professional with a highly developed personal style of comic book storytelling, but more about that in the next chapter.

Carmine Infantino was born in Brooklyn in 1925 and attended the School of Industrial Arts (now called the School of Art and De-

Lee Elias, pencils and inks, original artwork, *Beyond Mars*, June 22, 1952, ©1952 Lee Elias.

good."[12]   Giacoia went right to work, but Infantino spent the next six months honing his skill, and when he returned, Mayer kept his word. Infantino would now work in an environment populated by Barry, Toth, and Kubert which had a significant impact on the development of his style and approach to storytelling. During the late 1940s, Infantino's work was strongly derivative of Caniff's style. As the 1950s moved forward, his focus on design became more acute and his cartooning began to take on a much more individual tone. By the end of the 1950s, he had evolved a very singular style of drawing, layout, and design which came into full bloom in the 1960s.

The last of these three artists, Gil Kane, while the slowest to develop, ultimately became one of the most influential storytellers of the second generation. Kane, who started out life as Eli Katz, was born in 1926 in Riga, Latvia. In 1930 he and his family moved to New York where he grew up in the Jewish immigrant neighborhood of Brownsville in Brooklyn. Kane, like many of his fellow artists got his first exposure to art through reading newspaper funnies and comic books. He started shopping his samples around when he was 15, and one year later during his summer vacation, he finally landed a job in the production department at MLJ. The job was not glamorous, finishing artwork by putting in word balloons and borders on panels, but it got his foot in the door. Within three weeks, Kane had been dumped, and he quickly got a job working as a penciler for Jack Binder. Within a week, however, Kane was reoffered employment at MLJ, this time with an increase in salary. This began the typical odyssey of comic artists: bouncing from one shop or publisher to the next.

As we have seen, these youthful and aspiring artists who populated the second generation all gained experience in the same venues. Indeed, Kane observed that as he found new jobs he would always run into many of the same artists, which created a strange camaraderie.[13] Kane has acknowledged that his youthful work was extremely rough, but he was dedicated to improving and aggressive in

finding as much work as he could handle. Through this persistence and the improvement of his level of competence, he had an opportunity to work for Simon and Kirby, with assignments pencilling stories for their DC Comics strips. This gave him an inside look at Kirby's composition dynamics and allowed him to pick the older and more experienced artist's brain. Kane, while not socially friendly with Kirby, talked with him at length about a range of things, including the art of the comics. It was through this association that Kane became familiar with Mort Meskin which further added to his education. Kane also found work in Bernard Bailey's shop which precipitated his team-up with Infantino. Kane and Infantino produced strips, Kane penciling and Infantino inking, for several different shops and for DC Comics. The partnership was

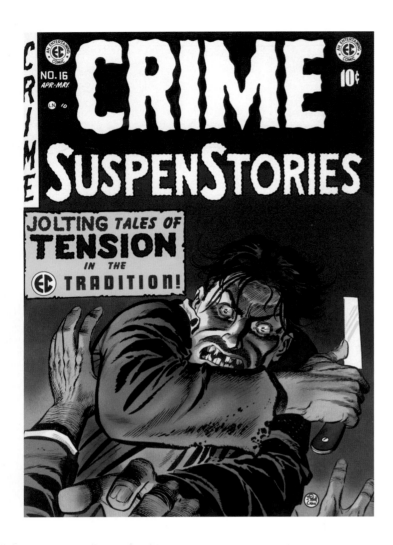

without the finesse or elegance. Kane was trying to consciously improve his craft, but that would come in the 1960s.

The late 1940s and early 1950s witnessed an influx of new blood into the ranks of aspiring comic book artists. Many of these artists had grown up reading comic books but had no connection to the shops or the first generation. The artists who began to field work in the business in the late 1940s/early 1950s included John Buscema, Steve Ditko, Jerry Grandenetti, Russ Heath, Joe Maneely, and John Romita. Many journeyman, too numerous to mention, also started grinding out undistinguished work for the many titles filling the racks at newsstands, drug stores, and airports. There were also artists who had their heyday during this time working in one genre, turning out products that were attractive but narrow in breadth and scope.

The most interesting of these artists were Matt Baker and Walt Kelly. In content and style, Baker and Kelly represented the extreme

short-lived due to competitiveness and clashing personalities. By 1943 Kane had quit The School of Industrial Arts, even though he was in his senior year, to dedicate himself to work, full time, as an artist of comic book stories. By 1944 Kane, like many of his colleagues, was drafted. After nineteen months in the service he returned to start anew in December, 1945. His work ever improving, Mayer hired Kane at All American in 1947, which only lasted for six months. By 1949 Kane began a relationship with DC Comics editor Julius Schwartz, which would last for the rest of his career and which would propel him to star status as a comic book artist.[14] During the 1950s at DC Comics, he pencilled stories in the mystery/detective, western, science fiction, and adventure genres. Kane occasionally did a story or two for others publishers as well, but the majority of his output was for DC Comics. The development of Kane's style was due in no small part to his exposure to the influence of Toth and Barry. His work in the 1950s also showed the influence of Lou Fine, but

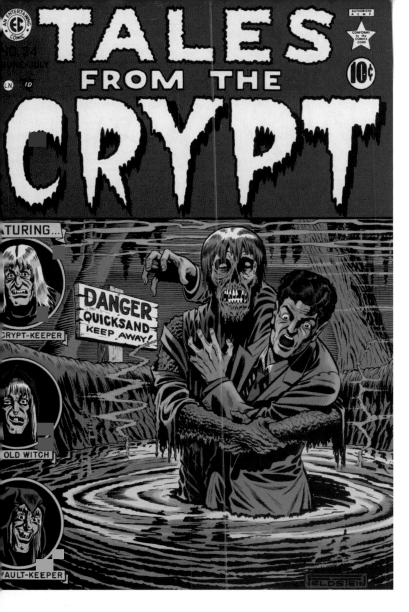

Left: Al Feldstein, pencils and inks, cover, *Tales from the Crypt* #24, June/July, 1951. Below: Al Feldstein, pencils and inks, cover, *Weird Fantasy* #13, May/June, 1952, ©1951 and 1952 William M. Gaines.

and slogans, such as "The Greatest Name in Comics," and stories full of violence and bloodletting, complete with sexy girls and unusual methods of dispatching characters. After the war, Biro hired Dan Barry, and the result was some extremely handsome work. Biro was impossible to work for, and he and Barry were constantly at odds. Alex Toth reports that the two were, "two monumental egos clashing like thunderheads."[15] Despite the backbiting atmosphere at Gleason, Barry turned in inspired work on a number of stories. In 1952 Lev Gleason got in touch with Toth and pitched him the idea of doing a comic book to simulate CinemaScope. The result was an odd comic book with panels with a slightly distorted aspect ratio. The storytelling, using double-tone craftint paper was another of Toth's effective homages to Sickles and more evidence that Toth had developed an independent and individual voice as a storyteller. The artwork on page 62, is an example from that book, *Crime and Punishment* #66. Toth's

diversity of what was available to readers of the comics. Baker drew pretty "good girls" in a variety of adventures, usually with as little clothing as was allowable by the standards of the time. Kelly was the creator of the philosophic possum, Pogo. Pogo and his friends from the swamp eventually found their way to newspapers as a strip, but they had their first exposure in a solo-only comic book in 1946.

Publishers were looking for the next hot genre, and for a while crime and mystery comics seemed the ticket. The move away from fantasy/superhero stories gave many artists an opportunity to develop their craft more completely than with costumed crime fighters. One publisher infamous for its crime, western, and romance comics was Lev Gleason (Gleason named his company after himself). At Gleason, artist and editor Charles Biro was a dominant voice in making successful such books as *Daredevil* and *Crime Does Not Pay*. Biro was famous for his bombastic headlines

use of cinematic angles, coupled with the shadowing given by the double-tone paper, creates a film noir feel in comic book form. With such work, comic books were clearly reaching well beyond their origins as pabulum for kids and into new territory.

Since artists were constrained by the material they were hired to produce, there were few avenues available for any type of experimentation. The comic book business was about getting a product on newsstands, not fostering creativity. Despite this reality of the business an interesting experiment was on the horizon, which due to the politics of the era and the missteps of its publisher would fail, but which would serve as an example of what comic books might someday aspire to be: EC Comics.

Max C. Gaines had been in the comic book business from its beginning but had ambitions of being completely independent. In 1945 Gaines sold his interests in All American to

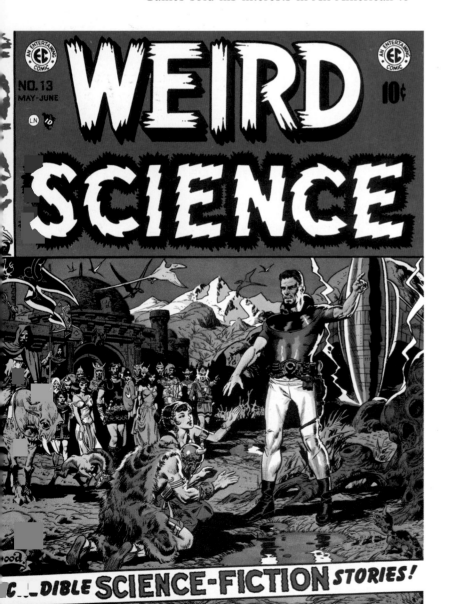

DC Comics for $500,000 after taxes. Within two weeks after closing the deal, he created a new company called Educational Comics, identified by the bulleted letters EC, to sell a new line of comic books.[16] Gaines did keep some of his non-superhero titles from the sale of All American which included *Tiny Tot Comics* and the *Picture Stories* series. Unfortunately these wholesome comic books did not prove attractive to kids having to plunk down their dimes at newsstands or drug stores. Gaines' greatest successes had been based on the advice and instincts of Shelly Mayer, who stayed on at DC Comics. In 1947, Gaines died accidentally in a boating mishap which thrust his then 25-year-old son, William, into the family business. Fortunately for William Gaines, artist Al Feldstein soon came on board at EC. It was through Feldstein and his close relationship with Gaines that the small debt-ridden company would rise to a unique position as an innovator in the business.

Feldstein, who was born in 1925, started work for the Jerry Iger shop while a student at the High School of Music and Art. After high school he attended the Art Students League and Brooklyn College. With the looming threat of the draft, he enlisted in the Air Force where he wound up painting cartoon military road signs and pretty girls on airplane noses. After the war he returned to work for Iger and then freelanced and packaged entire books. Through his letterer he heard that the business manager at EC, Sol Cohen, was looking for an artist for a teenage comic book. Feldstein took his samples and met with Gaines, who liked what he saw. Out of this meeting came an unusual deal: Feldstein would write, draw and deliver three complete comic books and in exchange he would receive a fee and a percentage. The contract was signed, and Feldstein began work. He then received a call from Gaines that they had to talk. Feldstein went down to EC's offices and Gaines told him, "The bottom is falling out of the market for these kinds of books, even though we have a contract it would be bad for both of us if you continue working and we can't make any money." Gaines explained that if he put out the books with no market, it would be a financial drain for him, and "it would be an end to our association." Feldstein considered his options, told Gaines he felt comfortable with him and wanted to work with him, and tore up the contract.[17]

Up until Feldstein's coming on board, EC had been following the trends in the comic book industry, but now that would change. Feldstein and Gaines were now working closely everyday on new concepts and ideas. After work they would socialize and continue to share opinions. Gaines would reminisce about how he was a science fiction and horror fan, and Feldstein would in turn talk about his great affection for horror movies and radio shows. Feldstein remembers, "...so I said to Bill, we should set the trends not follow them, why are we always copying someone else's ideas when we could be leading the way, let's do a real horror comic book that will really scare the pants off kids, like Arch Oboler's old radio programs like *The Witch's Tale*, *Lights Out*, or *Inner Sanctum*."[18] After reflect-

...OR MY WORLD CAN BE UGLY. IT CAN BE A WORLD OF INVASIONS FROM OUTER SPACE BY HORRIBLE INTELLIGENT ALIENS BENT ON CONQUERING MY WORLD... COMING ACROSS SPACE IN FLEETS OF FLYING SAUCERS...

...LANDING AT NIGHT AND ENTERING MY CITIES AND KILLING AND MAIMING AND DESTROYING...

MY WORLD IS WHAT I CHOOSE TO MAKE IT. MY WORLD IS YESTERDAY...

...OR TODAY...

...OR TOMORROW...

FOR MY WORLD IS THE WORLD OF SCIENCE-FICTION... CONCEIVED IN MY MIND AND PLACED UPON PAPER WITH PENCIL AND INK AND BRUSH AND SWEAT AND A GREAT DEAL OF LOVE FOR MY WORLD. FOR I AM A SCIENCE-FICTION ARTIST. MY NAME IS WOOD...

THE END

ing on Feldstein's recommendation, Gaines gave him a green light. Feldstein accordingly created characters to introduce and tell his stories: The Crypt-Keeper, The Old Witch, and The Vault-Keeper. These characters appeared in EC's new line of horror comic books, which debuted in 1950. Gaines would work on concepts called "springboards," which he and Feldstein would then flesh out. Feldstein, then, without a script, would completely develop the idea, creating the dialogue and narration, directly writing it onto the art boards used by

the artists. More importantly, Feldstein conceptualized the stories with specific artists in mind, taking into consideration the graphic strengths and weaknesses each artist might bring to a story. Feldstein also assembled a sterling cast of artistic talent many of whom helped to define the genres they worked in. The artists who contributed artwork for EC's stories included Feldstein, Wally Wood, Johnny Craig, Reed Crandall, Al Williamson (who was assisted occasionally by Roy Krenkel and Frank Frazetta), Harvey

Kurtzman, Bernie Krigstein, John Severin, Will Elder, Graham Ingels, Jack Davis, Jack Kamen, Joe Orlando, and George Evans. Alex Toth, Russ Heath, and Joe Kubert also contributed artwork on occasion.

EC began converting its existing crime, romance, and western titles to horror, suspense, science fiction, and war features. First came EC's horror titles with such memorable names as the *Crypt of Terror* (renamed *Tales from the Crypt*), *The Vault of Horror*, and *The Haunt of Fear*. Also added were *Crime SuspenStories* and *Shock SuspenStories*. Two science fiction anthology titles were additionally added: *Weird Science* and *Weird Fantasy*. EC's roster of features was also supplemented by two war books, edited, written, and laid out by Kurtzman: *Frontline Combat* and *Two-Fisted Tales*. All of these books were christened EC's "New Trend" line.

In 1952, when Kurtzman complained to Gaines that he was not making enough money editing his war titles, the solution was he edit another feature. Kurtzman suggested a humor book, and Gaines and Feldstein agreed.[19] Feldstein even suggested a title based on the Crypt-Keeper's monologue introduction of "…welcome to EC's MAD MAGAZINE…" Kurtzman picked up part of this suggestion and *Mad* was born.[20]

What distinguished EC's (now renamed Entertaining Comics) books from all the others were their tongue-in-cheek humor, intelligence, diversity of style, and consistent quality. Feldstein and Gaines challenged the notion that comic books only had to appeal to children. Their comic books had stories and artwork that appealed to a broad audience and which could be enjoyed by kids as well as by adults.

EC took the unusual step of adapting serious science fiction by one of the most creative authors in the field. This move, however, came about, at least to begin with, unintentionally. To come up with his springboards, Gaines read horror, mystery, and science fiction stories and used a semblance of the plots as starting points for his story sessions with

Feldstein. In one of their sessions, Gaines pitched ideas from a Ray Bradbury short story, which after being modified and retitled, found its way into *The Haunt of Fear* #6. March/April, 1951. Gaines relied upon Bradbury stories two more times until Bradbury was informed that his work was turning up in a comic book without his receiving credit and a royalty. The story in question, *Here to Stay*, turned up in the May/June, 1952 issue of *Weird Fantasy* #13 and had been based on two Bradbury short stories, *Kaleidoscope* and *The Rocket Man*. Bradbury wrote to Gaines, and in a matter-of-fact tone, advised him, "Just a note to remind you of an oversight. You have not as yet sent on the check for $50.00 to cover the use of secondary rights on my two stories THE ROCKET MAN and KALEIDOSCOPE…I feel this was probably overlooked in the general confusion of office work, and look forward to your payment in the near future."[21] In the P.S. of the letter, Bradbury inquired as to whether Gaines had ever considered adapting his stories into an entire issue using as source material *Dark Carnival*, *The Illustrated Man* or *The Martian Chronicles*. Gaines, never one to ignore a good idea, did not quibble with Bradbury and paid his fee. Thereafter EC entered into an agreement, after going through the legal niceties, to adapt more Bradbury stories.[22] While EC never devoted a whole magazine to adaptations of any of Bradbury's books, Feldstein was now free to adapt a number of Bradbury's stories for EC. Even after fifty years, Bradbury feels that these adaptations ring true to his source material with artwork which "wonderfully conveys the stories."[23] What is revealing about EC's use of Bradbury's material is that other comic book companies had an opportunity to use the same material but passed on the chance. Bradbury had approached his old agent Julie Schwartz, then an editor of two science fiction titles at DC Comics, and asked him if he would be interested in adapting his stories; the answer was no.[24] This example is indicative of the difference between EC and the other companies churning out comics at the time, EC was much more inclined to take

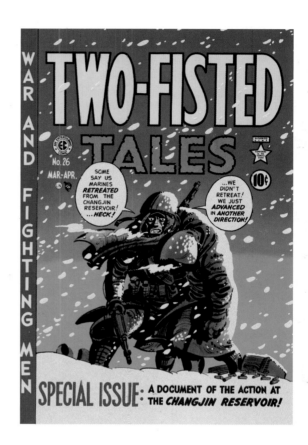

chances. This philosophy also applied to the artwork created for the company.

One of the artists charged with interpreting Bradbury's stories, as well as numerous, horror, war, and science fiction yarns for EC, was Wally Wood. Wood was, perhaps, the most talented artist to work for EC, and some of his strongest work was done during his association with the company. Wallace Wood was born in Menahga, Minnesota in 1927. Wood, who was a quiet, skinny kid, grew up in a constant state of flux, moving from town to town as the family followed his lumberjack father as he went from one job to the next. Wood's childhood was spent living primarily in Michigan and Wisconsin. His passion for comic strips developed early, and he got a great deal of his art education reading and copying his favorite titles. His teenage sketchbooks demonstrate an attraction to Will Eisner's *Spirit,* which is clearly the influence of one prominent composition in his journals. Wood also professed an attraction for Raymond, Foster, Caniff, and Crane. As soon as he was old enough, he joined the Merchant Marine. After his discharge in 1946, in an act befitting an adventurer, he enlisted in the Paratroopers where he saw duty in Japan. After completing his hitch, he returned to Minnesota where he briefly tried a go at art school. Wood, however, wanted to be a cartoonist, so he moved on, with his mother and brother in tow, to New York. By 1948 Wood had swung work, lettering for the Fox Features Syndicate and then for Will Eisner's *Spirit*.[25] He also attempted to get more formal training under his belt at the Cartoonists and Illustrators School. It was there that he took classes with Burne Hogarth, but after a year he dropped out. By 1949 he was getting his first regular work in comics, and his style was beginning to gel. He set up a small studio working with, among others, Harry Harrison and Joe Orlando. Some of his earliest efforts were done with Harrison. Wood benefited greatly when the association ended, as Harrison had very little to contribute artistically. Wood's great opportunity came when he began working for EC. By 1950 his work had hit its stride with the horror and science

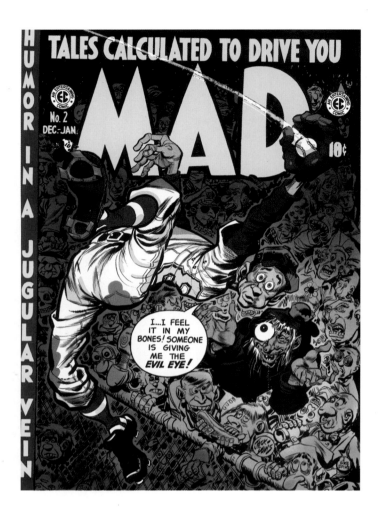

fiction material he was producing for Feldstein and Gaines. Wood was developing a style which merged Hal Foster type illustration with cartooning, and the result was storytelling with an aggressive line and a sexual edge never found in *Prince Valiant*. Wood may have been unassuming in his daily outfit of blue jeans and flannel shirts, but his comic book storytelling had an aggressive and active libido. Wood's artwork not only had obvious sexual tension but he decorated his backgrounds with intricate detail and shadowing. Wood's voice as a comic artist became easily identifiable and attracted the interest of readers, editors, and other artists. Wood's work as a storyteller was ideally suited for non-superhero fare, and his work during the 1950s was an eloquent example of the other, not-so-heroic side of the comics. Woody, as he became known, also excelled at parody and lampoon and became a regular contributor to *Mad*. By 1952, Woody was back working for Will Eisner; now, however, he was drawing the *Spirit* in outer space, and this time there was

no mistaking his artistic fingerprints all over each story. Wood's style had become so strong that his *Spirit* stories became an extension of his work for EC.

Of the many stories Wood created for EC, the one most representative of his work during the 1950s was *My World,* which appeared in *Weird Science* #22, November/December, 1953. Feldstein, who wrote the story, remembers that "I kind of wrote *My World* with myself in mind, telling a story of the different types of worlds I created in my work but when I decided to have Woody do the art it made sense to use him in the story and not myself."[26] The story, which presents vignettes of the different types of stories told by an artist ends with Wood, as the artist, drawing the story and appearing in the last panel. The story and the panel would be identified with Wood for the rest of his career. Wood's storytelling during his work at EC was distinguished primarily by the imagery he created, coupled with his technique. His ability to shadow and give depth to his drawings immediately highlights

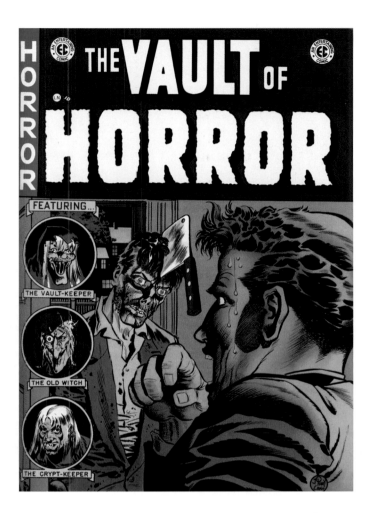

his compositions with words and pictures. Wood would go on to produce comic book stories for another twenty-five years, but his most artistically successful work was created in the 1950s, primarily for EC.

The environment created at EC by Gaines and Feldstein also encouraged its artists to turn in work which was uncharacteristic of mainstream comics of the era. Of the artists working at the company, Harvey Kurtzman not only took advantage of this freedom, but in the process acquired a reputation of being one of the decade's most creative humorists. While Kurtzman was talented and influential, his impact has been greatly exaggerated and overestimated by his zealous admirers who have elevated him to almost cult status. Kurtzman was born in New York in 1924. He attended, as did so many of the artists already detailed in these pages, the School of Music and Art. After graduation he was awarded a scholarship to Cooper Union, but he only stuck around for a year and left to pursue a career in cartooning. He began looking for work in

comic books early and his first fledgling effort found print in 1939. On the advice of one of his teachers Kurtzman landed work in Louis Ferstadt's shop. Ferstadt was a portrait painter and muralist, who due to a lack of work in his chosen profession during the Great Depression found employment supplying stories for the comic book business. Kurtzman started out in standard fashion: first erasing pencil lines from inked pages, then inking, finally graduating to pencilling.[27] His work at the time was undistinguished and gave no hint as to what was in store. In 1943 he was drafted and served a hitch in the service. After his return he started a small studio with Charlie Stern, and his friend and schoolmate Will Elder. The studio was called, appropriately enough, the Charles William Harvey Studio.[28] It was at the Studio that Kurtzman's signature style began to emerge and where he began to distinguish himself as a humorist with the strip *Hey Look!* The strip ran as a one-page filler in various Timely comic books, and editor Stan Lee gave Kurtzman free reign with the fea-

Below and opposite page top: Al Williamson, pencils, Roy Krenkel, inks, original splash page and interior page artwork, *Weird Fantasy* #19, May/June, 1953. Opposite page bottom: Al Williamson, pencils, Frank Frazetta, inks, cover, *Weird Fantasy* #21, September/October, 1953, ©1953 William M. Gaines.

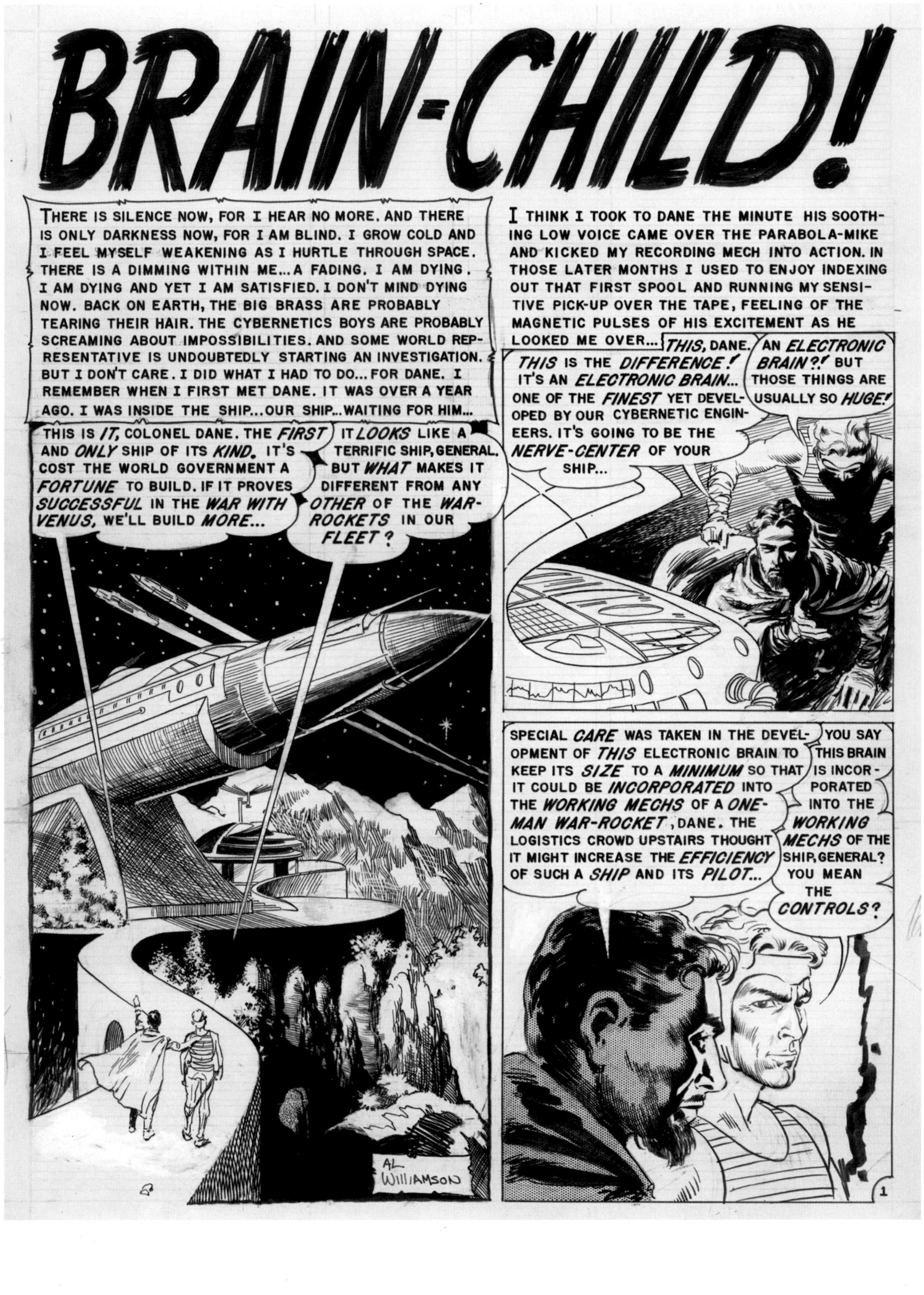
BRAIN-CHILD!
THERE IS SILENCE NOW, FOR I HEAR NO MORE. AND THERE IS ONLY DARKNESS NOW, FOR I AM BLIND. I GROW COLD AND I FEEL MYSELF WEAKENING AS I HURTLE THROUGH SPACE. THERE IS A DIMMING WITHIN ME... A FADING. I AM DYING. I AM DYING AND YET I AM SATISFIED. I DON'T MIND DYING NOW. BACK ON EARTH, THE BIG BRASS ARE PROBABLY TEARING THEIR HAIR. THE CYBERNETICS BOYS ARE PROBABLY SCREAMING ABOUT IMPOSSIBILITIES. AND SOME WORLD REPRESENTATIVE IS UNDOUBTEDLY STARTING AN INVESTIGATION. BUT I DON'T CARE. I DID WHAT I HAD TO DO... FOR DANE. I REMEMBER WHEN I FIRST MET DANE. IT WAS OVER A YEAR AGO. I WAS INSIDE THE SHIP... OUR SHIP... WAITING FOR HIM...
THIS IS IT, COLONEL DANE. THE FIRST AND ONLY SHIP OF ITS KIND. IT'S COST THE WORLD GOVERNMENT A FORTUNE TO BUILD. IF IT PROVES SUCCESSFUL IN THE WAR WITH VENUS, WE'LL BUILD MORE...
IT LOOKS LIKE A TERRIFIC SHIP, GENERAL. BUT WHAT MAKES IT DIFFERENT FROM ANY OTHER OF THE WAR-ROCKETS IN OUR FLEET?
AL WILLIAMSON
I THINK I TOOK TO DANE THE MINUTE HIS SOOTHING LOW VOICE CAME OVER THE PARABOLA-MIKE AND KICKED MY RECORDING MECH INTO ACTION. IN THOSE LATER MONTHS I USED TO ENJOY INDEXING OUT THAT FIRST SPOOL AND RUNNING MY SENSITIVE PICK-UP OVER THE TAPE, FEELING OF THE MAGNETIC PULSES OF HIS EXCITEMENT AS HE LOOKED ME OVER...
THIS, DANE. THIS IS THE DIFFERENCE! IT'S AN ELECTRONIC BRAIN... ONE OF THE FINEST YET DEVELOPED BY OUR CYBERNETIC ENGINEERS. IT'S GOING TO BE THE NERVE-CENTER OF YOUR SHIP...
AN ELECTRONIC BRAIN?! BUT THOSE THINGS ARE USUALLY SO HUGE!
SPECIAL CARE WAS TAKEN IN THE DEVELOPMENT OF THIS ELECTRONIC BRAIN TO KEEP ITS SIZE TO A MINIMUM SO THAT IT COULD BE INCORPORATED INTO THE WORKING MECHS OF A ONE-MAN WAR-ROCKET, DANE. THE LOGISTICS CROWD UPSTAIRS THOUGHT IT MIGHT INCREASE THE EFFICIENCY OF SUCH A SHIP AND ITS PILOT...
YOU SAY THIS BRAIN IS INCORPORATED INTO THE WORKING MECHS OF THE SHIP, GENERAL? YOU MEAN THE CONTROLS?
1

ture. Kurtzman also got the New York *Herald-Tribune* to pick up his newspaper strip, *Silver Linings,* which was drawn in a similar vein. *Silver Linings* was composed like a daily strip, in one tier, but ran in color in various Sunday sections. It was on the strength of *Hey Look!* that Kurtzman got a favorable recommendation, but no work from Gaines and Feldstein when he took his samples to EC. Although the referral was to another company for an educational feature on avoiding syphilis, Kurtzman was soon working for EC. As we already have seen, he was given the responsibility of helming EC's two war books. What distinguished these books was their uncharacteristically anti-war sentiment. Kurtzman was a fanatic for controlling every aspect of the stories, but few of the artists complained because of Kurtzman's habit of brainstorming with his staff. He was, however, inflexible in the layout and design of the stories.

As an artist, Kurtzman's style brought the frenetic action of cinema cartoons to the pages of comic books. Much like Jack Cole, Kurtzman was able to translate the maniac energy of big screen cartoons onto paper. The page from *Hey Look!* illustrated on page 75, does not carry with it the sophisticated undertones of the best cartoons; it is just old fashioned slapstick humor. Kurtzman's style, an in-your-face, aggressive, cartoon style of drawing, coupled with his thick, heavy inking, gave his work an undeniable energy rarely found in comic books. Kurtzman's forte, however, was in his use of design. The splash page from the story *Atom Bomb Thief,* from *Weird Fantasy* #14, July/August, 1950, illustrated on page 74, demonstrates how Kurtzman could design a page and tell a story simply and effectively. The page uses two vertical rows of three panels, horizontally side-by-side, with a long shot, horizontal panel at the bottom of the page. The story cuts back and forth, cropping much of the detail away, leaving a simple truncated image in each panel. These panels are juxtaposed against a black background so they stand out and are more graphically assertive. Unfortunately, Kurtzman's

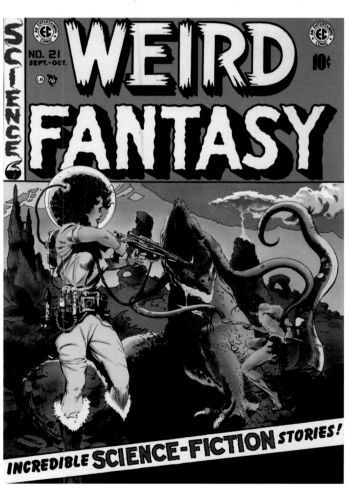

Al Williamson, pencils, Roy Krenkel and Angelo Torres, inks, cover, *Weird Science-Fantasy* #25, September, 1954, ©1954 William M. Gaines.

work in comic books was short-lived, as he spent most of his energies conceptualizing and editing. Kurtzman agonized over each story and was never able to produce work on a regular schedule. After the creation of *Mad,* he remained with the magazine for only 28 issues before leaving. He attempted to recreate *Mad* (with slightly different names and concepts), but due to various reasons he was never successful. It should also be noted that the *Mad* that became famous and synonymous with irreverent lampoon was the product of a different staff and another editor who took over after Kurtzman's departure. It was only under Al Feldstein that *Mad* finally became a nationally recognized instrument for thumbing its nose at the mundane idiocies of American culture.

EC gave a host of other talented artists a chance to push the limits of comic book storytelling, which produced varying degrees of success. Jack Davis, who would become one of the dominant commercial cartoon and character illustrators in America, got his start with the company working on every title put out by EC. Davis, born in Atlanta, Georgia in 1926, "always wanted to be a cartoonist."[29] During the Second World War, while serving his hitch in the Navy, he did cartooning for the *Navy News.* After the war he went to the University of Georgia on the G.I. bill to study art, and during the summers he worked inking and doing backgrounds for artist Ed Dodd who had a strip called *Mark Trail.* It was on Dodd's recommendation that he traveled east, to New York to seek out work as a serious cartoonist. There he attended the Art Students League and looked for work, but none was to be found. Finally, after seeing an ad looking for an inker at the New York *Herald-Tribune,* he swung a job inking for *The Saint* strip. That did not last for long, and again he was out on the street looking for work. Then, he got his lucky break; he went to EC and Al Feldstein gave him a script. Davis brought back the finished story and he had a job.[30] From the beginning, Davis' work had a facility for cartooning that gave his work an extremely animated quality. As his work matured it became more assured and jocular, which is why Davis' cartooning lent itself so well to satire.

Although Davis turned in competent work on EC's horror, crime, and science fiction titles he really hit his stride with his work for *Mad.* Davis also developed a knack as a caricaturist which is quite evident in his work for *Mad.* Davis would eventually go on to be recognized for his work all over the world, but much of his growth as an artist can be attributed to his work and the environment at EC.

Harvey Kurtzman's friend and protégé, Will Elder, also turned in work on a number a features for EC. Initially he teamed up with John Severin, with Elder providing the inks to Severin's pencils. Later, he found his own voice as a cartoonist at *MAD* working with Kurtzman. Elder's collaboration with Kurtzman would continue after Kurtzman left *Mad* and would result in a long term partnership which would produce, among other things, their long run on the *Annie Fanny* strip for *Playboy*.

Right: Joe Orlando, pencils and inks, splash page, *Weird Science-Fantasy* #27, January/February, 1955. Bottom: John Severin, pencils, Will Elder, inks, splash page, *Weird Fantasy* #18, March/April, 1953, ©1955 and 1953 Wiilliam M. Gaines.

Artists came to EC in a variety of ways. Some came in looking for work while others were steered there by artists working for the company. A number of EC artists formed "studios," and many of the artists connected with these ateliers found work as a natural product of their associations. Both John Severin, who had worked in Kurztman's Studio, and Al Williamson, who knew Wally Wood, got in the door this way.

Severin, who was born in 1921, graduated from the School of Music and Art. In 1942 he enlisted in the army and since he was color-blind found himself working in a camouflage unit stateside. Eventually he decided he wanted to see some action and became a machine gunner in the Pacific theatre. He attended art school for a while on the G.I. Bill and then looked for work ultimately winding up in the Charles William Harvey Studio. Soon he was working for EC, as we have already seen, teamed up with Will Elder. Severin had a straightforward, clean style. He greatly admired Roy Crane which is evident from his uncluttered storytelling.[31] Severin's figures were not heroic but looked like real people,

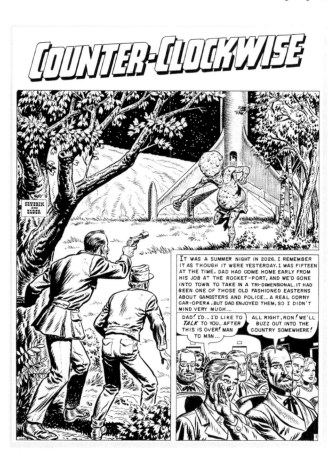

and his work had a simplicity of line and clarity of composition which served his fantasy, science fiction, and war tales well. Severin developed an inking style which resembled the line and crosshatch of an etching.

Williamson, who was the "young kid" on the staff, started work at EC when he was twenty years old. Williamson, unlike a majority of the artists at EC, preferred to have someone else ink his work and frequently teamed up with Roy Krenkel, Frank Frazetta, and Angelo Torres to finish his stories.[32] Williamson saw his working for EC as an adventure. He felt that the stories he produced were "for the fun of it."[33] For whatever reason, Williamson and his collaborators turned in intelligent, elegant work. While not on the cutting edge of storytelling, there is an undeniable grace and refinement to be found in his EC stories. Williamson's work embraced the style espoused by illustrator/storytellers rather

HIS MISSION FORGOTTEN, HE BEGAN TO TRY KEY AFTER KEY... PICKING THEM FROM THE PILE AND INSERTING THEM IN THE FRONT DOOR LOCK...FAILING... TRYING AGAIN...FAILING..GROWING MORE AND MORE DESPERATE...

FEAR GRIPPED HIM. HE FROZE AS THE FOOTSTEPS RETURNED. THE COP AGAIN! UNGER COWERED IN THE SHADOWS...

THE POLICEMAN PASSED. UNGER'S SLEEVE CAUGHT THE HANDLE OF A BENCH DRAWER, PULLING IT OUT, SPILLING ITS CONTENTS UPON THE FLOOR. MORE KEYS...

FOR A WILD MOMENT, HE ALMOST SMASHED THE GLASS BUT THE FOOTSTEPS RETURNED. HE COULDN'T DO THAT! THE COP WOULD HEAR IT...

HE GROVELED AMONG THE MASS OF KEYS ON THE FLOOR...TRYING ONE... DISCARDING IT ONTO THE BENCH... TRYING AGAIN...

HE TRIED AND FAILED FOR AN HOUR...

HIS LEGS ACHED FROM HIS CRAMPED POSITION. HE STOOD UP, SWAYING, STUMBLING AGAINST THE BENCH, KNOCKING THE KEYS HE'D TRIED BACK ONTO THE FLOOR...

THE KEYS GLITTERED. THE WALLS SEEMED TO CLOSE IN. UNGER GIGGLED. HE STARTED ALL OVER AGAIN...TRYING... FAILING...TRYING...

THE OLD MAN FOUND HIM IN THE MORNING, SITTING IN THE MIDDLE OF THE TINY SHOP'S FLOOR. EVERY DRAWER HAD BEEN OPENED AND EMPTIED... EVERY KEY IN THE SHOP SPILLED OUT. UNGER SAT AMONG THEM... CRYING SOFTLY... HIS EYES GLAZED AND STARING...

(SOB...SOB...)

THEY CAME AND TOOK HIM AWAY. HE NEVER HEARD THE OLD MAN REMARK...

I FIGURED HE WAS UP TO SOMETHIN', HANGIN' AROUND LIKE THAT LAST NIGHT. I MADE BELIEVE I LOCKED UP. THOUGHT I'D DISCOURAGE HIM. WHEN HE PICKED MY POCKET, I FIGURED HE WAS DESPERATE. WHAT WOULD A GUY WANT IN AN OLD LOCKSMITH'S SHOP ANYWAY? 'SPECIALLY ONE WITH A BUSTED FRONT DOOR LOCK THAT DON'T EVEN WORK...

THE END

than attempting to develop a simplified and individual language to depict his tales. Williamson was an obvious disciple of Alex Raymond, which comes through loud and clear in almost all of his work. Williamson provided many highly attractive illustrations for his stories, but he was never able to outgrow his influences.

Another artist to find work at EC was Reed Crandall, whose work in the Golden Age had been so exciting and fresh. Unfortunately, Crandall attempted to make his work more akin to illustration rather than proceeding in the direction of his earlier efforts. The result, while highly competent, was usually juiceless and uninspired.

While Williamson may have qualified as the youngest artist to work for EC, the artist who had been with the company longest and was one of its most dependable stalwarts was Johnny Craig. Craig started out as a letterer for Shelly Mayer at All American while still in high school. After returning from the service in 1946, he started an extended relationship with EC Comics, first under Max C. Gaines and then with William Gaines. His clean, Caniff-inspired style can be found on a variety of the line's crime and horror covers, including some of its most infamous (or famous, depending on your perspective) products. He became editor of one of the line's titles, *The Vault of Horror* with issue #35. Craig's work was competent and rarely inspired.[34]

EC had other dependable artists turning in work who ranged from journeymen to proficient craftsman. Graham Ingels turned in countless horror and crimes tales, which gave many young readers nightmares for weeks after reading his yarns. George Evans produced stories for a number of EC titles, but his work involving airplanes always proved eye-catching. Evans, who had been an aviation mechanic but could not become a pilot because of problems with his vision, excelled in stories of dogfights, biplanes, and gallant pilots.[35]

During its brief foray into the business, EC acquired a reputation for being a different kind of comic book company. Gaines, who became more and more paternalistic as the company became more successful, was liberal in the editorial freedom he gave Feldstein and Kurtzman. Gaines frequently socialized with his artists and even threw Christmas parties where he gave extravagant presents to his staff. It was in this milieu that Bernie Krigstein became the last artist to start working for EC before it became the scapegoat for the comic book industry and was put out of business only to be resurrected as the publisher of one title which would make the company world famous.

Krigstein came on board at the suggestion of Harvey Kurtzman, although a majority of his work was done for Feldstein. Krigstein, who was born in Brooklyn in 1919, studied art at Brooklyn College and after his graduation worked for the Works Progress Administration (WPA) painting and teaching. Through a relative, he later found work in Bernard Baily's shop despite his distaste, as a serious artist, for comic books. After his hitch in the army, he returned to the Baily shop. He then floated between several publishers. His work came to Kurtzman's attention in 1951, and he was offered work with EC, but Krigstein was making more money churning out work for Atlas, so he demurred. Later, in 1953 he reapproached EC, and even though they had a full compliment of artists, with Kurtzman's help, he got the job.[36] Krigstein, as with many of the second generation of comic book artists, had severe misgivings about developing a voice as an artist in such a pedestrian craft as the comics. As an artist, Krigstein was a competent commercial artist with aspirations and pretensions which exceeded his abilities. His work for EC brought his talents as a comic book storyteller to their peak. Krigstein developed a simple, angular style of drawing and inking for his stories which is immediately identifiable and visually striking. His reputation, however, lies with a gimmick of breaking down a page into multiple panels, reducing a moment in time down by, in some cases, moments. While this proved effective in many of his EC stories, panel breakdown on its own does not a great storyteller make. As Toth proved with his eloquent work for Standard, simplicity and straightforward storytelling are the key. Krigstein's multiple panel pages are in some cases fascinating, in some cases make for good drama but ultimately appeal more on a theoretical level. Illustrated on page 82, is example of Krigstein's use of dissecting time panel by panel, stretching one moment in time out over several frames on the page. After a disagreement with Feldstein and Gaines over a story Krigstein had altered the ending on, he left EC for good.[37] He worked in comics for a while longer and then labored in illustration.

As EC was breaking new ground and being imitated by other companies, Simon and Kirby were not sitting idly by but were coming up with new concepts to sell more comic books. After they each returned from their service in the war, they kept busy producing the first romance comic book, *Young Romance* #1, September, 1947.[38] Kirby's artwork was strong, as usual, but nothing had changed since his efforts for DC Comics. During the late 1940s and 1950s, Kirby would venture into several genres with varying degrees of success. He would try his hand at westerns, horror, mystery, science fiction, and he even tried to revisit superhero territory. Business was booming for the partnership, and to keep up with the demand for material, they set up a shop which included experienced hands in the business as well as a host of young up-and-comers. The list of Simon and Kirby's staff included Mort Meskin, Jerry Robinson, Bruno Premiani, Ross Andru, Steve Ditko, Carmine Infantino, Bob Powell, John Prentice, John

Severin, and George Tuska.[39] Kirby's greatest accomplishments as a comic book storyteller would manifest themselves shortly.

Generally, the fare offered by the majority of comic books during the 1950s was undistinguished. Martin Goodman's Timely, which became Marvel, took the moniker of Atlas in the 1950s. Atlas cranked out dozens of titles under editor Stan Lee, Goodman's cousin-in-law, most of which followed the trends of the era. The company even tried to resuscitate its superheroes from the Golden Age with no success. Atlas boasted several freelancers who were developing diverse styles and approaches to comic book storytelling. John Buscema, Gene Colan, Bill Everett, Russ Heath, and John Romita, all turned in work for the company which hinted at their future promise. As we have seen, Bernie Krigstein had worked for Atlas as well, as did Harvey Kurtzman, who contributed his signature brand of humor for the company before he enlisted with EC.

One particularly interesting artist, who helped set the tone for Atlas but who tragi-cally died in an accident in 1958 was Joe Maneely. Maneely was born in 1926, and grew up in Philadelphia. When he dropped out of school, his mother ordered him to shape up or ship out, and he accomplished the latter by joining the Navy. After his tour of duty he returned to Philadelphia and attended art school on the G.I. Bill.[40] By 1948 he got his first work in the business and eventually wound up at Marvel. At Marvel and then Atlas, Maneely did everything, including instructional sessions with younger artists on layout and composition.[41] He turned in work on hundreds of stories and covers, many of which are strikingly unusual. Maneely's work was distinguished by its quirky, primitive tone. His was an individual voice in a pedestrian craft.

Up until the mid-1950s, the primary concerns of comic book publishers had been to sell enough titles to make a living and keep in step with the changing trends in the industry. In crafting their wares, the largest publishers established internal controls on the content of their material to avoid difficulties with church and parents' groups. In their desire to keep revenue flowing, the publishers did not want to run afoul of public opinion. The atmosphere after the war, however, put the publishers on notice that intolerance for their product was on the rise. With the Second World War over, juvenile crime and delinquency became the focus of concern for civic groups, associations of parents and teachers, and politicians. The 1950s were a time of uncertainty and anxiety. In perspective, comic books were hardly of legitimate relevance to the American public. Larger, more threatening portents loomed before the public every day: nuclear war, the Korean conflict, the execution of Julius and Ethel Rosenberg for giving away America's secrets, and the never-ending parade of televised House and Senate investigations. This was the litany which became daily fodder for the media and the public. It was in this climate that rock 'n roll was born, that television became a household commodity bringing Jackie Gleason, Sid Caesar, Lucy and Ricky, and Lassie into just about everyone's home. It was also a time when America became the

Jack Kirby, pencils and inks, original ad artwork, reused as the table of contents page,
Western Tales #32 and #33, March, 1956, July, 1956, ©1956 Harvey Publications.

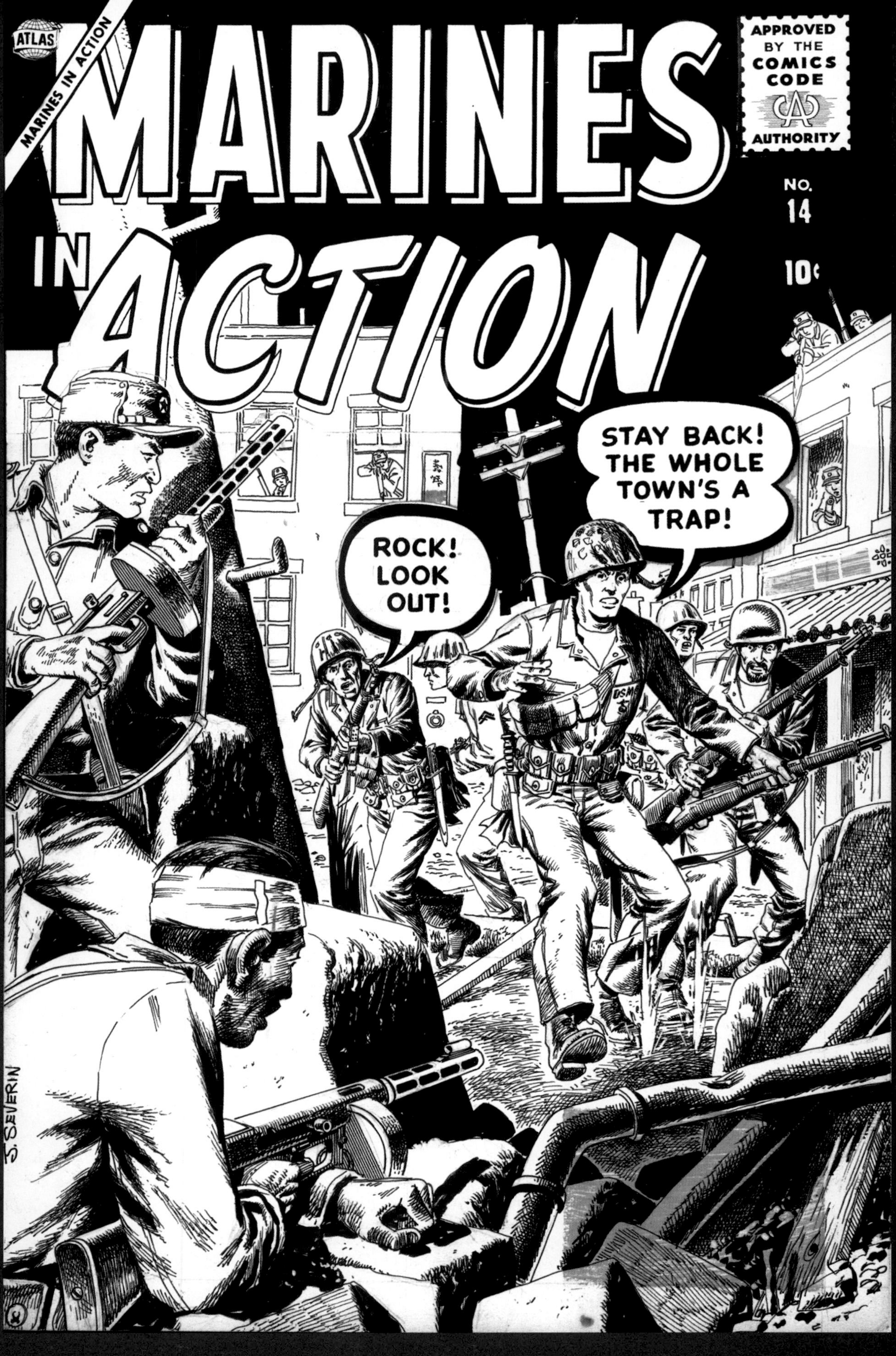
ATLAS
MARINES IN ACTION
MARINES IN ACTION
APPROVED BY THE COMICS CODE AUTHORITY
NO. 14
10¢
STAY BACK! THE WHOLE TOWN'S A TRAP!
ROCK! LOOK OUT!
USMC
J. SEVERIN

dominant force in modern art with the growth and maturity of the New York School. Nevertheless, comics became the focus of groups that attributed many of the societal ills of children to the content of the comics.

Since kids were the primary buyers of comic books, cursory attempts were made by the industry to assure parents that content was being reviewed and overseen by experts. Criticism was mounting that comic books were a negative influence on American youth. This theory was advanced by a psychiatrist named Fredric Wertham, who authored a book entitled *Seduction of the Innocent*. Wertham was born and educated in Germany and came to the United States to take a position at the psychiatric clinic at Johns Hopkins University in Baltimore. In 1932 he moved to New York City to take a position as the senior psychiatrist in the Department of Hospitals. It was at this time that he became interested and involved in the study of how crime and criminals related to diseases of the mind. As a byproduct of his work in forensic psychiatry, he began to advocate the use of censorship of the media to protect the public from exposure to the lurid details of sensational crimes. His

position was that the media had a responsibility to educate the public to the evils of crime and not to titillate readers with irresponsible reporting.[42] This concern also lent itself to the dangers of children being improperly influenced by the content of crime and horror comic books. While it appears that Wertham's concerns were well motivated, the connections he made between comic books and juvenile delinquency were unsubstantiated and misguided. Censorship rarely works as a solution to general societal ills, and Wertham's prescription, that eliminating undesirable content in the mass-media would make a better society, was simplistic and naïve.

Seduction of the Innocent was published in 1954 and was used as the centerpiece for televised hearings of the United States Senate Subcommittee to Investigate Juvenile Delinquency. The thesis of *Seduction of the Innocent* was that comic books inspired anti-social behavior and had to have their content reviewed and regulated. Instead of an honest overview of comic books, however, Wertham relied on taking images out of context, misrepresenting the pervasiveness of the content

of comic books, and in the use anecdotal analysis of the effects of comics on their readers. Wertham's analysis was intellectually dishonest and intentionally mendacious. Wertham even insisted that the comic book publishers were out to get him as a result of his efforts to regulate the content of the industry.[43] *Seduction of the Innocent* was not Wertham's first salvo at the industry though. Earlier in 1948 he had convened a symposium dealing with "The Psychopathology of Comic Books" at the New York Academy of Medicine which resoundingly attacked comics as an evil, malevolent influence that had be eradicated. Wertham conducted his inquisition with unrelenting zeal and self-righteous indignation.

His take on comic books was picked up by the press and received consideration in magazines, newspapers, and even on television. As a result of the pressure brought to bear by these efforts, the Association of Comics Magazine Publishers created the first comics code for the industry which was never seriously followed.

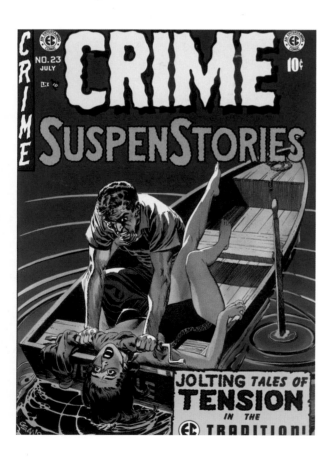

The Senate Subcommittee hearings had a radically different impact and effect. The hearings, chaired by Senator Robert Hendrickson, were held in New York, the center of the comic book world, for maximum impact. The hearings, however, are usually credited to Senator Estes Kefauver, who was looking for a vehicle to bolster his political ambitions.[44] Kefauver had previously used such investigations to gain national notoriety which helped propel him to an unsuccessful bid for the Democratic Presidential nomination in 1952. He was accordingly hopeful that his involvement with cleaning up comic books would recharge his political standing. The hearings' most memorable moments, however, came with the testimony of William Gaines. Due to inadequate preparation and the use of weight loss medications which made it difficult for him to concentrate, Gaines inadvertently, became the poster child for the evils of the comics.[45]

In preparation for the hearings, the Subcommittee staff called Feldstein for a private interview. Nothing came of this meeting. Gaines, on the other hand, insisted on voluntarily appearing before the Subcommittee and reading a carefully drafted statement.[46] The statement, which Gaines read on April 21, 1954, was eloquent and carefully refuted many of the points Wertham had made before the Subcommittee earlier.[47] The problems started when Subcommittee members started to ask Gaines questions for which he was obviously unprepared. Gaines' most widely publicized exchange with Kefauver reads almost like a bad comic book:

> Kefauver: Here is your May 22 issue (*CrimeSuspenStories* #22). This seems to be a man with a bloody ax holding a women's head up which has been severed from her body. Do you think that is in good taste?

> Gaines: Yes sir: I do, for the cover of a horror comic. A cover in bad taste, for example, might be defined as holding the head a little higher so that the neck could be seen dripping blood from it and moving the body over a little further so the neck of the body could be seen to be bloody.

> Kefauver: You have blood coming out of her mouth.

> Gaines: A little.[48]

Kefauver could not have arranged a more perfect colloquy to point to the obvious naïve insensitivity of Gaines if he had written the words himself. Despite Gaines' intelligent defense of comic books, freedom of expression, and the danger of censorship, he damned his cause in several minutes before a television audience of tens of thousands. Among the viewers watching Gaines' performance were many of the artists of EC's staff at the company's editorial offices. Al Feldstein, Harvey Kurtzman, Will Elder, Joe Orlando, Marie Severin (the staff colorist for EC), and John Severin all watched Gaines' performance. John Severin remembers, "They laughed. They were amused by the whole thing…all of us – we took it very lightly."[49]

The industry did not take the hearings lightly. By August, 1954, an organizational meeting of comic book publishers and distributors met which led to the formation of the Comics Magazine Association of America and the Comics Code. Self censorship was not new to commercial ventures; the motion picture studios had earlier implemented self-control of content which did not significantly stifle Hollywood's creativity. The industry would just have to look for another trend. They also acted punitively against Gaines by drafting a code that made him change the titles and content of his line to the point where he had to completely revamp his products, first with the New Direction line and then with the Picto-Fiction comic books, neither of which were financially successful.

By the beginning of 1956, EC Comics was gone with the publication of its last comic book, *Incredible Science Fiction* #33. The eccentric Gaines continued to publish *Mad* and, with the help of Kurtzman and then Feldstein, eventually had the last laugh with a magazine that influenced kids to behave badly, which to this day is still going strong.

The comic book industry was hit hard by the changes wrought by these hearings, which cast comic books in a negative light nationally. Another less talked about contributing factor to the decline of the industry was the abrupt disappearance of one of the main distributors of comic books, the American News Company, and its subsidiary the Union News Company. The Justice Department had filed an antitrust lawsuit against American News, alleging that publishers were coerced into signing exclusivity agreements requiring that their products be handled by American News to be distributed solely by Union News. As a result of this litigation, Union News settled the suit in 1955 and agreed to no longer give preference to American News customers. American News no longer had national distribution which left the many comic book publishers the company handled without an outlet for their books.[50]

The companies that emerged strongest from all these events were Dell, DC Comics,

Harvey, Charlton, and Archie. Dell, which never would subscribe to the Comics Code, became the largest comic book publisher in the world and also created its own distribution network, becoming more independent than before.[51] By the end of 1955, there were less than three hundred plus titles being printed, down from the over six hundred in 1954.

The classic argument made in response to censorship of free speech in the marketplace, that such attempts have a chilling effect, contrary to traditional American values, fell on deaf ears. This hardly came as a surprise to anyone, as the bottom line was, as it always had been, the final arbiter of policy in the industry. The major comic book publishers calculated that by creating a system of controls, they could avoid legal regulation and entanglements. The cost of this compromise was a chilling effect, of sorts, but it should be remembered that a majority of the comic books and companies that fell after the great purge did not represent the publishers producing the best or most ground-breaking art or stories. EC was the great casualty in the ranks of those who went under; they had tried to produce material with legitimate quality. It should be noted that even before the hearings, EC's best titles, its science fiction anthology magazines, were being financially subsidized by its horror titles. Nevertheless, comics became far less interesting after the imposition of the Comics Code.

DC Comics, never a company to push the envelope of creativity, kept churning out stories. Dell, which sold tens of millions of comic books a year, mostly so-called funny animal strips, notably with Disney characters, continued unaffected by the hearings. The best artists of the second generation may have been shaken by the developments of 1954, but they continued telling stories in comic books and developing their art. The Comics Code was not an impediment to the further development of the artists and their art; it was merely a detour.

NOTES

[1] John Benton, *The Comic Book in America.*

[2] Interview with Gil Kane.

[3] Ibid.

[4] Interview with Joe Giella. Correspondence with Alex Toth.

[5] Ibid.

[6] Correspondence with Alex Toth. See: Vincent Davis, Richard Kyle, and Bill Spicer interview with Alex Toth, *The Comics Journal*, #98, May, 1985.

[7] John Benton, *The Comic Book in America.*

[8] Gary Groth interview with Joe Kubert, *The Comics Journal* #172, November, 1994.

[9] Ibid.

[10] Gary Groth interview with Carmine Infantino, *The Comics Journal* #191, November, 1996. See also: Bob Koppany interview with Carmine Infantino, *Alter Ego* #10, September, 2001.

[11] All American had its offices in the same building as DC Comics, on 480 Lexington Avenue in New York.

[12] Gary Groth interview with Carmine Infantino, *The Comics Journal* #191.

[13] Interview with Gil Kane. See also: Daniel Herman, *Gil Kane: The Art of the Comics*, Hermes Press, 2001.

[14] Ibid.

[15] Davis, Kyle, and Spicer interview with Alex Toth, *The Comic Journal* #98.

[16] Frank Jacobs, *The Mad World of William M. Gaines*, Bantam Books, 1972.

[17] Interview with Al Feldstein.

[18] Ibid.

[19] Jacobs, *The Mad World of William M. Gaines.* Interview with Al Feldstein.

[20] Ibid. There are a number of stories as to who was responsible for naming *Mad*. Kurtzman always said that he came up with the name. His wife, Adele, clearly corroborates this, as she was there when her husband came up with the the the title's moniker. See: "A Talk with Adele Kurtzman," *Tales of Terror*, Fantagraphics Books, 2002. It should be noted that Adele Kurtzman's interview is refreshingly candid and should be considered a highly

credible account of her experiences with the gang at EC Comics. In any event, it is clear that *Mad* was Kurtzman's show. He clearly was the one who conceptualized the magazine and carefully and completely supervised its content until his relationship with the magazine was severed.

[21] Correspondence between Bradbury and Gaines dated April 19, 1952.

[22] Interview with Ray Bradbury.

[23] Ibid.

[24] Ibid.

[25] Shel Dorf, "An Interview with Woody," *The Comic Book Artist* #14, July, 2001. Also see: James Steranko, *Wally Wood Sketchbook*, Vanguard, 2000; Cat Yronwode, "Introduction," *The Outer Space Spirit*, Kitchen Sink Press, 1983.

[26] Interview with Al Feldstein.

[27] Harvey Kurtzman with Michael Barrier, *Harvey Kurtzman's Visual History of the Comics*, Prentice Hall Press, 1991; Harvey Kurtzman with Howard Zimmerman, *My Life as a Cartoonist*, Pocket Books, 1988; Harvey Kurtzman and Bill Elder Interview, *Squa Tront* #9, 1983.

[28] Ibid.

[29] Will Eisner interview with Jack Davis and Harvey Kurtzman, "Shop Talk," *Will Eisner's Quarterly* #6, September, 1985.

[30] Ibid.

[31] Gary Groth interview with John Severin, *The Comics Journal* #215, August, 1999.

[32] Frazetta later worked in commercial illustration, toiling only briefly in comic books and newspaper strips. As an inker and illustrator he turned in work on a very high technical level. His work in illustration is problematic as he has used crude clichés repeatedly to the delight of his small but loyal legion of followers.

[33] Stave Ringgenberg interview with Al Williamson, *The Comics Journal* #90, May, 1984.

[34] Roger Hill interview with Johnny Craig, *Comic Book Marketplace* #80, July/August, 2000.

[35] Paul Wardle interview with George Evans, *The Comics Journal* #177, May, 1995.

[36] Greg Sadowski, *B.Krigstein*, Fantagraphics, 2002.

[37] The Krigstein story most often cited by comic book historians is *Master Race* from the EC New Direction comic book *Impact* #1, March, 1955. *Master Race* is not the most representative of Krigstein's efforts, nor is it the masterpiece fans insist it is. It is an effective, but overly melodramatic story, with an obvious ending, even by the standards of 1950s comic books. Krigstein's take on Feldstein's script adds dimensions to the story which do ratchet up the drama of the parable, but it is hardly Krigstein's most inspired work.

[38] Another Simon and Kirby comic book, *My Date* #1, July, 1947 has also been credited with being the first romance comic, but its tone is different, and it is clearly not a part of that genre.

[39] Ray Wyman and Catherine Hohlfeld, *The Art of Jack Kirby*. Blue Rose Press, 1992.

[40] Michael J. Vassallo, "What if...Joe Maneely had lived and drawn in the Marvel Age of Comics?," *Alter Ego* #28, September, 2003.

[41] Interview with John Romita.

[42] Amy Nyberg, *Seal of Approval the History of the Comics Code*, University Press of Mississippi, 2002.

[43] Wertham even attacked Superman, Batman, and Wonder Woman. He insisted that Batman and Robin's relationship "may stimulate children to homosexual fantasies."

[44] Ibid.

[45] Jacobs, *The Mad World of William C. Gaines*. Interview with Al Feldstein.

[46] Ibid.

[47] Transcript of the Hearings before the Senate Subcommittee on Juvenile Delinquency, 83rd Congress, 2nd Session, April 21-22 and June 24, 1954.

[48] Ibid.

[49] Gary Groth interview with John Severin, Part 2, *The Comics Journal* #216, October, 1999

[50] Nyberg, *Seal of Approval the History of the Comics Code*.

[51] Ibid. See also: Benton, *The Comic Book in America*.

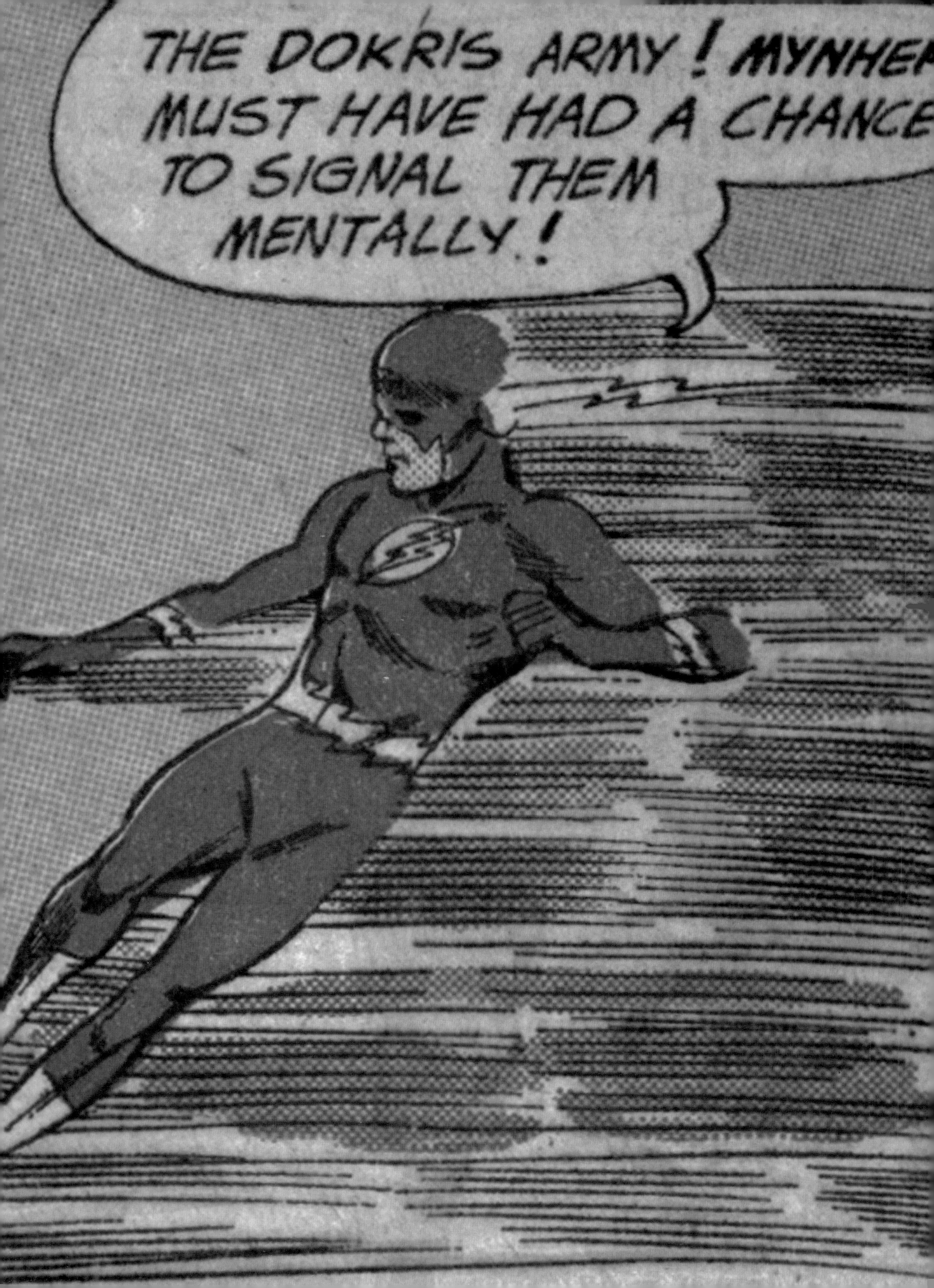
THE DOKRIS ARMY! MYNHER MUST HAVE HAD A CHANCE TO SIGNAL THEM MENTALLY!

4 THE INDUSTRY AFTER THE PURGE; THE SILVER AGE OF SUPERHEROES BEGINS; INFANTINO, KANE, AND KUBERT TO THE FOREFRONT; JACK KIRBY, ACT III; THE JOURNEYMEN; THE INDUSTRY IS HOT AGAIN AND MAINSTREAM AMERICAN LOVES THE COMICS

The major powers of the business came through the imposition of the Comics Code shaken, but unscathed. Artists and writers had to conform to the guidelines of the Comics Code which required rewrites and changes to artwork. Even with the new caution being exercised by editors, sometimes even the most innocuous artwork was now being returned with an "approved" stamp on it and with the hand-written notation, "subject to corrections." No more horror and suspense. No more science fiction with a cutting edge. No more ghouls and corpses. The comic book publishers would have to look to another genre to revitalize the industry. The trouble was to find the right one. The company in the best position to take this step forward after the hearings of 1954 and which had attracted the best up-and-coming artists in the field was DC Comics. Since the beginning of the 1950s, DC had been bringing aboard a number of talented artists. DC's editors continued this trend after the Subcommittee hearings, adding to its talent pool both established and new artists.

With so many publishers gone, work was at a premium. Many artists would leave the industry and take up work in advertising and illustration. Atlas, which had produced a spate of titles, was reduced to a mere eight, not due to the code, but because of a bad business decision. Owner Martin Goodman distributed his own magazines, but by 1957, he decided to abandon this aspect of his business as unprofitable, in favor of using American News. Unknown to Goodman, when the decision was made; American News was about to go under. Without any way to get his magazines to newsstands, drug stores, train stations, and airports, Goodman was forced to go to DC Comics to use its distribution. DC would only distribute less than a handful of his titles, reducing Atlas to almost a one-man operation.[1] Ever quick on his feet, Atlas editor Stan Lee was back within a year, bringing new artists aboard who would help define the line in the coming decade.

Despite the atmosphere created by the aftermath of the Subcommittee hearings, many of the artists who had established themselves kept working. Carmine Infantino kept churning out westerns, science fiction, and mysteries under editor Julie Schwartz. Infantino began to pull away from his dense, Caniff-inspired style and started to loosen up his artwork. When he was allowed to ink his work, it was clear his drawing was exhibiting an energy rarely found in the pages of comic books. He was also developing a sense of design which juxtaposed empty rectangles of space against his foreground characters, creating a figure and a clearly defined background which served as a design element rather than as an actual landscape. Infantino, who was never concerned with perfect anatomy or proportion, was more interested in creating images that caught the eye and used the frequently banal plots given him as devices to come up with new and novel ways to use intelligent composition to make his point. In addition to Infantino, Schwartz was building an impres-

A gallery of four Flash covers. All Carmine Infantino, pencils. Clockwise, covers from: *Showcase* #8, June, 1957; *The Flash* #125, December, 1961, Joe Giella, inks; *The Flash* #135, March, 1963, Murphy Anderson, inks; and *The Flash* #146, August, 1964, Murphy Anderson, inks, ©1957, 1961, 1963 and 1964 DC Comics.

sive roster of artistic talent to pencil and ink the stories for his books.

Gil Kane, who primarily worked for Schwartz, spent his time pencilling similar fare. Kane was reducing the detail in his compositions to only what was necessary, ever mindful of what he had learned from Barry and Toth. Kane was constantly studying his craft, refining his use of anatomy. He was now drawing panels which used this facility – thrusting his figures into and off the comic book pages he was composing.

Also coming to the forefront at DC Comics was Murphy Anderson. Anderson's first

work for DC was stiff and sometimes clumsy. Unfortunately, even as his work matured, he was not always able to overcome these deficiencies. Anderson, who was born in North Carolina in 1926, was an early fan of pulp science fiction, comic books, and newspaper strips. He attended the University of North Carolina hoping to study art. Impatient with the academic world, he convinced his father to lend him $100 so he could go to New York to try his hand as an artist. Fortunately, right before his money ran out, he swung a job for Fiction House on the basis of a strong portfolio of science fiction artwork and a helping

hand from Harry "A" Chesler. Anderson had gone to Chesler's shop looking for work, but none was available. Chesler, obviously impressed with the youngster's samples, sent Anderson over to Fiction House for an interview, and he got his lucky break.[2] Soon though, Anderson enlisted in the Navy, but by 1947 he was back working on the *Buck Rogers* strip. By 1950 he was working for Julie Schwartz on his *Mystery in Space* title.

Anderson's keen interest and affection for science fiction made him a natural to collaborate with Schwartz, and the two worked comfortably together. Anderson had even provided illustrations for one of Schwartz's old friends, Ray Palmer, the editor of the sci-fi pulp magazines *Amazing Stories* and *Fantastic Adventures*. Schwartz used a number of pulp writers as scripters for his titles including John Broome, Gardner Fox, Otto Binder, and Edmond Hamilton.[3] They all turned in scripts for which Anderson provided the artwork.[4] Anderson's artwork was problematic as it was

graphically bold, but his figures were often rigidly posed. Anderson could churn out eye-catching covers, but frequently his stories, while assertively drawn and strongly inked, were not particularly well structured. Anderson went on to work primarily as an inker for Schwartz for the next decade.

Inker Joe Giella also joined DC Comics in 1950, again working primarily for Schwartz. Giella had, like many of his peers at DC, attended the School of Industrial Art but was forced to drop out before graduating due to the necessity of having to help his family financially. Giella made the rounds in the business, and, through the insistence of his friend and classmate Frank Giacoia, went to work for DC in 1950. It was at DC that he came under the influence of Barry and Toth. He remembers that Schwartz wanted "clean, honest inking" and that his primary inspiration was

Left: Carmine Infantino, pencils, Murphy Anderson, inks, cover, *Mystery in Space* #86, August, 1963. Below: Carmine Infantino, pencils, Joe Giella, inks, original splash page artwork, *Mystery in Space* #84, June, 1963, ©1963 DC Comics. Opposite page: Carmine Infantino, pencils, Murphy Anderson, inks, original splash page artwork, *Mystery in Space* #85, August, 1963, ©1963 DC Comics.

the style "established by Barry."[5] Giella would serve almost exclusively as an inker for Schwartz's artists and he gave Kane and Infantino's strips a slick, homogeneous look. Giella did not overpower either artist's pencils; he was not skilled or dynamic enough to echo the drawing without interfering with it. He was inadequate at capturing the dynamics of Kane's pencils and was unable to leave Infantino's quirky anatomy and slightly-off figures alone. It should be noted that much of this interference was at Schwartz's insistence. Giella removed the spontaneity both artists gave to their work and replaced it with competent consistency.

Schwartz additionally used Sid Greene to pencil strips and to contribute inks for his stable of artists. Greene had been working in the business since 1941 and had worked for a number of publishers. By 1955, he had found work with DC. Although Greene had a strong personality as a penciler, as an inker, he was able to successfully submerge his style and to highlight the pencilers he was embellishing.

Joe Kubert was back at work for DC by 1955 and was one of the bright lights of editor Robert Kanigher's stable. Kanigher edited many different non-superhero titles and *Wonder Woman* and was a voracious writer to boot. Kanigher was another of Shelly Mayer's recruits, and his personality and manner evoked two responses – admiration or irritation – and sometimes elicited both.[6]

Kubert focused on such strips as *Viking Prince* and on DC's war titles.[7] By the late 1950s Kubert had developed a virtuoso style with a pen and brush which was bold and easily identifiable. Kubert had been working in comics for what must have seemed like his whole life. He had been involved in numerous aspects of the business, ranging from working as a freelance artist to running his own business supplying finished comic book material. After a five-year stint working for All American and its successor, DC Comics, he went out on his own in 1949. He then took the initiative to start up his own shop, creating stories and artwork as a complete package for St. John Publishing. After returning from

service in the Korean War, he became partners with his boyhood friend, artist Norm Maurer, and they opened another shop, again supplying material for St. John Publishing.[8] Work was picking up, so Kubert called on his old All American colleagues Infantino and Toth to help out.[9] Due to the economic uncertainties of the business, he finally went back to work for DC Comics.

Kubert had a singular voice as a draftsman and could create a tableau which appeared, on the surface, to be deceptively simple but which required both technical skill and a sophisticated sense of design to pull it all off. Kubert drew figures loosely with a blue pencil and then polished his compositions as he inked. He created atmosphere rather than detail, and his compositions had a natural flow. As his characters were connected to the real world, his style was ideally suited for tales of ordinary men and women, not super human musclemen. His Viking Prince may have been a heroic figure, but he had a human dimension grounded in fantasy, which made the strip and its main character easy to accept as being *almost* real.

Russ Heath also started his association with DC Comics in 1950. Heath, who was born in New York in 1926, grew up in New Jersey. He had aspirations of becoming an artist from early childhood and his father, a former cowboy, brought him up with a fascination for the American west. By 1942 he was working in the comics, and by 1946 he found steady work

Carmine Infantino, pencils, Batgirl, Batman, and Robin model sheet, 1966, ©1966 DC Comics.

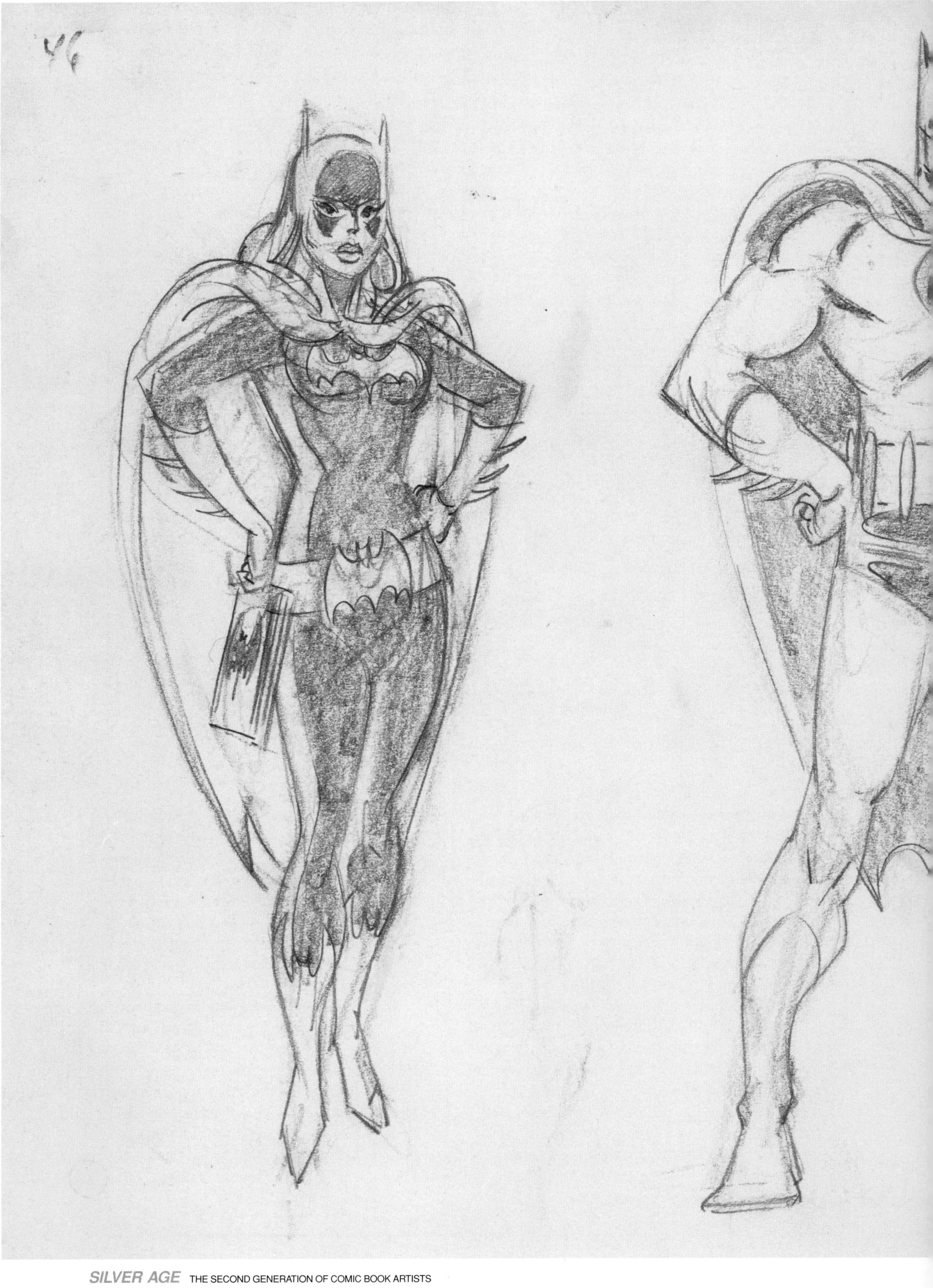

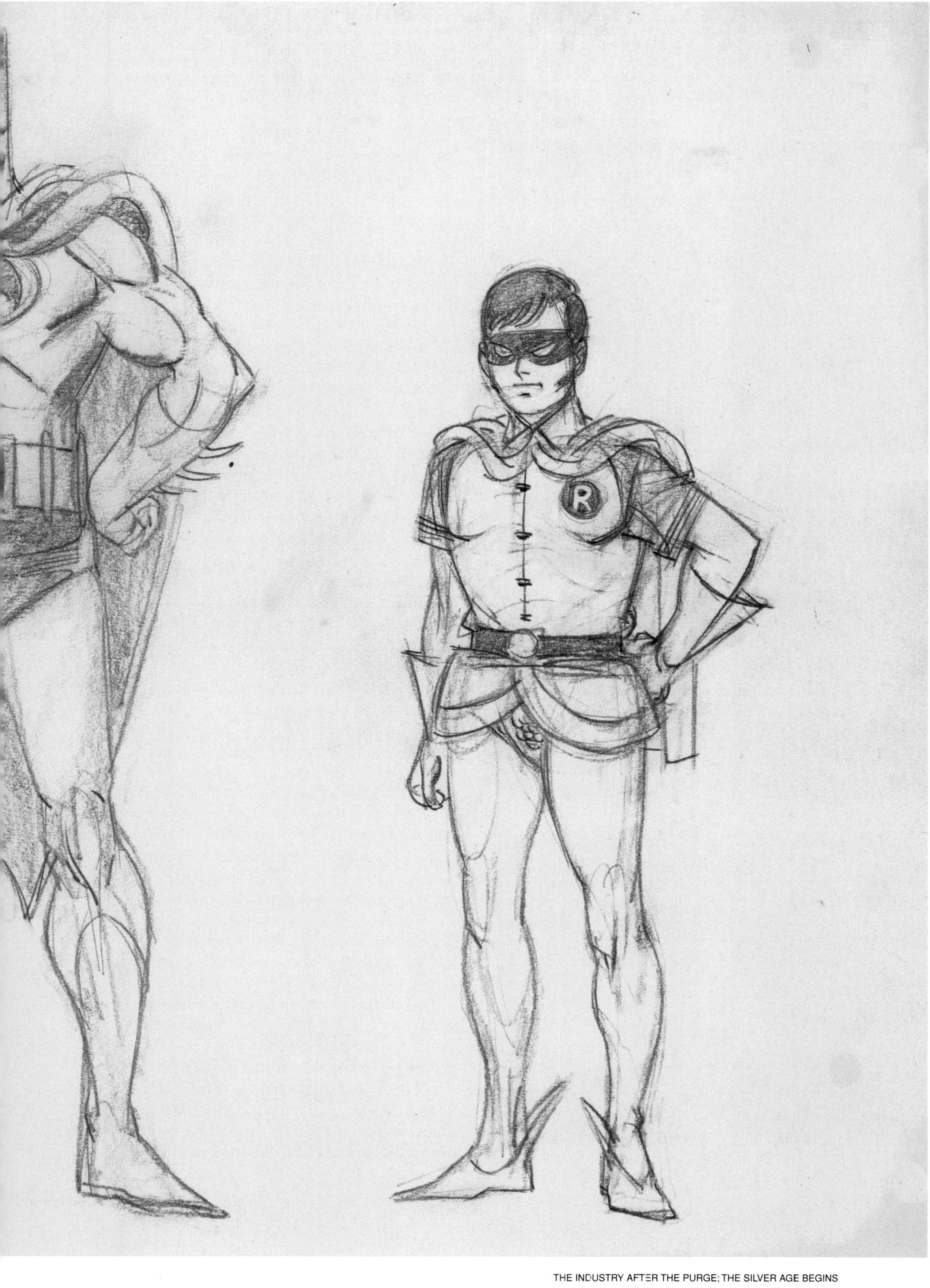

A gallery of *Batman* and *Detective* covers, all pencilled by Carmine Infantino. Clockwise: *Detective* #355, September, 1966, Joe Giella, inks; *Detective* #351, May, 1966, Murphy Anderson, inks; *The Brave and the Bold* #67, August/September, 1966, Joe Glella, inks; *Detective* #342, August, 1965, Joe Giella, inks; *Detective* #359, January, 1967, Murphy Anderson, inks; and *Batman* #169, February, 1965, Joe Giella, inks. Opposite page: Carmine Infantino, pencils, Murphy Anderson, inks, original cover artwork, *Detective* #364, June, 1967, ©1966, 1965, and 1967 DC Comics.

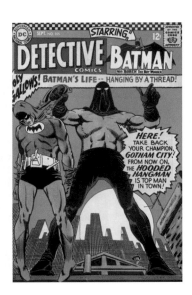

in the business. At DC he worked for Kanigher, turning out war comics as well as the *Shining Knight* and *Gladiator* strips in *The Brave and the Bold*.[10] Heath's work, as with Kubert's, was at its best in his depiction of real people thrust into extraordinary situations. Heath was an excellent draftsman and inker and could effortlessly and convincingly stage stories, which ranged from westerns to war stories to adventure tales.

Two others artists, or an artistic team, who worked primarily in Kanigher's stable and added their names to the roster of DC artists in 1952, were Ross Andru and Mike Esposito. Of the two, Andru was the quiet, reserved member of the team who provided the pencils, and Esposito was the inker and dealmaker. Both had been students at the School of Visual Arts and by the mid-1950s were turning out work for a number of publishers. They also went out as entrepreneurs and published their own magazines. By the end of the 1950s they were back with Kanigher, turning out war comics and *Wonder Woman*.[11] Generally they were dependable journeymen, but with one strip they created something unusual and memorable and for a brief moment turned out truly engaging work, as we shall see.

During the 1950s, DC's number one character, Superman, limped along with competent artwork by the same artists who had been with the strip for years. Clark Kent's alter ego was ably drawn by Wayne Boring and Al Plastino, but neither artist was able to put much pizzazz into Supes, and the character began to look tired. Boring is frequently credited with defining the look of the character, but by the mid-1950s his work was no more than a pastiche of his earlier efforts. Al Plastino did nothing more than turn out an easily distinguishable imitation of Boring's work.

This all changed when the editor of the Superman line, Mort Weisinger brought artist Curt Swan in to take over the comic book adventures of the man of steel. Swan hailed from Minneapolis, Minnesota and was born in 1920. He never gave comic books any consideration until during his service in the Second World War, when he met comic book writer France

Herron.[12] Swan, who had studied at the Pratt Institute, was working as a cartoonist for the army newspaper *Stars and Stripes*. After the war, at Herron's suggestion, Swan interviewed with Weisinger and Whitney Ellsworth, and he was put to work on *The Boy Commandos* strip. For the next ten years, Swan fielded a number of assignments, including *Superboy*, until he was picked to draw a 3-D Superman comic book.[13] Swan would go on to become the chief Superman artist and to define the look of the character for thirty years. Swan brought an attractiveness to the man of steel that had been missing from the strip since Jack Burnley had pencilled *Superman* in the 1940s. Swan's version of the character, while still a cartoon, had a smooth simplicity which echoed illustration. Swan was never a cutting edge storyteller; he just produced attractive, consistent, and beautifully crafted work. Swan would never be in the forefront of comic book storytelling, but his work was solid and always skillfully executed.

Another artist, who started with DC in the 1950s and produced competent work but sparkled in the 1960s, was Ramona Fradon, one of the few woman artists in the business. Fradon, who was born in 1926, hailed from Chicago and attended the Art Students League. She was never particularly interested in comic books but needed a job, so after interviewing around found employment with Atlas. She did not stay there long, and by 1952 she was working at DC on the *Shining Knight* strip. She then started pencilling the *Aquaman* strip for nearly a decade.[14] Her work on the feature was efficient and got the job done, but it never really gave Fradon a chance to flex her artistic muscle nor did it give a her an opportunity to impart any sense of humor to her work. Fortunately, she got an opportunity to demonstrate these attributes with her work in the 1960s.

The 1950s witnessed a number of competent craftsmen coming on board at DC. The ranks of these artists included a number of veterans from the Golden Age as well as newcomers just starting in the business. Each of DC's editors would usually use the same art-

ists to give their strips consistency. In addition to Kubert, Heath, and Andru and Esposito, Kanigher also called upon, among others, Jack Abel, Mort Drucker, Jerry Grandenetti, Irv Novick, and Alex Toth to craft his tales. Julie Schwartz would use six-foot-three-inch "Big" Mike Sekowsky and inker Bernie Sachs with increasing frequency. Mort Weisinger would turn to George Papp, John Forte, Win Mortimer, Kurt Schaffenberger, and John Sikela.

DC also assigned artwork chores to a legion of other artists: Tony Abruzzo, Bob Brown, Joe Certa, Nick Cardy, Dick Dillin,

Lee Elias, Bill Ely, Mort Meskin, Shelly Moldoff, Jim Mooney, Bob Oksner, Bruno Premiani, Howard Purcell, John Romita, Dick Sprang, and Jack Sparling. Some of these artists would go on to distinguish themselves while others just punched the clock as journeymen. Gil Kane commented that for the most part "very little thought or craft was put into the art, it was just being pumped out to make a living."[15]

By 1956 the stage was set for something which would change everything for comic books. Things were cooking at DC Comics which would revitalize the industry and the tired and listless superhero genre. Since the end of the war, Superman, Superboy, Batman and Robin, and Wonder Woman had listlessly

glided along. For the most part these were the only superheroes available in comic books, and at best the artwork and stories found in the pages of these DC titles were uninspired. In 1956 DC premiered a new comic book title called *Showcase,* which would use its pages as a trial balloon for new characters to see if they generated adequate sales to merit their own separate magazines. The first several issues of *Showcase* were duds and fired little enthusiasm; kids were not lining up to buy titles about frogmen and firefighters. At the editorial meeting to decide the fate of the fourth issue of *Showcase*, Julie Schwartz remembers, "I suggested we try to revive the Flash, who died with the demise of the other superhero titles…some of my coworkers were incredulous and asked me why I thought Flash would succeed now, having failed so dismally a few years before…"[16] Schwartz reasoned that another go with the Flash might give the superhero a new lease on life as all the youngsters who had lost interest in costumed heroes had since grown up and there was a whole new crop of kids looking for something more interesting than the staid likes of DC's remaining super/wonder/bat-titles. Schwartz was right.

Editorial Director Irwin Donenfeld, son of the company's founder Harry, was so impressed with the idea that Schwartz was charged with coming up with something. Things had changed significantly since Schwartz had edited the original Flash who had last run at super speed before being sent out to pasture in 1949 with *Flash Comics* #104. The artists who had crafted the first incarnation of the Flash at his end, who included Infantino, Toth, and Kubert, had now spent seven years developing and maturing as art-

ists. These artists were no longer just up-and-comers; they were ready to take on something interesting and give it a new twist. Schwartz called on Robert Kanigher, who shared an office with him, to come up with a script. The backup story was written by John Broome. Both Kanigher and Broome worked under Schwartz's close supervision. More importantly, he picked Carmine Infantino to pencil and design the character and Joe Kubert to ink the feature. Almost eighteen years before, when Superman had premiered in *Action* #1, it took four issues before the company knew it had a hit; the same was true with the reintroduction of the Flash. After four tryouts, superheroes would re-emerge, but with a difference.

The second incarnation of the Flash presented an origin story where police chemist Barry Allen is hit by lightning and bathed in

Left: Jack Kirby, pencils, *House of Secrets* #12, September, 1958. Below: Jack Kirby, pencils, Wally Wood, inks, original interior page artwork, *Challengers of the Unknown* #7, April/May, 1959, ©1958 and 1959 DC Comics.

chemicals from his lab, turning him into the fastest man alive. He takes as his inspiration the comic book character from the Golden Age, adopting his moniker. Alan dons a red outfit with a yellow lightning bolt and takes up crime fighting as a sideline.

The artwork for Infantino's Flash was sleek and crafted with unmistakable panache. The experience Infantino had gained from his assignments with tales of westerns, mysteries, and science fiction, coalesced as his work headed into the 1960s, resulting in storytelling that pushed established conventions in new directions. While the design of the panels and layout on a page had always been a consideration for comic artists, by and large most artwork was designed using a standard grid layout, providing for two panels on the top, three panels below, and two panels in the last tier, with standard variations. Infantino subtly experimented with his page breakdowns but never allowed the design to detract from the storytelling. The interior page artwork from *Flash* #135, illustrated on page 95, is a perfect example of Infantino's dramatic use of design. The first panel is horizontal and occupies roughly one-third of the entire page. Infantino uses a clever but simple effect to simulate the lightning fast speed of Kid Flash as he runs toward his mentor, the Flash. In the tier below, of two equal panels, Infantino focuses on both characters and develops the exposition by cutting from one angle in the left hand panel to another angle in the next panel to prevent the story from becoming static. Infantino also uses sparse, simple, black backgrounds to keep the page uncluttered. The third tier consists of a thin horizontal rectangle with a long shot showing both characters to keep the story moving and to give the page more visual diversity. The last panel is a close-up of the Flash against a black background which crops much of the character's face away. This dramatic use of black and white and of the figure of the Flash juxtaposed across from a word balloon makes the dialogue an element in the composition of the panel   In the space of one page, Infantino uses an arsenal of storytelling techniques for a visually effective

essay in the use of intelligent and artful page design.

Infantino was Schwartz's favorite artist.[17] Schwartz used him frequently and well on other projects which further defined DC's newly invigorated line of super and not-so-super characters. By the August, 1959 issue of *Mystery in Space*, Infantino also took on the duties of pencilling the *Adam Strange* strip, a yarn about an anthropologist from earth, the namesake of the feature, who is mysteriously transported to the planet Rann, located in the galaxy Alpha Centuri, via the zeta-beam. Strange not only had unearthly adventures, but also fell in love with the exotically named Alanna, daughter of a prominent scientist on the far-away world Strange visited in each episode. In the *AS* strip, Infantino composed covers which got kids to look inside and stories which were handsomely and aggressively designed. The plots for *Adam Strange*, as with the *Flash* series, were whimsical, innocent and are still naïvely amusing.

Perhaps Infantino's most successful work was on a character called the Elongated Man. As his name implied, the Elongated Man could stretch himself to any length necessary to help solve the puzzles and mysteries he was investigating. The Elongated Man stepped into the DC universe in a *Flash* story presented in issue #112 in 1960. The character was a guest star in the *Flash* series until he got his own feature as a backup in *Detective* #327 in 1964. EM was a superhero, who, unlike most crime fighters, did not have a secret identity and was named Ralph Dibney. He solved mysteries with his wife in tow, in the style of Myrna Loy and William Powell in the *The Thin Man*. During the Elongated Man's tenure as a second banana to the Flash, he was pencilled by

Infantino with inks supplied by Joe Giella. As usual, Giella removed Infantino's personality from the feature and provided a consistent, bland gloss. When the Elongated Man was promoted to his own strip, Infantino, on occasion, provided both pencils and inks. It is clear from Infantino's efforts that he not only had fun with the strip, but also let loose creatively with inks that were spontaneous, lively, and in some cases, off-the-wall. Unfortunately, the scripts by Gardner Fox never matched the improvisational feel of Infantino's artwork.[18] Fox never had a wry sense of humor, and, although he presented the strip's mysteries as light fare, the feature never really took advantage of EM's ability to bend and stretch every part of his body á la Plas. While Jack Cole may have been the inspiration for the strip, the maniacal tone necessary to make the feature click never materialized. Because of his ability to ink the strip and make it completely his own, *Elongated Man* was Infantino's favorite effort.[19]

Infantino's last major effort and best known strip, to the non-comic book fan audience, was *Batman*. DC's management knew that the strip was in trouble and reasoned a makeover might help boost sales. Schwartz was called in to give the feature a face-lift. He performed his usual intelligent job and brought in Infantino to pencil the strip. For years Bob Kane had signed the strip and had a number of other artists ghost for him.[20] The primary artist had been Shelly Moldoff, whose work was sometimes just barely competent. Infantino's redesign brought the character up-to-date and added a sheen to the caped crusader missing for years.

Infantino's version of Batman and Robin gave them a contemporary feel with artwork that was as slick as anything he had ever produced. The covers created by Infantino quickly helped to boost sales and the general appeal of the dynamic duo. When the *Batman* television show hit the tube, sales of DC's battitles, *Batman* and *Detective*, went through the roof.

Infantino has candidly confessed that he had no particular love for superheroes; nevertheless, he gave the strip a new lease on life. By 1964, Infantino had firmly established design conventions for his pages that he used as

Gil Kane, pencils, Joe Giella, inks, original interior page artwork, *Green Lantern* #8, September/October, 1961, ©1961 DC Comics.

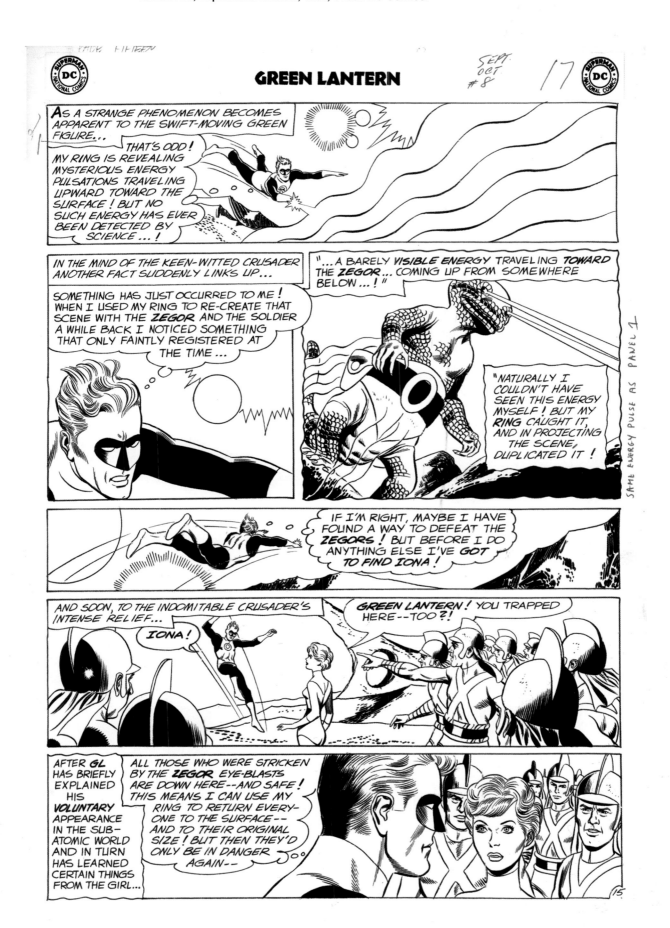

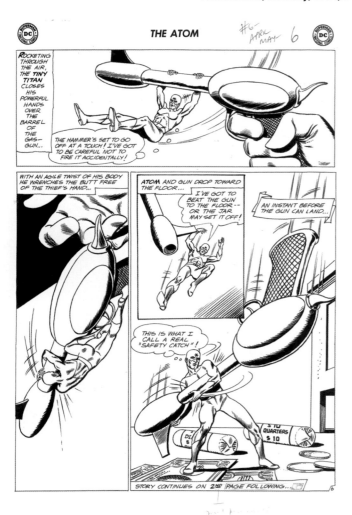

Anderson also added weight to the drawing which was never intended by Infantino's pencils. Pages 98 and 99, display a model sheet of Infantino's uninked pencils of Batgirl, Batman, and Robin. A comparison of the model sheet with Anderson's inking of the cover clearly demonstrates the flavor removed by Anderson when he inked over Infantino's spirited and animated pencils. Anderson replaced Infantino's spontaneity with solid, heavy inking and correct anatomy.

Infantino was not content to work solely as an artist. With Schwartz's help, he pitched himself to DC's management and swung the job of art director. Now, Infantino had a hand in the cover artwork for all of the company's books.[21] Infantino owed as much to his talent as he did to DC's not wanting to lose him to Marvel. Infantino had received an offer, at a higher rate of pay, to jump ship to Marvel. Stan

a template for all of his layouts. The interior page artwork from *Detective* #327, on page 102, is clearly a variation on his *Flash* page previously discussed; the layout is merely rearranged. The second panel of the page is yet another example of how Infantino was using design to highlight his storytelling. Two horizontal rectangles, one with text, the other empty, serve as a counterpoint to the cropped figures of Batman and Robin, who are asymmetrically placed in the panel to give it more visual interest. This page was inked by Joe Giella who turns in a competent effort, again giving a slickness to Infantino's work that was never intended. Compare this page with the cover to *Detective* #364 on page 101, which was inked by Murphy Anderson. Anderson clearly altered the figures' anatomy, making it more attuned to illustration and less cartoony.

Gil Kane, pencils, Murphy Anderson, inks, original cover artwork, *Green Lantern* #60, April, 1968, ©1968 DC Comics.

Lee had pitched an offer for him to come over to Marvel; Infantino advised Irwin Donenfeld of the situation. The end result was Infantino stayed with DC and started his trip up the executive ladder. By 1967 he became editorial director of DC Comics.[22] Infantino would spend a majority of his time for the foreseeable future in management, and his art would suffer for it. When he finally actively returned as an artist, the spark which had made his artwork hot was gone.

Just as *Showcase* #4 had thrust Infantino into the limelight, *Showcase* #6, released in late 1956, gave comic book veteran and the industry's presumptive preeminent artist, Jack

Kirby, another vehicle to show off his stuff, again. Only two years before, Kirby was still going strong; he and Joe Simon had been setting trends and turning out some of the best work in the business. The aftermath of the Subcommittee hearings left them beached, scrambling for work and income. Their company, Mainline Publications, which had published the comic books *Bullseye*, *Foxhole*, *In Love*, and *Police Trap*, was pulled down when its distributor, Leader News, which had also distributed EC Comics, became insolvent.[23]

Kirby rather melodramatically described the atmosphere after the Subcommittee hearings and its effect on the partnership to his biographer, Ray Wyman, observing, "It was like walking into a house that was burned to the ground…everything is where you left it, but there's nothing left of what it was like. Like the atom bomb in Japan, all that was left of the people were shadows on the sidewalks and walls. All you can do is pick up what's left and move on. I guess that's what happened to Joe and me."[24] Simon went off to work for Harvey; Kirby went to work for Atlas and DC, and finished outstanding commitments to several other companies, including Harvey.

With the dissolution of the partnership, Kirby had taken his share of unrealized projects, including the concept that became *Challengers of the Unknown*, which was used in *Showcase*.[25] Kirby refined the idea for the strip over a several month period and then sold it to DC Comics.[26] *Challengers* was another variation on a team of adventurers pioneered in the pulps in such titles as *Doc Savage*, but with a flavor and point of view only Kirby could bring to such a concept. Since Kirby's breakthrough with *Captain America*, fifteen years before, he had been strongest telling stories which focused on mythical, archetypal characters. Kirby was in his element with superheroes, but the times had dictated that he focus on other genres. Now, superheroes and adventurers were being reconsidered for rejuvenation, and with *Challengers of the Unknown*, Kirby was able to turn in a virtuoso performance. Under the editorial control of

Top: Gil Kane, pencils, Wally Wood, inks, original interior page artwork, *Captain Action* #2, December/January, 1969, ©1969 DC Comics. **Bottom:** Gil Kane, pencils and inks, original cover artwork, *Tales of Suspense* #88, April, 1967, ©1967 Marvel Characters, Inc.

Jack Schiff, the editor of the Batman line of comic books, with a script by Dave Wood, Kirby turned in a full twenty-four page story with characters and a plot which would put the most recent season of *Alias* to shame.

The Challengers were a group of four men who had miraculously escaped a jet crash and were living on "borrowed time." Their survival binds them together as a team who challenge the unknown, hence their moniker. In their first adventure, the Challengers confront a puzzle of mythological proportions and search for a secret which will give its possessor something eternally desired. Obviously, the general plot outline for this story, *The Secrets of the Sorcerer's Box*, is required reading for all television scripters and screenwriters today. As a storyteller, Kirby relished his ability to spin this yarn, and his artwork moves the story along without missing a beat. After three more tryouts, *Challengers* received its own title in 1958. Kirby turned in other efforts at DC, but it was with *Challengers* that he established he could turn in topnotch material on his own. His composition, pacing, and breakdown of the action throughout this story is a near perfect example of comic book storytelling.

Kirby did not limit his efforts solely to comic books; he was also actively pitching newspaper strips. Nothing seemed to click, and just when it looked as if Kirby would never get an opportunity at a syndicated feature, he met in the DC offices with Jack Schiff and Dave Wood. Schiff had been approached by a syndicate wanting to do a space-related strip. The George Matthew Adams Syndicate had approached Schiff, looking to buy a prepackaged product. Schiff queried management, but DC was unwilling to oblige. Schiff nevertheless was given the green light to proceed on his own with the project. Schiff naturally turned to his freelance staff for talent, hence the involvement of Wood and Kirby.[27] The subject of the strip was the current national fascination – the space race. Space travel had always been a mainstay of science fiction, but with Sputnik orbiting the earth every ninety-eight minutes and the United States space pro-

Gil Kane, pencils, Sid Greene, inks, original cover artwork,
The Atom #37, June/July, 1968, ©1968 DC Comics.

gram struggling to keep up with the Russians, outer space was now on everyone's mind. The result was a beautifully crafted product, inked by EC veteran and science fiction specialist, Wally Wood, called *Sky Masters*. Wood additionally lent a hand with the inking chores over Kirby's pencils in several *Challengers* books. *Sky Masters* premiered in over three hundred newspapers on September 8, 1958. The strip was a blessing and a curse for Kirby, however.

When it was assured that *Sky Masters* would make it into syndication, a dispute broke out between Kirby and Schiff over royalties. Schiff filed a lawsuit against Kirby and the strip's writers, Dave and Dick Wood. Kirby vehemently opposed Schiff's claim, and the case came to a head with a favorable verdict being rendered for Schiff.[28] For years, Joe Simon had successfully handled the business aspects for the partnership, but now Kirby was on his own. The message from the *Sky Masters* debacle was clear: Kirby should stick to his art. Even though Kirby had been turning out mountains of artwork for DC, he left the publisher and went back to Stan Lee at what would become Marvel. Even though at the time Kirby never suspected it, this would be his lucky break. His move to Marvel would revolutionize comics and assure Kirby's place as the industry's preeminent storyteller.

Julie Schwartz was on a roll. Energized by the reception of the new and improved Flash, he decided to follow up with the reintroduction of another mothballed character, Green Lantern. This time he turned to Gil Kane for artwork and design chores. For the last ten years, Kane had been turning in competent work on westerns, science fiction, mystery titles, and even on some romance stories. Kane was also making a conscientious effort to develop as an artist and as a storyteller. He was aware that comic books were as much about art as they were about craft. Kane had spent the 1950s honing his skills as a draftsman, developing his sense of design and layout. Looking back at his pre-Green Lantern efforts on the *Johnny Thunder* strip in *All-Star Western*, a clear progression can be seen in

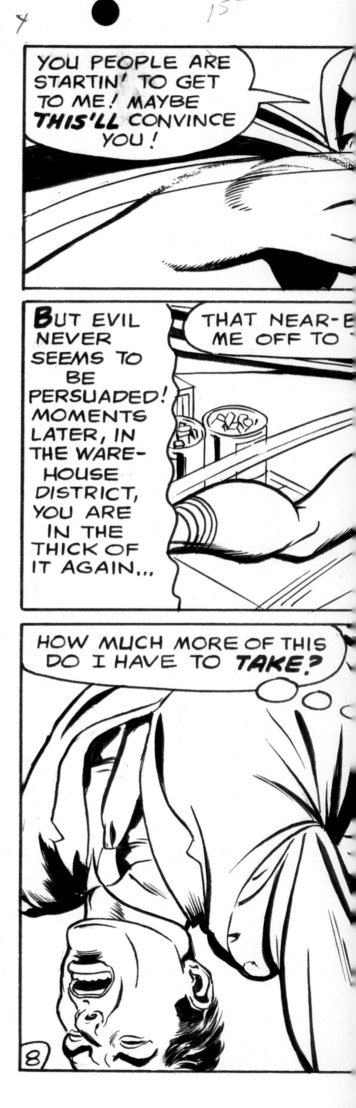

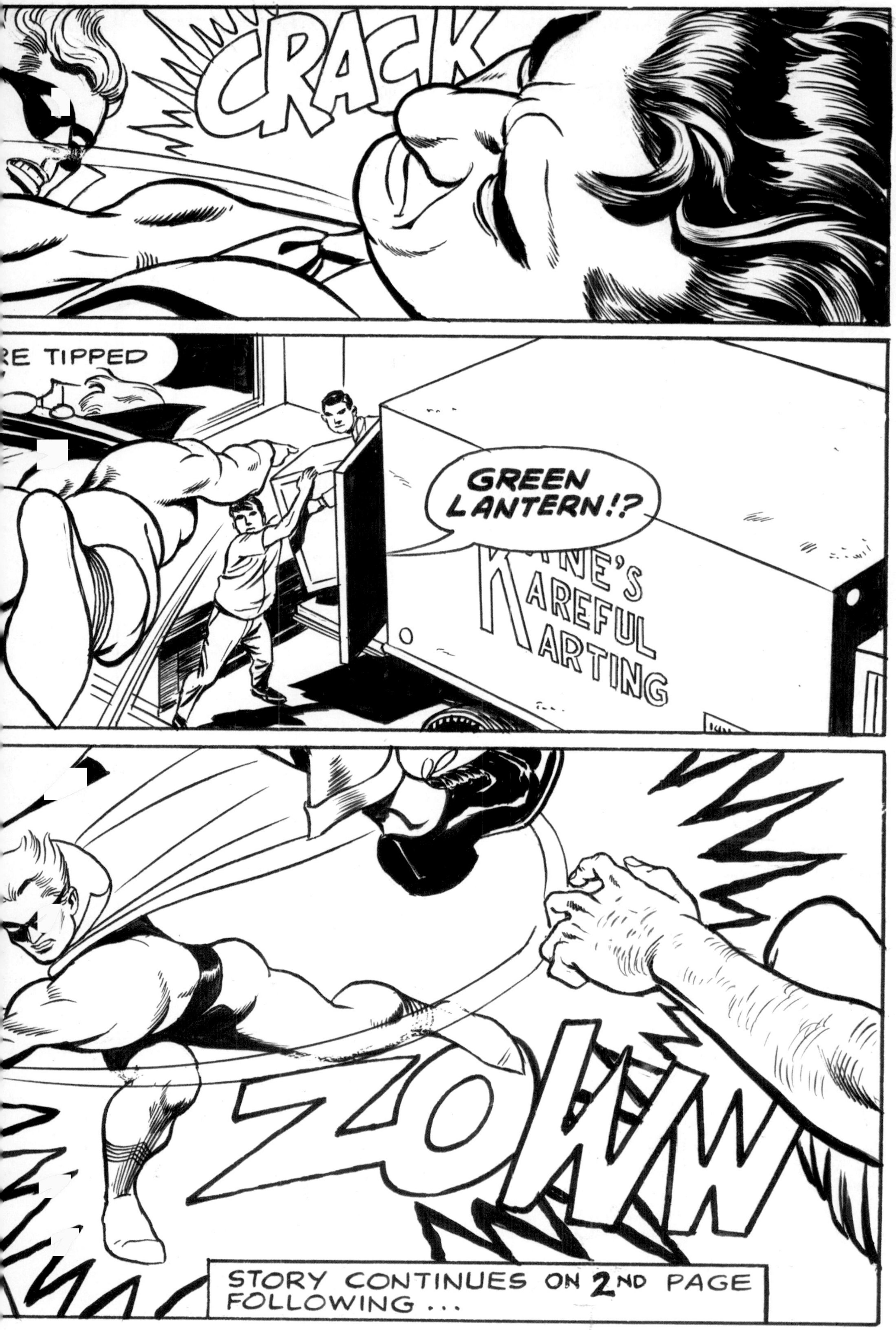
CRACK
RE TIPPED
GREEN LANTERN!?
K NE'S AREFUL ARTING
ZOWW
STORY CONTINUES ON 2ND PAGE FOLLOWING . . .

Mike Sekowsky, pencils, Bernie Sachs, inks, original interior page
artwork, *The Brave and the Bold* #29, April/May, 1960, ©1960 DC Comics.

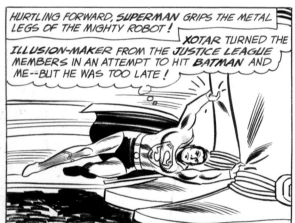

Kane's handling of his figures. He was even allowed, on occasion, to ink some of these stories, and when he did, it was clear Kane was coming into his own as an artist with a distinguishable voice, which had something to say about action/adventure storytelling. Kane's work on DC's western strips gave hints as to what was brewing with his art and what might be in store.

Green Lantern made his re-debut in *Showcase* #22, with a release date of September/October, 1959. Kane's art got off to a solid start with an inking assist from Joe Giella. Schwartz drew on the dependable talent of John Broome for the plots, which propelled Green Lantern into action. Green Lantern, as with the Flash, was given a fresh update. GL was now a test pilot, who, when he put on his green, white, and black formfitting suit, doubled as a member of an intergalactic police force. Instead of the magical powers the first GL possessed, the space age version of the character enforced the laws of the cosmos with a power ring, which had to be charged every twenty-four hours with a green glowing power battery, a green lantern.

The new GL was athletic, handsome, and owed a lot of his grace to Kane's conscious attempts to inject some Lou Fine-ish elegance into the strip.[29] Kane's efforts, at first, were not entirely successful due to Giella's inking, which failed to adequately translate the acrobatic energy of Kane's pencils. Kane was also paired with inker Murphy Anderson, which was not a significant improvement. Anderson, who was also a big fan of Fine, was incapable of imparting the sense of movement Kane was striving for. Despite the incongruent inking of the strip, it was, nevertheless, charming, fun, and good looking to boot; after all, lackluster and stiff inking cannot suppress spirited, creative pencilling.

Kane was not entirely content with his initial contributions for the strip, either. He understood where he wanted to take it but needed to improve; in retrospect, Kane noted that he was working hard to hone "his facility to impart grace to the human form in action."[30] A rather high-sounding sentiment, but Kane's

steady, disciplined quest to further refine his figures paid off with work that exploded off the pages of his comic books, right into the imaginations of the kids reading the stories.

Help was around the corner when Schwartz assigned inker Sid Greene to embellish the strip. Finally, Kane had somebody who could keep up with his frenetic pacing and full-bodied anatomy. Kane's art was also forced to mature with the demands made by the strip, which he freely admitted.[31]

While Infantino's work had focused on design, with the anatomy and choreography of the characters taking a back seat, Kane focused on giving the action in his stories a tangible presence through his skilled depiction of his highly styled, idealized version of the human form. In summarizing his work on the strip, Kane observed:

> I think a lot of my work on *Green Lantern* was very primitive...the one quality that I'm always trying to push through in my work is grace and power. The sort of primitive lyricism that I've been capable of. I thought that that's the one quality that sort of saved me and permeated my work and gave me any kind of legitimate status. Finally I could support it with better drawing and better understanding of my craft.[32]

With superheroes on the rise, other genres that had offered work and put bread on the table for artists were vanishing. Western genre comic books, which had been Kane's main money makers during the 1950s, were now being cancelled. Even though Kane had a steady gig with *Green Lantern* (the strip received its own title in 1960), he needed to drum up more work to pay the bills. In his effort to solve this dilemma, Kane pitched the idea to revive a Golden Age superhero with a twist: combine two heroes into one.[33] When Quality had gone under in 1956, DC purchased its characters, including Blackhawk, Plastic Man, and Doll Man. The latter character, who had been created by Will Eisner with artwork by Lou Fine, was the first step in Kane's amalgam. Doll Man was a costumed crime-fighter who could reduce his size to 6 inches, which permitted him to get into interesting situations using giant props.[34] Kane combined Doll Man with DC's Golden Age Atom, who was a short but mighty, mortal crime-fighter with an "atomic" punch. Kane's new Atom could reduce himself from normal size to any dimension. This allowed the character to become subatomic and travel through telephone lines.

Kane did several concept drawings, including an illustration which showed the diminutive Atom in a formfitting red-and-blue outfit

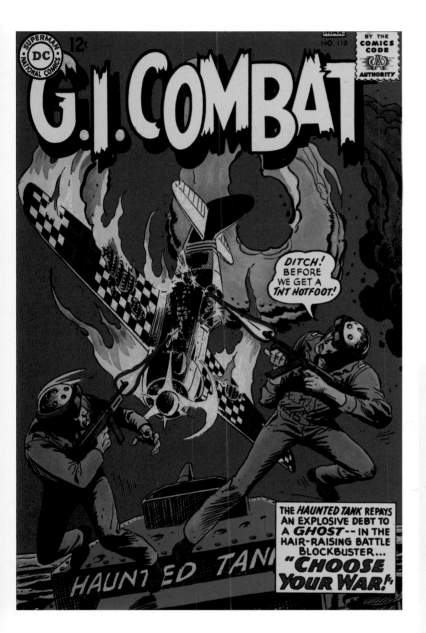

own book in 1962, assuring Kane more income and an opportunity to further tweak his skills.

By the mid-1960s Kane's work on GL was really cooking. His staging was now more confident and assured; his figures boasted a new energy and elegance. Kane's artwork for GL oozed with élan. Kane attributes part of this development to his methodical analysis of the anatomy treatises of George Bridgman. Kane remembered, "…I practiced every day, I kept going back to Bridgman."[36] Kane also went back to basics and reassessed the work of Roy Crane and revisited Reed Crandall's early work for Quality. Kane's persistent, critical analysis of his own work, coupled with refocusing on his craft, paid off; he was quickly approaching the top of his game as an artist.

(most of the new heroes favored formfitting attire without the ornament of a cape), sitting atop a German Shepherd, presumably Rex the Wonder Dog, one of Kane's signature characters from the 1950s. Julie Schwartz tweaked the character, adding a familiar science fiction twist; the Atom was able to "get small" by the use of white star matter. The strip premiered in *Showcase* #34 with a cover date of September/October, 1961. As an inside joke and a tribute, Schwartz named the Atom's alter ego after his friend, Ray Palmer, who due to a childhood injury was never able to grow to adult size.[35] After doing time as a *Showcase* feature, the Atom was promoted to his

The advances made by Kane are readily apparent by comparing the interior page artwork from *Green Lantern* #8, inked by Joe Giella, on page 107, with the page from *Green Lantern* #61, inked by Sid Greene, on pages 112-113. Six years separate the artwork on these pages, and the differences between both of these examples is immediately obvious.

The page from *Green Lantern* #8 is skillfully designed, but Kane does not take advantage of the full potential offered by the format of an entire comic book page. This page does not go beyond standard storytelling methods of the early 1960s. Kane conservatively breaks down the narrative and keeps all of the action within the confines of the panels. He effectively crops some of his shots but never pushes the action outside of the panel borders. The panels on the page act as a border to confine the action. The frame used on comic book pages is, obviously, an artificially constructed boundary and accordingly has infinite uses not explored by this page. In film, movement and action take place outside the frame of the screen. Sometimes it can be a sound off screen that signals something is going to happen. In other instances, action can literally fly out of the picture frame or into the frame from off

screen. These techniques were used, with varying degrees of success by comic artists during the 1950s, notably, as we have seen, by Toth. When used skillfully, "shooting" a comic book page can become as effective as the theatrical devices used in film, but on paper.

The page from *Green Lantern* #61 is frenetic, spirited, and cinematic in its handling of the action. This page contains an array of devices Kane would use for the rest of his career and is an excellent example of his mature style. The inking by Greene perfectly captures Kane's fluid and animated pencils. The first panel throws the head of the bad guy out toward the viewer, with Kane cropping the shot to the narrow horizontal perspective of the frame within the panel. Kane forces the perspective of the shot out, toward the viewer, to the right hand side of the frame. The bottom panel throws the top and bottom of the next villain's body out of the frame (as he is confronted by the Golden Age GL) and only shows the arm of the second bad guy that GL has already dispatched flying out of the frame on the right (notice the name on the truck). Not only is this page more fun to look at, it is more lively and actually animates the action of the story so that the page hardly needs any

Joe Kubert, pencils and inks, original splash page artwork, *The Brave and the Bold* #35, April/May, 1961, ©1961 DC Comics.

Russ Heath, pencils and inks, original splash page artwork, *Sea Devils* #9,
January/February, 1963, ©1963 DC Comics.

text or word balloons to make its point. While, admittedly, the plots of most action comic book stories do not require much exposition, neither did most action/adventure movies of the 1960s. Sometimes the action is an end unto itself. Archetypal comic books tell stories which focus on battles between the good and the not-so-good, and Kane was a master of concisely chronicling these adventures in pages such as this.

Kane's covers also show the same evidence of his increased sophistication as an artist and his developing design sense. The cover from *Green Lantern* #26, with Murphy Anderson, inks, on page 108, was created in 1963. This cover boasts a solid layout with a clever hook to get kids to buy the comic book before reading the story. Covers were designed much like movie posters, to attract the buyer and make a quick sale. Contrast this cover with the cover from *Green Lantern* #60, created in 1967, on page 109. This comic book poster-cover, ably inked by Anderson, is dramatic and theatrical. It crops GL's face which takes up half of the cover, with the issue's nemesis shown in outlines, only as a design element. This cover is worlds apart from the *GL* #26 cover which is standard fare, and hardly exceptional. Graphically, the *GL* #60 cover, with its asymmetrical design is completely at home with the best motion picture advertisements of the era and would definitely have hooked kids, or maybe even a grown-up or two, to buy the book.

Unlike many of his colleagues, Kane was intellectually restless and always trying to push the envelope of his own limitations. By 1966, he was 40, his hair was streaked with flecks of silver, his six-foot-three frame was still athletic, and he almost always sported a jacket. He was also mixing with non-comic book writers and artists. New York City was now the pop capital of the world, despite what Londoners would have you believe. Kane circulated in the mix between comic book artists and those who would not even look at one. He also had aspirations to do more than just pencil GL and the Atom for DC. It was during this time, the early-1960s, that he made

Ross Andru, pencils, Mike Esposito, inks, original interior page artwork, *Metal Men* #25, April/May, 1967. Below: Ross Andru, pencils, Mike Esposito, inks, cover, *Showcase* #38, May/June, 1962, ©1967 and 1962 DC Comics.

the acquaintance of one James Warren. Warren wanted to be a mover-and-shaker in the world of comics, and he had both the aspiration and the drive to give his ambition a try.

Warren hailed from the City of Brotherly Love, Philadelphia, where he got his start in the publishing business. In 1957, he started a *Playboy* simulacrum called *After Hours*, which had a run of four issues before Warren was arrested for peddling pornography. The charges put the publication out of business and got the local District Attorney, who had brought trumped up allegations against Warren, reelected. When the case finally went to court, it was quickly thrown out. Warren had not published anything really indecent; he was just in the wrong place at the wrong time, as the publicity-hungry D.A. needed a hometown boy as a target to maximize his press coverage.[37] By 1960, Warren had relocated in New York in an attempt to inject some excitement into his products. He was now publishing a number of off-beat magazines, none of which were comic books, which consisted of *Famous Monsters*, *Favorite Westerns of Filmland*, *Help!*, and *Wildest Westerns. Help!* was an adult humor magazine helmed by Harvey Kurtzman, who also had a financial stake and creative control of the publication. Unfortunately, *Help!*, which premiered in 1960, folded after only twenty-six issues in 1965. Kurtzman was involved with other Warren magazines as well, but without any ownership interest.

Warren ran his business from a duplex penthouse in midtown Manhattan at 47th Street and 2nd Avenue called Embassy House.[38] It was at this locale that Kane made Warren's acquaintance. Kane also became friendly with another Warren mover-and-shaker, editor-writer, Archie Goodwin, a relationship which would artistically blossom later. Warren was trying to develop comic book properties, and one of Kane's friends, cartoonist Dick Hodgins, put in a good word for him. Warren and Kane hit it off, and work was started on a comic book which was to be in the vein of *Archie*. To get Kane moving on the project, Warren gave him a studio in his building to focus on turning out

his artwork. Warren lived in the penthouse of the building and still fancied himself a Hefneresque figure, walking around in a bathrobe by day and hosting many spirited parties, after hours. Kane's work on the project never amounted to anything, but he did have a lot of fun and got the itch to publish his own magazine, which he would get around to doing shortly, raising some eyebrows and making some comic book history in the process.[39]

In addition to his DC efforts, Kane turned in work for Wally Wood's line of superhero comic books put out by Tower Comics. Kane's stories for Wood's *Thunder Agents*, *NoMan*, *Undersea Agent,* and *Dynamo* let loose with a level of action less restrained than his DC efforts, but these tales were hobbled by inane plots even by the standards of the day. He also started to contribute artwork for DC's main rival, Marvel, at first using the pen name Scott Edward (the first names of his son and adopted son). Kane's efforts at Marvel, where Stan Lee dubbed him Gil "Sugar lips" Kane and "Gregarious" Gil Kane (Stan loved catchy nicknames), were exercises in unbridled action and were animated, exciting, and fun.

Kane also had an unusual opportunity to write, pencil, and ink an entire comic book story. Kane had become the artist on a strange title, which was created as a tie-in with a boy's action doll. The strip, which only ran for five issues, was called *Captain Action*. Kane's involvement started with issue #2, release dated December/January,1969, which teamed him with inker Wally Wood. Kane, who at the time was reading George Bernard Shaw's *Man and Superman*, took the third act of the play, *Don Juan in Hell*, as his inspiration for issue #4 of the feature, which he scripted, pencilled and inked. Despite Kane's general reliance on Shaw, the story is pure, archetypal, pulp fantasy, charged by Kane's frenetic artwork. Kane recalls that he never "had so much fun" working on a comic book and his enthusiasm is clearly in evidence.[40]

During the late 1960s, Kane's work evolved to the point where he found a voice and rhythm for his storytelling that was uniquely his own. The time he spent with Julie Schwartz pencil-

office and he takes the check out of his drawer and looks at it, knowing what the amount is, and looks at me and tells me my page rate is too high. I told him, 'That's the same rate I've been getting for couple of years.' So, Carmine tells me he was cutting my rate."[41] The incident stood out in Schwartz's mind over thirty years later, and he remembered that Kane came back to his office with the check and "announced he wasn't working for DC anymore."[42] Kane saw the writing on the wall: his tenure with DC for the time being was effectively at an end. Kane jumped ship, or was thrown, over to Marvel, which ironically turned out to be his lucky break. His work at Marvel for the next five years gave him more freedom, frequently teaming him with a collaborator who shared many of his sensibili-

ling *GL* and *The Atom* were the final steps in Kane's development, which led to his surpassing his influences. Kane's ascendance to the top ranks of his profession did not go unnoticed, and his work was admired by fans as well as by other artists.

This did not help him maintain his established rate of pay per page for artwork with DC, however. As we have seen, by 1967 Carmine Infantino had ascended to the exalted position of editorial director; he then was promoted to publisher and finally became president of DC. When Infantino had the chance, he arranged for Kane to pick up his check in his office rather than from Julie Schwartz. Kane remembers, "So I went into Carmine's

Ramona Fradon, pencils and inks, original cover artwork, *The Brave and the Bold* #58, February/March, 1965, ©1965 DC Comics.

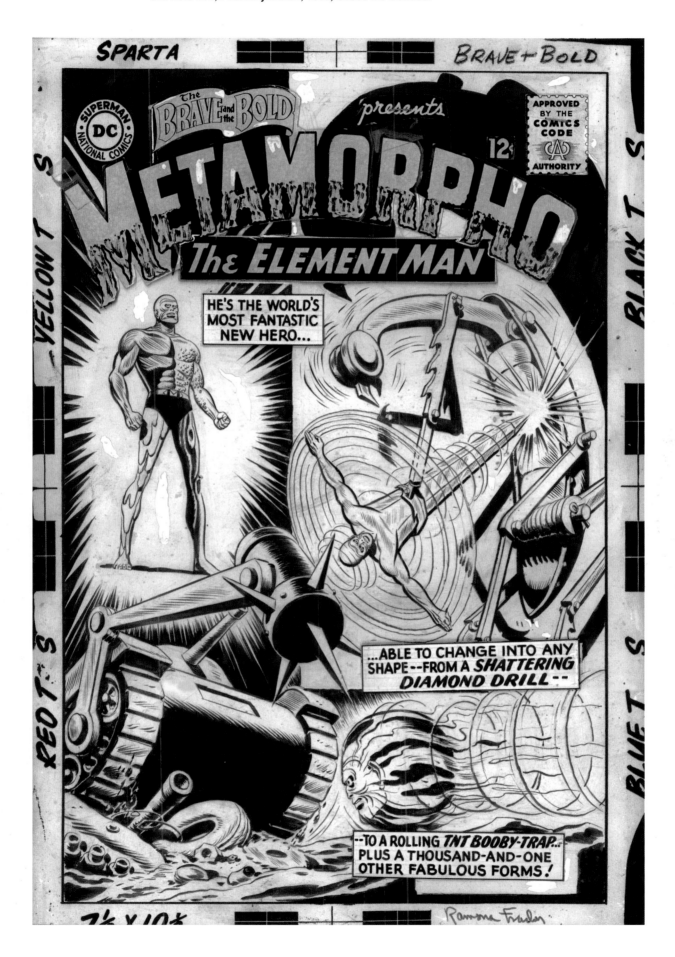

ties, Roy Thomas. This partnership produced some inspired storytelling. Kane also became the company's chief cover artist and influenced the look of the entire Marvel line of comic books and a whole new generation of artists and kids reading comic books.

After Julie Schwartz's successes with *The Flash* and *Green Lantern*, he considered what to do next, as superhero titles were once again flying off the comic book racks. In the 1940s, All American had successfully pioneered the idea of teaming its various heroes together in an organization called the Justice Society of America. The first such "team-up" occurred in the pages of *All Star* #3, with a release date of Winter, 1940. *All Star* brought together such colorful characters as the original Flash, Green Lantern, Hawkman, Spectre, Atom, Hourman, Dr. Fate, and the Sandman. Of course, as DC had instigated Max C. Gaines to produce the All American line of comic books and distributed them, occasionally Superman and Batman joined in as well.[43] For Schwartz's next trick, he took it upon himself, as he described it, to

"Silver Age the Golden Justice Society of America." Schwartz changed the name of the new superhero association though, because he thought, "it sounded too much like a club name like 'high society' or something…the readers were more familiar with 'League' from the National League and the American League."[44] For this new incarnation of DC's superhero team, Schwartz picked Gardner Fox, who had written the strip in the 1940s, to script the feature and drafted artist Mike Sekowsky to pencil. The JLA's roll call included as its members: Flash, Green Lantern, Wonder Woman, Aquaman, Martian Manhunter, and an irritating teenager named Snapper Carr. Superman and Batman put in guest appearances. The strip premiered in *The Brave and the Bold* #28 with a release date of February/March, 1960. After three tryouts, the *JLA* proved to be so popular that it was given its own title by the end of the year.

Sekowsky proved an interesting, if not unusual, pick. He was born in 1926 and attended the School of Industrial Arts. By the early

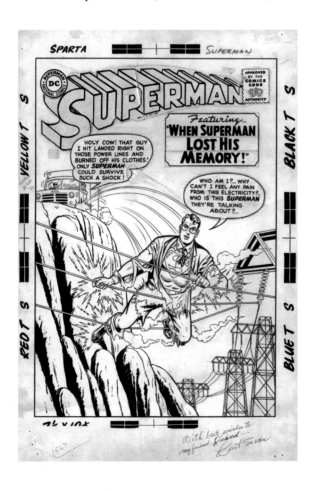

1940s, Sekowsky had found work on super-hero strips the like of *Captain America* and the *Human Torch*. He also spent considerable time punching the clock, turning out funny animal strips. In the 1950s he worked all around the industry in virtually every genre. Sekowsky developed an intelligent and thoughtful style of storytelling which helped get him in the door at DC in 1954. His work was an interesting mix of action/adventure storytelling told in a more cartoony style, which clearly owed a debt to Alex Toth. The un-Tothlike aspect of his work was that many of his superheroes looked as if they needed to go on a diet. Sekowsky was light years away from the artists at DC who were trying to define the medium. He was, simply, an extremely competent journeyman, who could, on occasion, turn in work that was well designed and fun. He did just that with the *JLA* strip. Today, he is primarily remembered for the eight years he put in pencilling the *Justice League*, with inking assists first from Bernie Sachs, and later from Sid Greene.[45] He moved on to other assignments, including the chore of editing and drawing *Wonder Woman*.

The superhero revivals engineered by Schwartz had almost run their course. There would be others, but they never achieved both the popularity and the artistic success of the work turned in by Infantino and Kane. Joe Kubert was given the chance to try his hand at a superhero update with Schwartz's next effort, the *Hawkman* strip. Kubert had worked on the strip when he was a teenage newcomer recruited by Shelly Mayer. Schwartz and Fox's new take on Hawkman changed the character from a reincarnated Egyptian prince to an alien policeman from the planet Thanagar, who comes to earth in hot pursuit of an evil-doer. He brings his wife, his partner in business and pleasure, along to assist him. On Thanagar, all the police sport wings and formfitting uniforms, so when the Hawk-duo need to investigate an intergalactic crime being carried out on earth, they just don their hawk outfits, and away-they-go. Kubert drew the strip and inked it, as he did with almost all

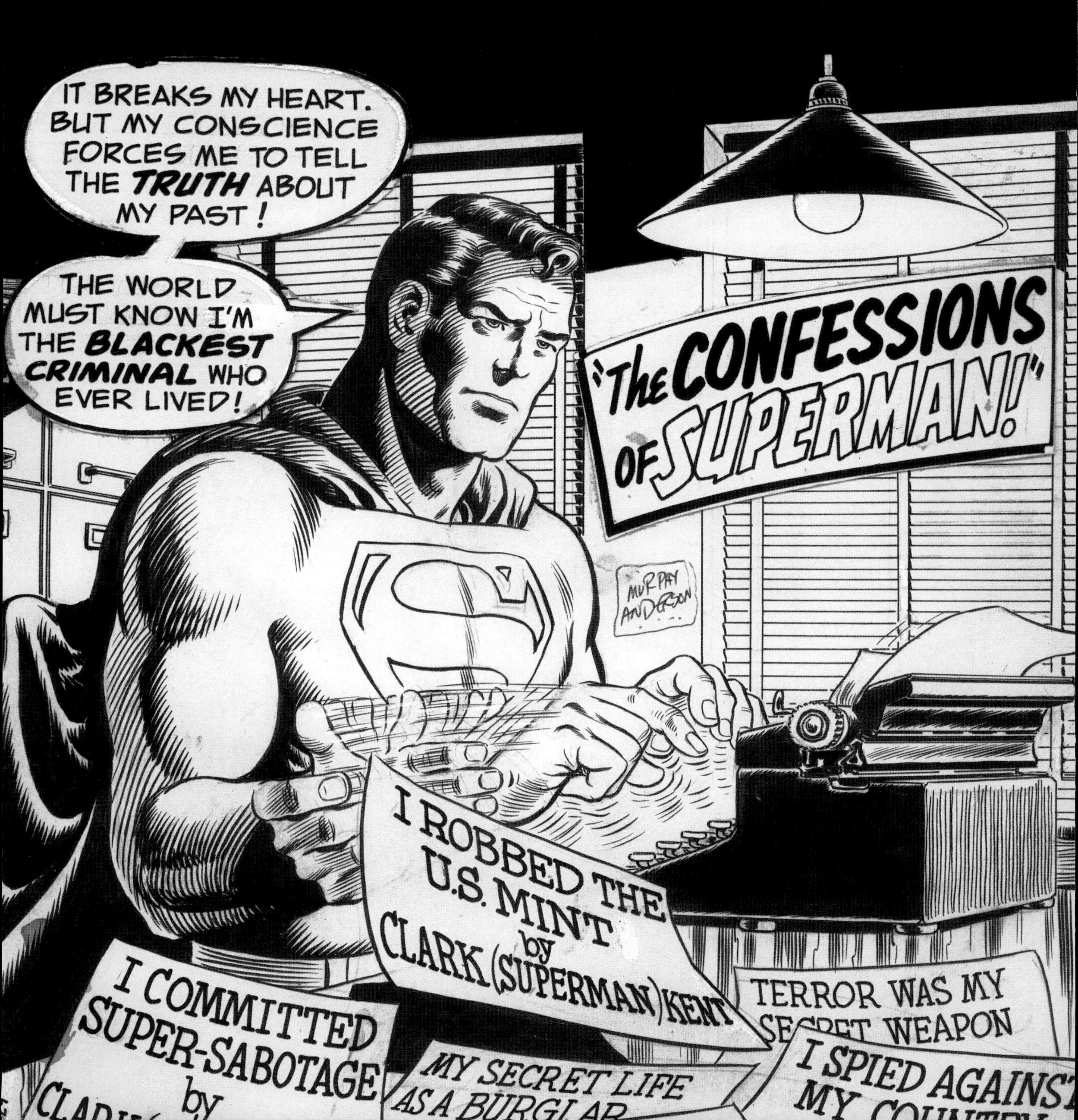

IT BREAKS MY HEART. BUT MY CONSCIENCE FORCES ME TO TELL THE **TRUTH** ABOUT MY PAST!
THE WORLD MUST KNOW I'M THE **BLACKEST CRIMINAL** WHO EVER LIVED!
"The CONFESSIONS OF SUPERMAN!"
MURPHY ANDERSON
I ROBBED THE U.S. MINT by CLARK (SUPERMAN) KENT
I COMMITTED SUPER-SABOTAGE by
TERROR WAS MY
WEAPON
MY SECRET LIFE AS A
I SPIED AGAINST

Opposite page: Curt Swan, pencils, Murphy Anderson, inks, original cover artwork, *Action* #380, September, 1969. Bottom: Curt Swan, pencils, original cover layout drawing, *World's Finest* #186, August, 1969, ©1969 DC Comics.

his work. He gave the hawk couple's strip a look of spontaneity not usually found in superhero features. Gone was the chiseled, musclebound look, replaced by lean energy. Fox's scripts were, as usual, solid, and Kubert's storytelling did not miss a beat.

Kubert's take on the character, a man who flies around fighting bad guys with ancient weapons (that was the hook of the strip; Hawkman's alter ego was a museum curator who used weapons from the collection's inventory) was played tongue-in-cheek, and Kubert's artwork gave the feature a perfect balance. The strip had its premiere in *The Brave and the Bold* #34, with a release date of February/March, 1961. All did not go as planned, however, and the strip failed to attract sufficient interest to receive its own title. Schwartz tried again a year later. Kubert's artwork was still strong and assured. It was still, nevertheless, grounded in fantasy-reality rather than in musclebound caricature. The strip failed again. Finally, Murphy Anderson was selected to try the feature, this time as a team-up in Schwartz's science fiction title, which featured Infantino's Adam Strange in *Mystery in Space* #87, with a release date of November, 1963. Finally after three more tries, Hawkman got his own title under Anderson's wing. The artwork was flashy, attractive, and uninspiring.

Kubert returned to work on war books for Kanigher. By the early 1960s, Kubert looked upon his work as nothing more than a job, which included his long tenure on comics, telling tales of soldiers and their day-to-day experiences. Kubert explained that "…I've never had any special affinity for the war stuff at all." He found pleasure only in spinning stories involving mythical characters and adventurers, especially his own stone age Tarzan, Tor, which saw print in the 1950s during Kubert's work for St. John Publishing.[46]

By the end of the 1950s, Kubert's approach to comic book storytelling had crystallized; his technical facility was now fully mature. His style and handling of his storytelling chores never significantly changed after that. Throughout the 1960s his work remained con-

sistent; he maintained a high level of quality, which was rarely inspired. A majority of the war material Kubert was given was predictable and resembled Hollywood's version of war and combat. There were occasions when Kanigher's scripts and Kubert's artwork gelled. When Kanigher would challenge Kubert with an unusual and intriguing concept, the artist could still deliver with satisfying results, as with the *Enemy Ace* strip first presented in the comic book *Our Army at War* #151, with a release date of February, 1965. The *Enemy Ace* stories threw readers a curve with the presentation of an existential German World War I ace. The ace, Hans von Hammer, went on to be featured in stories which emphasized the futility and tragedy of war. Kubert's artwork was completely sympathetic to the stories and the character.

On occasion, Kubert kept his hand in the superhero genre by turning in work for Schwartz on covers for such titles as *Detec-*

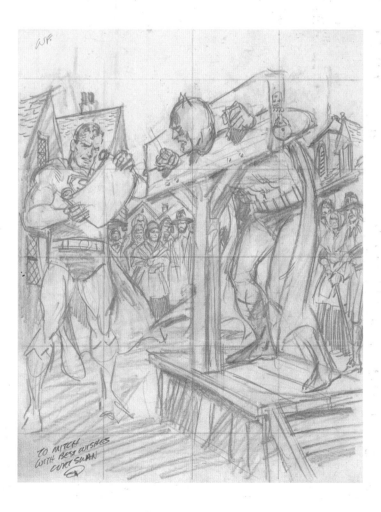

tive featuring Batman. His artwork was strangely out-of-sync with superhero strips as Kubert's forte was with mortal heroes rather than with the more-than-mortal variety. Kubert cruised through the 1960s almost on auto-pilot, taking time to provide artwork for a newspaper strip called *The Green Berets*, which was a disaster on just about every level. The strip quickly became preachy and turned into a polemic for the Vietnam War, as the conflict spun out of control, dividing the country. Kubert disagreed with the direction the strip was going and withdrew his involvement.[47]

After Carmine Infantino became publisher of DC, Kubert became an editor in late 1967, replacing Kanigher, who had stepped down

due to illness.[48] Kubert had spent his time away from DC on a number of assignments, including the *Green Berets*. As part of Kubert's return, he adopted the slogan "make war no more," which became the acknowledged sentiment of DC's war strips. As an artist, Kubert's strongest work, though, was for the strips produced in the late 1950s through the mid-1960s, before his attentions began to turn in other directions.

Julie Schwartz was not the only editor at DC pitching new concepts. Robert Kanigher had been creating scores of characters and plot lines since his first association with DC in 1943. In *Showcase* #3, release dated July/August, 1956, he created the *Frogmen*. The title went nowhere, but Kanigher recycled the idea, giving it a new twist by creating a team of underwater adventurers called the Sea Devils. The title, *Sea Devils*, premiered in *Showcase* #27, with a release date of July/August, 1960. As with his *Frogmen* strip, Kanigher turned to Russ Heath for artwork. Heath had been one of the other bright lights in Kanigher's stable of artists, and his artwork made the strip a pleasure to look at. The stories were, at best, standard fare, but Heath's artwork for *Sea Devils*, which he inked himself, really distinguished the strip's look and tone.

The splash page from *Sea Devils* #9, on page 120, is an eye-grabber. The page dramatically sets the pace for another episode of *Sea Devils*, and the story, which fills up the entire comic book, uses an encyclopedia of storytelling effects utilized by Heath throughout the 1960s.[49] This splash page was censored by the Comics Code Authority, which felt that the creature's left hand was too close to catching the Sea Devils and thus too scary for kids. The final version of the page had the hand photostatted over and moved down to be less threatening. The artwork on display here is the original version composed by Heath, on view in its uncensored form for the first time, which even by the standards of 1962, is hardly threatening. Heath, who usually inked his own work, turned in scores of war tales for Kanigher with consistent panache and

Murphy Anderson, pencils and inks, original splash page artwork, *Mystery in Space* #88, December, 1963, ©1963 DC Comics.

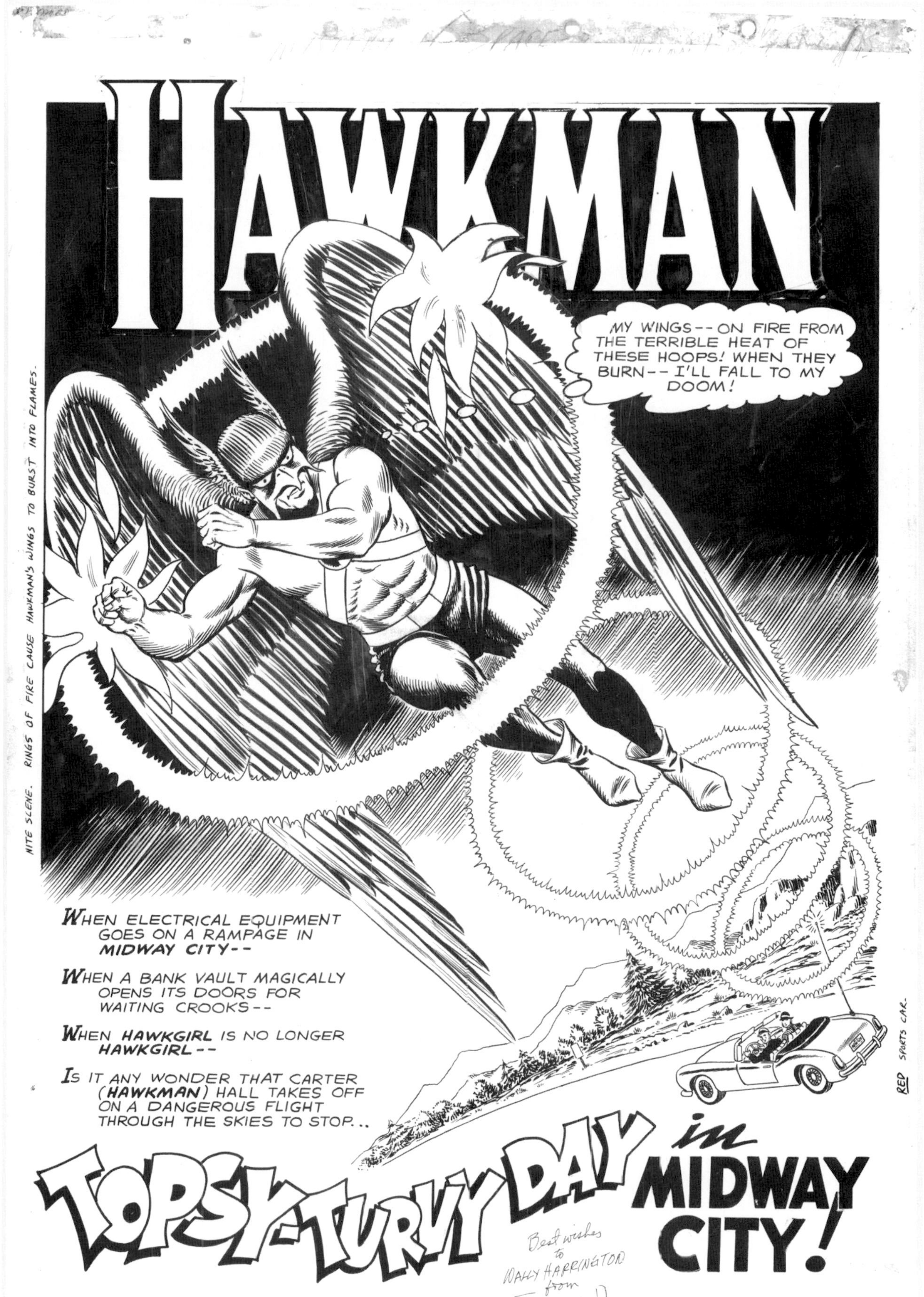

HAWKMAN
MY WINGS--ON FIRE FROM THE TERRIBLE HEAT OF THESE HOOPS! WHEN THEY BURN--I'LL FALL TO MY DOOM!
NITE SCENE. RINGS OF FIRE CAUSE HAWKMAN'S WINGS TO BURST INTO FLAMES.
WHEN ELECTRICAL EQUIPMENT GOES ON A RAMPAGE IN MIDWAY CITY--
WHEN A BANK VAULT MAGICALLY OPENS ITS DOORS FOR WAITING CROOKS--
WHEN HAWKGIRL IS NO LONGER HAWKGIRL--
IS IT ANY WONDER THAT CARTER (HAWKMAN) HALL TAKES OFF ON A DANGEROUS FLIGHT THROUGH THE SKIES TO STOP...
RED SPORTS CAR.
TOPSY-TURVY DAY in MIDWAY CITY!
Best wishes to WALLY HARRINGTON from MURPHY ANDERSON GREENSBORO 1984

Left to right: Irv Novick, pencils and inks, original cover artwork, *Wonder Woman* #174, January/February, 1968; Joe Certa, pencils and inks, original splash page artwork, *House of Mystery* #173, March/April, 1968; Shelly Moldoff, pencils, *Batman* #172, June, 1965; and Al Plastino, pencils and inks, *Action* #294, November, 1962, ©1968, 1965, and 1962 DC Comics.

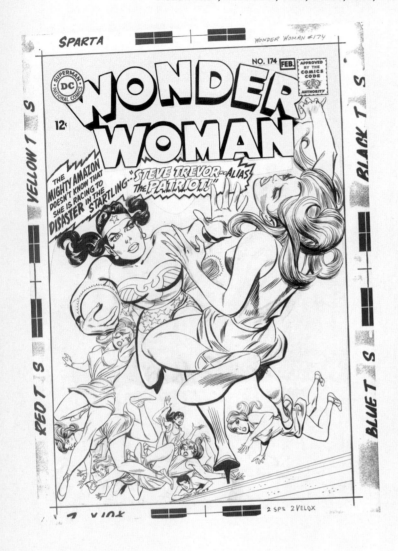

quality. Because Heath did not venture into superhero territory, having little affinity for such larger, bigger, and better heroes, he has frequently been overlooked, but his work in many respects is on par with Kubert's.

Kanigher also regularly depended on the Andru/Esposito team for artwork on *Wonder Woman* and on his war fare. The duo were dependable: Andru was a solid storyteller and Esposito's inking did little harm to the dynamics of his partner's composition. Andru's style was looser than many of Kanigher's regulars and was decidedly more cartoony than the slick styles usually associated with DC. Andru and Esposito had tried their hands at Kanigher's answer to an earth-bound adventure team, the Suicide Squad, but the strip never achieved adequate popularity to merit its own title. *Suicide Squad* had its premiere in *The Brave and the Bold* #25, release dated August/September, 1959. The strip had all the touches Kanigher used in his books and focused on a team of government agents described as "America's top secret weapon." The formal name of the group was "Task Force X," but their nickname, appropriately enough, was the Suicide Squad, as they tempted death in each exciting installment. The plots for the strip came right out of B-sci-fi movies, complete with dinosaurs, communists, and atom bombs. The strip was drawn in the team's loose, characteristic style which would be put to better use with Kanigher's next attempt at creating a new strip, *Metal Men*.

If the story surrounding the strip is to be believed, Irwin Donenfeld came into Kanigher's office late on a Friday afternoon, with a dilemma; he needed a story for the next issue of *Showcase*, fast. Someone had neglected to schedule a story for the next issue of the feature. Donenfeld asked Kanigher if he could come up with something, and by Monday the requested story was complete. Upon arriving at the DC offices on Monday morning, Kanigher called Ross Andru to start work on the art for the strip. Kanigher handed Andru the script, typed by Kanigher's wife from his handwritten notes, and twenty-five pieces of typing paper to prepare the breakdowns: a rough, loose layout of each page. By the end of the day the whole story had been

designed, tweaked, and fine tuned and was ready for Andru to do the final pencils on art board.[50] The strip turned various metals into characters: Lead, Gold, Mercury, Tin, and Platinum, with personalities to match their mettle. The strip was quirky, unusual, and fun. Andru's pencils and Esposito's inks perfectly match the light fantasy of *Metal Men*. Andru's storytelling moves the plot along effortlessly, and the origin episode of the strip is appealing to kids of all ages. With fantasy tales such as *Metal Men*, a more realistic or illustration oriented approach would have completely failed; the feature had to be drawn in a loose, fluid, almost surreal style to keep the right tone.

The Metal Men had their premiere in *Showcase* #37, release dated March/April, 1962.

Novick. Grandenetti started searching for work in the business in 1946. After an interview with Busy Arnold, he was referred to Will Eisner who was looking for additional hands to assist on *The Spirit*. Grandenetti hurried over to Eisner's office and was offered a job, on the spot.[51] His tenure with Eisner had an obvious impact on his layout and composition, but Grandenetti was clearly intent on developing beyond his influences. His stories always had an attention to detail and design which makes his work easy to identify. He worked for a number of publishers and regularly turned in well-crafted work for Kanigher's titles.

He also briefly tried his hand at superheroes, when DC attempted to revive another of its Golden Age characters, the Spectre. The strip started out in the hands of Murphy Anderson, was then passed to a young kid named

Kanigher ended the origin story with a characteristic touch: he killed all the Metal Men off. As everyone knows, though, death never counts in comic books, and the Metal Men returned in the next three issues of *Showcase* and received their own feature by 1963.

Andru's style and storytelling perfectly complemented the strip, and it stands, even today, as an enchanted collaboration between Andru and Kanigher. The first issues of the strip work so well because the light fantasy of the feature captures the innocence and attitude of the early 1960s.

Kanigher also relied upon the skills of other tried-and-true stalwarts for artwork, including the ever dependable Jerry Grandenetti and Irv

inset panel at the beginning of the page). Grandenetti lingered turning in comic book work until the mid-1970s, then, he left for good, lured into advertising.

Irv Novick had been in the business since the beginning. He had worked with Kanigher at MLJ and their association continued at DC. Novick was dependable and competent. By the late 1960s, Novick began working for Julie Schwartz, turning in stalwart duty on the *Batman* and *Flash* strips.

His war comics were, in many respects, archetypal of middle-of-the-road storytelling. Novick understood the established conventions of page design and storytelling, and he stuck to them. His pages are textbook examples of solid, if not particularly inspired,

Neal Adams and then assigned to Grandenetti. The interior page artwork from *Spectre* #6, on page 130, which dates from 1968, displays his unusual layout and page design. The page, ably inked by Murphy Anderson, amply demonstrates how much a talented storyteller can cram into one page and still keep a reader's interest. Grandenetti moves the figure of the Spectre within the top frame from the far left to the right without breaking up the panel. In the bottom, borderless panel, he continues the frenetic action, pulling the camera back from a different angle. This page is exciting and creates an illusion of action and movement, using only two large panels (with one small

storytelling. Many of his panels are so attractive that they were cribbed by pop artist Roy Lichtenstein for his paintings. Lichtenstein also used panels from other Kanigher regulars, including Heath and Grandenetti. [52] These paintings clearly pay homage to the attractiveness of the images they appropriate. When Lichtenstein finished with his series of comic panel-inspired paintings in the mid-1960s and applied his ben day, color saturated style to other subjects, he was never again able to recapture the visual success of his funny book and newspaper strip derived work.

Of all the strips to come out of DC during the Silver Age, perhaps the more interesting creations were two off-beat features which had short but memorable runs. The first of these strips was called *Doom Patrol* and utilized the talents of artist Bruno Premiani and writer Arnold Drake. Premiani was born in Trieste, Italy in 1924. He worked as an editorial cartoonist in Italy in the early 1940s and due to his anti-fascist sentiments was forced to leave his native land, relocating in Argentina. His address may have changed, but not his politics; his anti-fascist sentiments continued to

Opposite page: Nick Cardy, pencils and inks, original interior page artwork, *Aquaman #22*, July/August, 1965. Bottom: Nick Cardy, pencils and inks, original cover artwork, *Teen Titans #19*, January/February, 1969, ©1965 and 1969 DC Comics.

be on display in his editorial cartoons in his adopted home which led to his being deported by the Peron regime, resulting in his relocation to the United States. Along the way he co-authored an authoritative text on drawing horses, *El Caballo*, which is still in print today. The thin, bespectacled, and thoughtful artist went on to find work for various comic book companies during the mid-1950s as a penciller and inker.[53]

By the early 1960s he had come to the attention of several DC editors including Murray Boltinoff. He edited a number of DC titles, including *The Adventures of Jerry Lewis*, *Challengers of the Unknown*, *Tomahawk*, *House of Secrets*, and *My Greatest Adventure*.[54] By 1963 the latter title was in need of some new blood, and Boltinoff enlisted the help of Drake to come up with something fresh. Drake was opinionated, sometimes off-the-wall, and intelligent. He had the audacity to think that comic books should address an audience which included teens and college students.[55] The results of Drake's ruminations was *Doom Patrol*, which premiered in *My Greatest Adventure #80*, release dated June, 1963.[56] Six issues later the book's title was officially changed to *Doom Patrol*. Drake's plots for *DP* featured grotesque characters and deformed villains which were uncharacteristically out-of-sync with DC's other titles. The DP's team of heroes were all outcasts, at odds with society because they had been changed by accidents and did not "fit in" anymore. The DP consisted of an ex-movie star, Rita Farr or Elasti-girl, who was transformed so she could expand and reduce her size. She was clearly not one of the strip's grotesque characters. Premiani drew her as an elegant, exotic beauty. The other members of the DP were Negative Man, Robotman, and the Chief. Negative Man, who had to live wrapped in bandages all the time, á la the "mummy," could turn himself into negative energy that left his body. The catch was, if the negative energy did not return to his body in sixty seconds, he was dead. Robotman, who was based on a Golden Age character, once had a human counterpart whose body had been "charred" in a racing accident, requiring a conveniently available brain transplant into a robot body. The leader of the group was the wheelchair-bound "Chief" who, of course, was a scientific genius.

Premiani's artwork created an off-kilter mood with an unreal quality which made the strip click. The art for the feature established a weirdness which set it apart from other titles in the DC family. Premiani was an unusually capable draftsman who almost always inked his own work. His drawing had a sure and deliberate, delicate line. Premiani's composition was balanced and nuanced with just the right amount of detail. He also used interesting layout and page design which never distracted from his storytelling. The interior page

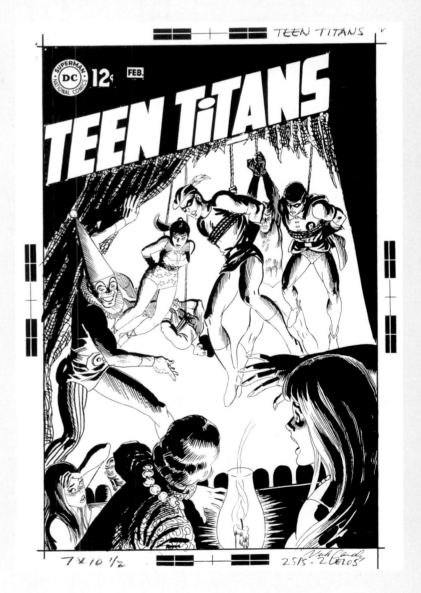

artwork illustrated on page 123, uses two thirds of the page as a splash and insets two panels for exposition, which keeps the story flowing and the page design balanced.

While the strip descended into silliness after the first dozen episodes, the art remained consistently strong. During the title's run, journeyman Bob Brown filled in for Premiani on occasion. The feature ended with issue #121, release dated September/October, 1968, with the entire DP being killed off by two of their archnemeses.

The other strip in question was *Metamorpho*. The artist who gave the strip its spirit was Ramona Fradon. She had left comics to raise her family and had been lured back to work on *Metamorpho*. She collabo-

rated with writer Bob Haney on the strip and both succeeded in creating a hero who was at odds with DC's line of squeaky clean characters. Fradon remembers that she and Haney "had a lot of fun bouncing ideas off each other," which is clearly in evidence in the first issues of the strip.[57] The namesake of the feature was another unfortunate mortal transformed into a superhero, whose power happened to be that he was a human chemistry set. Metamorpho could turn himself into any element he imagined, the trade-off was he was transformed into a somber, grotesque creature who looked like a cross between one of Alberto Giacometti's elongated alienated sculptures and a surreal nightmare. To make things more interesting, the strip attempted a slightly hip tone. The saving grace of the feature was Fradon's concept of the character and her execution of the stories. Her composition was imaginative and her drawing was on the mark, with just the right, light touch. The inks for the strip were provided by veteran Charles Paris who was clearly in tune with Fradon's pencils. Fradon's sense of design and cartoon style gave the feature a singular look and presence which still stands out almost forty years later.

Metamorpho's origin was chronicled in *The Brave and the Bold* #57, release dated December/January, 1965 under the stewardship of editor George Kashdan. After two tryouts the element man got his own title. After only four issues, Fradon was gone. Without her the strip aimlessly plodded along under less sympathetic and capable hands. Fradon clearly defined the feature and during her brief association with *Metamorpho,* it was a true standout.

DC had tried other odd-ball characters including another Bob Haney creation, Eclipso, who made his first appearance in *House of Secrets* #61, release dated August, 1963. Veteran penciller Lee Elias turned in artwork for the strip, but the whole concept fell flat. The main character had a classic split personality in the literal sense. During an eclipse, or anything remotely resembling one, our hero would split off into two characters, the nice one and his evil counterpart, and the hijinks would then ensue. The problem was, nothing really interesting happened with the strip. Alex Toth took the feature over for a few issues, lending his talents in an effort to pump a little life into the strip. Although the artwork was handsome, well paced, and skillfully inked, as was to be expected, the plots and the character went nowhere. After his return from service in the Korean War, Toth had come back to the business, but most of his output was for other publishers, as we shall see in Chapter Six. He turned in work for a handful of DC titles, but the bulk of his efforts went into non-comic related work, in animation.

Other forces outside the comic book industry would define the direction of comic books and their art, and would contribute to their decline as well. Bat-fever hit the United States with the release of the television show on the ABC network on January 12, 1966. For two consecutive nights, kids and their parents were mesmerized, for different reasons, by the show.

The show's share of the television audience was stratospheric, and sales of DC's *Detective* and *Batman* comic titles reached record numbers with sales of the latter exceeding over eight hundred thousand copies, an all time high for the decade. Comic books were now beloved by parents and kids, by the media, and the academic world. Superman was on Broadway, but not for long; the show crashed, but America was still hungry for more super-heroics. ABC television received thousands of complaints protesting the Bat-show's preemption for breaking news about an emergency during a Gemini space mission. Had it been just a little over a decade ago when Americans were excoriating the comics?

DC was rushing into the breach to use Batman in every title it could think of, and all seemed well for the moment. The television version of the dynamic duo did influence DC's strips, which became sillier and campier in an effort to capitalize on the success of the show. DC's other comic book titles continued to crank out products like a well-oiled machine. Artists the like of Joe Certa, who dependably turned in steady, if not very imaginative, work on the *Martian Manhunter* strip, churned out his feature every month. Certa had been diligently working on the Manhunter, a green guy from Mars, who is accidentally brought to earth and then stranded here, since his introduction in 1955. The strip had been a back-up in *Detective,* but when *Elongated Man* took over the back half of the book, Certa's character was bumped to *House of Mystery* where he bided his time until he was cancelled.

Throughout the 1960s, Mort Weisinger's crew on the Super-titles also continued to spin their yarns in *Action, Superman, Superboy, Jimmy Olsen,* and *Lois Lane.* Curt Swan continued to turn in beautiful stories exquisitely inked by George Klein. Swan's work on *Superman, Superboy, The Legion of Superheroes,* and *Jimmy Olsen* still looks elegant and assured forty years later. The other Weisinger regulars, George Papp, Kurt Schaffenberger, and Jim Mooney, did yeoman duty as well. Other less noteworthy contributors included journeymen Al Plastino and John Forte. Weisinger's super-factory of titles produced charming fare that presented a mythology carefully crafted by such writers as Otto Binder, Jerry Siegel, Leo Dorfman, and Robert Bernstein. Weisinger was notorious for the control he exercised over his titles and was considered by many a disagreeable tyrant. Swan, who was the star of the group, nevertheless labored productively pencilling his version of Superman's homeworld and of an imaginary, cleaner-than-clean future that is especially charming in today's cynical world.

DC drew on many hands for its books. Another dependable long-term veteran who saw duty during the 1960s was Nick Cardy. Cardy, who was born Nicholas Viscardi in New York in 1920, had attended the Art Students League. He spent the 1950s turning in work on a number of DC titles, including *Daniel Boone, Congo Bill, Gang Busters,*

House of Secrets, and *Tomahawk.*[58] When Ramona Fradon left the *Aquaman* strip, Cardy took over chores on the feature when it received its own title in 1962, and his smooth, elegant line helped complement an otherwise bland strip. Cardy went on to provide artwork for the popular *Teen Titans* strip which created a team of junior heroes, which kids could easily identify with. *Teen Titans* was a sidekick's delight, putting together every kid's favorite second banana: Robin, Kid Flash, and Aquaman's buddy, Aqualad.

By 1967 the gloss of the Bat-Super-boom was losing its shine. DC's sales were down, although they still dominated the industry. Many of the writers who had helped mold DC's identity during the boom years of the 1960s were now attempting to cash in on the profits being made by the company, lobbying together for health insurance, retirement benefits, and some protection from the abuse many of them had taken from slave driving editors. Their attempt failed to get them anything, except notice as troublemakers.[59] Within a short

time, these writers, who had given life to countless DC tales would be gone; they were no longer receiving any work from the company.

Nineteen sixty-seven also marked the year that DC began reducing the size of the art board given to artists to draw their stories on. While to the uninitiated this may not seem like a big deal, the reduction of the original artwork page size from roughly 12 inches by 18 inches to 10 inches by 15 inches meant a lot to the artists. The move, which has been attributed to cost cutting by DC, allowed less room to develop a panel and a story. Even though artists eventually adapted to the reduced size, the change clamped restrictions on the amount of artwork that could comfortably fit on a page, forcing the images to be scaled down or changed to fit into the new format.

Many of the artists who had been at the forefront of the second generation were now in their mid-40s. By 1967 not only were many of the artists feeling a little tired, but the titles that had made DC's Silver Age hot, *The Flash*, *Green Lantern*, *Detective*, *Justice League*, *Adam Strange*, *Elongated Man*, and *The Atom*, were running out of steam. The art was becoming matter-of-fact, and it was hard to keep the momentum of creative storytelling going month-after-month. The Silver Age was winding to an end, and DC was looking for fresh blood to reenergize itself.

Help came with Neal Adams. Adams, who was born in 1941 on Governor's Island, New York, was part of the next generation of artists to work in comic books. By the time he was 18, his work had been published in *Archie's Jokebook Magazine*. He cut his teeth working on the *Ben Casey* newspaper strip for four years starting in 1962.[60] Adams brought with him a different, illustration-oriented approach to comic book storytelling which proved popular and influential. In 1966 he started work at DC, inking Curt Swan's pencils, and turned in work on numerous DC covers. By 1967 he was pencilling the *Deadman* strip and *The Spectre*. *Deadman*, another quirky Arnold Drake concept, was one of the last projects pencilled by Carmine Infantino

AND IN THE MIND OF NICKY AS WELL AS IN THAT OF THE REST OF
THOUGHT OF THE TITANIC DOOM TICKING AWAY OVER THEIR

TICK··TOCK···TICK·TOCK···TICK··TO

before he completely turned in his pen and brush for a suit and tie. After *Deadman's* premiere in *Strange Adventures* #205, release dated October, 1967, Adams took over the strip and helped define the feature as one of the more interesting ideas to see light at the end of the Silver Age. The namesake of the strip was an aerialist who is murdered during a performance and whose spirit is given a second chance to find his killer by being given the power, by a sympathetic deity, to inhabit the bodies of the living. Adams' impact would be felt very quickly, but his influence would be on the next generation of fans and artists.

Another addition was a 13-year-old kid from Pittsburgh named Jim Shooter. Shooter had submitted a completely drawn and scripted comic book to DC and was given a shot with the company. He would go on to write the *Legion of Superheroes* strip. Together with Curt Swan, who replaced John Forte on the strip, the feature took on a new and interesting presence in the DC universe.[61] Shooter was another star who would rise and later cause considerable controversy in the industry as the editor-in-chief at Marvel in the late 1970s and through the 1980s, who could be the subject of an entire book.

By 1968, DC under Carmine Infantino, was rapidly changing in an effort to accommodate the times. The *Batman* television show, which had helped fuel the comic book boom, was on

SEA DEVILS, IS THE SAME s...

...TICK TOCK--

17

the skids. The last episode of the show aired on March 14, 1968 to dismal ratings. No one was watching anymore; the Bat-show was no longer hip, and kids and adults were looking for something more relevant and violent. *Hawaii Five-O*, *Rowan and Martin's Laugh-In*, *The Smothers Brothers Comedy Hour*, and *Star Trek* were the shows to watch.

Many of the writers who had started in the Golden Age and had helped create the Silver Age were gone. Gardner Fox, John Broome, Bill Finger, Otto Binder, all for different reasons, were no longer around to help create the fantasies to fuel the production of comic books. Many of the artists who had defined the Silver Age were gone or would move on

to other publishers. Carmine Infantino was now in management and was Julie Schwartz's boss. Gil Kane was putting the bulk of his effort into something revolutionary which we will focus on in Chapter Seven and would soon become a star at Marvel. Joe Kubert was focusing on editing, and Bob Kanigher was now working for him, churning out war tales as fast as usual. Ramona Fradon had left the business to raise her family. Murphy Anderson would now only provide inks and cover artwork and would never seriously return to pencil another strip again. Mike Sekowsky, like so many others, would be lured to Hollywood to work in animation. Many old hands would stay on to finish out the 1960s and work into the 1970s, but the spark was gone. It had been an exciting ride, but the torch was being passed to younger hands.

DC's artists and its strips did not exist in a vacuum. Other forces and talents were at work in the business, which influenced the artists and writers at DC and helped redefine comic book storytelling. When Jack Kirby left DC, after his legal run-in with Jack Schiff over *Sky Masters*, he started to devote his considerable energies collaborating with Stan Lee at Marvel. It was this partnership that would literally change the face of comics and influence every artist in the business. What happened at Marvel with Jack and Stan is, accordingly, our next stop.

NOTES

[1] Les Daniels, *Marvel*, Abrams, 1991.

[2] Gary Carter interview with Murphy Anderson, *Original Comic Art*, Avon, 1992.

[3] Schwartz, who had worked with Fox as an editor on comic book stories, was actually guilty of convincing Fox to try his hand at pulps.

[4] Ibid.

[5] Interview with Joe Giella.

[6] Rich Morrissey, Al Turniansky, Robin Snyder, and Gary Groth interview with Robert Kanigher, *The Comics Journal* #85 and #86, October and November, 1983. Kanigher began writing for All American in 1943. He wrote and edited *Wonder Woman*, went on to write and edit romance books and the *Johnny Thunder* strip for Julie Schwartz, and turned in hundreds of war stories as an editor and a writer.

[7] The *Viking Prince* strip was featured as a backup feature in the first twenty-four issues of the comic book *The Brave and the Bold*.

[8] Archer St. John, the company's owner, who was at least twenty years senior to Kubert, had a warm and productive relationship with the artist. Kubert and Maurer also brought the idea of doing 3-D comic books to St. John which initially proved extremely profitable for the company. Unfortunately, when St. John shifted to exclusively doing 3-D books, the market collapsed, putting him out of business.

[9] Gary Groth interview with Joe Kubert, *The Comics Journal* #172, November, 1994.

[10] Ken Jones interview with Russ Heath, *The Comics Journal* #117, September, 1987.

[11] Will Murray, "Of Robots, Amazons and Dinosaurs…Andru and Esposito," *Comic Book Marketplace* #78, May, 2000.

[12] Herron, who was called Eddie, and not France, had worked for Fawcett editing and scripting *Captain Marvel*. After the collapse of Fawcett, he found work at DC writing for the *Superman* strip.

[13] Richard Morrissey, Dwight Decker, and Gary Groth interview with Curt Swan, *The Comics Journal* #73, July, 1982.

[14] Interview with Ramona Fradon.

[15] Interview with Gil Kane.

[16] Julius Schwartz with Brian M. Thomsen, *Man of Two Worlds*. It should be noted that there are different versions of whose idea it was to reintroduce the Flash which will be debated by comic book cognoscenti forever. However, Schwartz edited *Showcase* #4, Kanigher wrote the lead or "origin" story, and Infantino designed the character and pencilled the strip. For a scintillating, in-depth discussion of the never-ending arguments as to who did what, see: Roy Thomas, editor, excerpts from various interviews and statements of Kanigher, Infantino, and Kubert, "Who Created the Silver Age Flash," *Alter Ego* #10, September, 2001.

[17] Interview with Gil Kane.

[18] The character was created by John Broome and Infantino; Fox took over writing when the strip became a feature in *Detective*.

[19] Gary Groth interview with Infantino, *The Comics Journal* #191, November, 1996.

[20] Schwartz with Thomsen, *Man of Two Worlds*.

[21] Ibid.

[22] Gary Groth interview with Carmine Infantino, *The Comics Journal* #191, November, 1996.

[23] Joe Simon with Jim Simon, *The Comic Book Makers*, Crestwood/II Publishing, 1990.

[24] Ray Wyman and Catherine Hohlfeld with Robert C. Crane, *The Art of Jack Kirby*, The Blue Rose Press, 1992.

[25] Gerard Jones and Will Jacobs, *The Comic Book Heroes*, Prima Publishing, 1992.

[26] Wyman and Hohlfeld with Crane, *The Art of Jack Kirby*.

[27] Jon B. Cooke, "The Story Behind Sky Masters," *The Jack Kirby Collector* #15, April, 1997. Also see: Greg Theakson, "King of the Comic Strips," *The Complete Sky Masters of the Space Force*, Pure Imagination, undated.

28 Ibid.

29 While Kane was designing GL, he decided to pattern the character after his next-door neighbor, actor Paul Newman.

30 Interview with Gil Kane.

31 Ibid.

32 Ibid.

33 Ibid.

34 When you are that small, everything becomes giant, and many things become menacing.

35 Interview with Julius Schwartz.

36 Ibid.

37 Jon B. Cooke interview with Jim Warren, "Forry, Harvey and the man called Flintstone," *The Warren Companion*, TwoMorrows, 2001.

38 Ibid; Interview with Gil Kane.

39 Interview with Gil Kane.

40 Ibid.

41 Ibid.

42 Interview with Julius Schwartz.

43 It should be remembered that Shelly Mayer was instrumental in the creation of the JSA, as well as with most of the aspects of All American. As we have seen, his judgment was responsible for bringing some of the most talented artists of the second generation to All American and thus to DC, when it acquired Gaines' stake in the company.

44 Schwartz with Thomsen, *Man of Two Worlds*.

45 Sekowsky's tenure ended on the *JLA* when he became an editor for DC. He also continued pencilling duties on other DC strips. Sekowsky worked for a number of publishers during the 1960s including Tower and Gold Key Comics.

46 Gary Groth interview with Joe Kubert, *The Comics Journal* #172, November, 1994.

47 Ibid.

48 Ibid.

49 Unfortunately, Heath's tenure on *Sea Devils* was short lived. He left after issue #10 and was replaced by several artists including Irv Novick, Joe Kubert, and Gene Colan until the book was passed to journeyman Howard Purcell with issue #16. Purcell held onto the assignment with staid competence, missing only one issue, until the strip's end.

50 Rich Morrissey, Al Turniansky, Robin Snyder, and Gary Groth interview with Robert Kanigher, *The Comics Journal* #85 and #86.

51 Ron Goulart, *The Great Comic Book Artists*, Volume 2, St. Martin's Press, 1989.

52 When Lichtenstein was in the army, he was assigned to an art unit, and his immediate supervisor was Irv Novick.

53 George Guay, "The Life and Death of the Doom Patrol," *Amazing Heroes* #6, November, 1981. Marc Svensson interview with Arnold Drake, *Alter Ego* #17, September, 2000.

54 Boltinoff had started off as a writer for DC working on such titles as *Action*, *Detective*, *House of Mystery*, *House of Secrets*, *Our Fighting Forces*, and *Sugar and Spike*.

55 Marc Svensson interview with Arnold Drake, *Alter Ego* #17.

56 For the first story of the series, Drake co-plotted with writer Bob Haney.

57 Interview with Ramona Fradon.

58 John Coates, *The Art of Nick Cardy*, Coates Publishing, 1999.

59 Interview with Gil Kane.

60 Interview with Neal Adams, *Comic Book Profiles* #3, Summer, 1998, As You Like It Publications, 1998.

61 Les Daniels, *Marvel*.

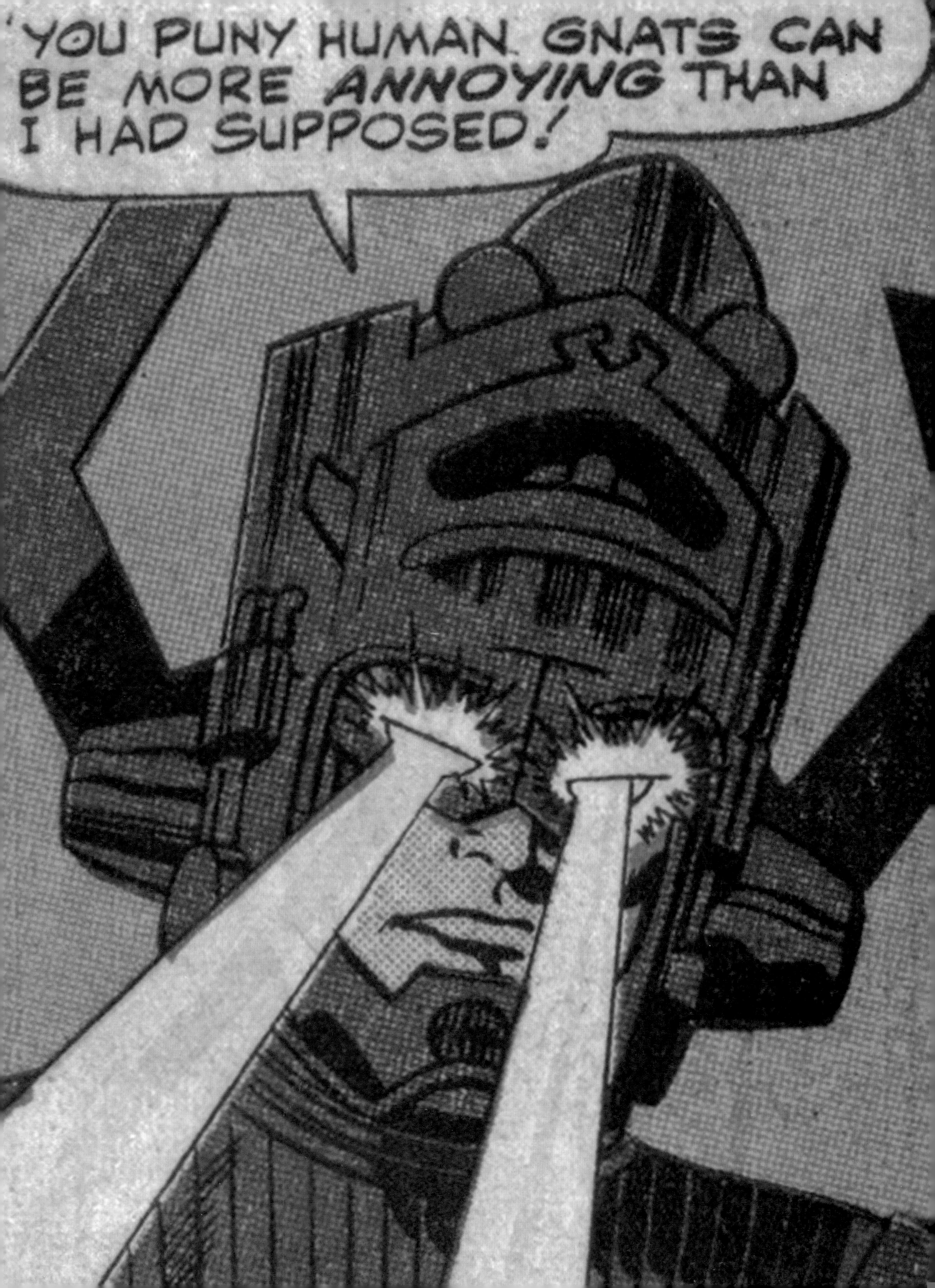
YOU PUNY HUMAN GNATS CAN BE MORE ANNOYING THAN I HAD SUPPOSED!

5 JACK AND STAN'S MARVELOUS ADVENTURE; THE WORLD'S GREATEST COMIC MAGAZINE HITS PAY DIRT; STEVE DITKO FINDS HIS VOICE; THE MERRY MARVEL MARCHING SOCIETY

By the end of 1960 everything at DC was humming like a finely tuned engine. Things were looking fantastic, sales were up, just about every new title was popular, and the second generation of artists and their superheroes could do no wrong. Over at Martin Goodman's Marvel, it was a different story.

Goodman's disastrous decision to unload his Atlas distribution company and throw in his lot with a distributor that pulled the rug out from under him by going out of business left him without any way to sell his comic books. In a corner, he had gone to Independent News, the distributor owned by DC, which cut a hard bargain with him, nearly chopping his company to pieces by limiting the number of titles he could publish to little more than a half-dozen books. Stan Lee laid off just about every artist working for him. Overnight, John Romita, Gene Colan, John Buscema, Russ Heath, and a host of others were cut off from further work. By 1958, Marvel, which was not yet the company's official name, had been reduced to producing practically nothing. But the news was not all bad; after all, they were still in business.

John Romita remembers that when the bad news came, he did not even get a call from Lee. Romita, who thought he had been close to the editor, was crushed.[1] Romita would quickly recover, finding work pencilling romance stories for DC, a job which kept him financially secure and occupied with work for the next eight years. Colan and Buscema would find work in advertising. Many of

Marvel's legion of other artists, artisans, and technical people who had toiled for Lee would find work in other venues and professions.

Lee was now relying on journeyman Dick Ayers and Don Heck for artwork. Jack Kirby was also hanging his hat at Marvel which would lead to some interesting developments, but that was on the horizon.

By 1960, the oft-told story goes, Lee was contemplating leaving the business for good.[2] He had two strong artists to turn to for work, Kirby and a young guy named Steve Ditko, but his heart just was not with the funny book business anymore. Before he had a chance to inform Goodman of his decision, however, he was given the assignment of coming up with a team of superheroes to capitalize on the success of DC's *Justice League of America*. It seems Goodman had just returned from a game of golf with Jack Liebowitz, who had been bragging how well his new *JLA* title was selling. Goodman wanted to test the waters with his own group of heroes. The problem was, Marvel was not in the superhero business any longer. Lee remembers that Goodman's solution was to use the heroes they had abandoned in 1954 and 1955: Captain America, the Human Torch, and Sub-Mariner. Kirby, Ditko, and the other artists working for Lee were now toiling with mystery, suspense, and monster material, not heroes. Kirby had been working on westerns and lots and lots of monsters with silly names, like Grogg and Monteroso. The stories were just as inane as the names of the monsters Kirby was forced to come up with

Jack Kirby, pencils, Dick Ayers, inks, original artwork from two interior pages, *Two-Gun Kid* #60, November, 1962, ©1962 Marvel Characters, Inc.

artwork for, but it was a job, just the same. So, Lee decided to stay with the company "and try one more book and then see what happens."[3]

This is where the story becomes complicated, as there is no clear and consistent recollection from anyone as to what happened next.[4] The comic book which was the product of Goodman's request was *The Fantastic Four*. *FF* was the vehicle which helped Marvel regain its footing in the business and contributed to further defining how a comic book story can be told. *FF* also helped further the perception, which was already growing, that comic books, far from being viewed as merely for children, were also worthy of consideration as entertainment for teenage and college age readers, also sometimes referred to as adults.

The Fantastic Four #1, release dated November, 1961, was written by Lee (most likely with assistance from Kirby) with pencils by Kirby. The cover and the story are not exceptional and recycle themes used by Kirby and Lee previously. Kirby's artwork is solid and sure and bears the unmistakable imprint of his experienced hand. By 1961, Kirby was 44-years-old. He, better than practically anyone in the business, knew how to tell a superhero story; after all, he had defined the genre a little over twenty years ago with his co-creation and work on *Captain America*. Kirby's work on *Sky Masters* and *Challengers of the Unknown* clearly presaged his work on *FF*. There are also close similarities between the look of the characters in *Sky Masters*, *Challengers*, and *FF*, which clearly points to Kirby's guiding hand on Marvel's first entry into the superhero sweepstakes of the 1960s.

FF was not the creation of one person but the collaboration of two experienced professionals at turning points in their careers. As comic book storytelling is a visual medium, Kirby's vigorous artwork was a key ingredient in the strip's success. The feature's origin episode presents the story of four adventurers who attempt a trip in a rocket only to be bombarded by mysterious cosmic rays, which transform each of the heroes. The characters are Reed Richards, Sue Storm, Ben Grimm,

A gallery of early 1960s Marvel covers, all with Jack Kirby pencils and various inkers. Clockwise: *Journey into Mystery* #109, October, 1964; *Journey into Mystery* #101, February, 1964; *Tales of Suspense* #40, April, 1963; *Sgt. Fury* #8, July, 1964; *Tales to Astonish* #61, November, 1964; *The Fantastic Four* #10, January, 1963; *The Fantastic Four* #6, September, 1962; and *The Fantastic Four* #3, March, 1962, ©1964, 1963, and 1962 Marvel Characters, Inc.

and Johnny Storm. Richards, a stuffy professor, is transformed with Plastic Man-esque stretching abilities. His girlfriend, Sue Storm, is able to turn herself invisible and later becomes capable of projecting force fields. The pilot, Grimm, an old high school chum of Richards', is transformed into a large orange creature resembling a muscular Michelin man and becomes known as the Thing. As the series progressed, the Thing developed as the most human of all the characters, despite his outward appearance. Many see the character as Kirby's alter-ego. Last but not least, Sue's teenage brother Johnny, is turned into the new version of the Human Torch, who can ignite himself into flame at will. Buoyed by the progress of the strip, the cover of the third issue of the magazine now proclaimed, "The Greatest Comic Magazine in the World."

Kirby's artwork became more elaborate and sharpened as the feature progressed. Kirby received inking assists from numerous hands, which gave the strip different looks as the feature grew and matured. The page from *The Fantastic Four* #15, on page 150, was inked by Dick Ayers, who regularly inked the feature after issue #6 until #20 (with the exception of issue #13, inked by Steve Ditko). After that, various hands inked the feature, ranging from finishes that were clearly in tune with Kirby's pencils rendered by Frank Giacoia in issue #39, an example of which is on display on page 151; to the barely competent inking of Vinnie Colletta. By issue #46 inker Joe Sinnott took over finishes for the strip. It was at this point in the feature that the plots, artwork, and finishes fulminated into something rarely seen in the popular/fantasy entertainment medium: science fiction and soap opera with a compelling edge, skillfully drawn, inked, and scripted.

By the time Kirby was creating these stories, Lee was using what has come to be called the "Marvel method" of producing comic book stories. Lee would meet with the artist, come up with a general outline of the plot and leave the rest to the penciler. As the workload picked up, Lee depended more and more on the "method." This left much of the story development to the artists. Lee's hand is clearly in evidence with the final dialogue used in the stories: his patented brand of banter is omnipresent and easily identifiable. Lee continued to exercise control over the cover artwork and production, but the method permitted Marvel's artists a degree of participation in stories unheard of at the time at DC.

During the 1960s, Kirby's style of storytelling was well established. He was not interested in experimenting with page design and panel layout; his ambition now was to create a modern comic book mythology. Kirby clearly felt that comic book storytelling was the medium for spinning such tales. He proceeded with his work in *FF* to try his hand at

creating a group of archetypes in a multiple book story arc to advance this ambition. Kirby's imagery and his visualization of his universe is what made his storytelling compelling. Up until this time, no artist working in comic books had ever tried to create an imagery with the coherent complexity attempted by Kirby with *FF*.

Kirby created a universe of characters that were troubled and ambivalent. His arch-evilguy character, Dr. Doom, who had made his first appearance back in issue #5, became more complex and interesting as the series wound forward. Doom, Kirby's variation on the man in the iron mask, is another of the series' tortured souls who strike out at everyone who

Jack Kirby, pencils, Frank Giacoia, inks, original interior page artwork, *The Fantastic Four* #39, June, 1965, ©1965 Marvel Characters, Inc. This page features the FF's diabolical archnemesis, Doctor Doom.

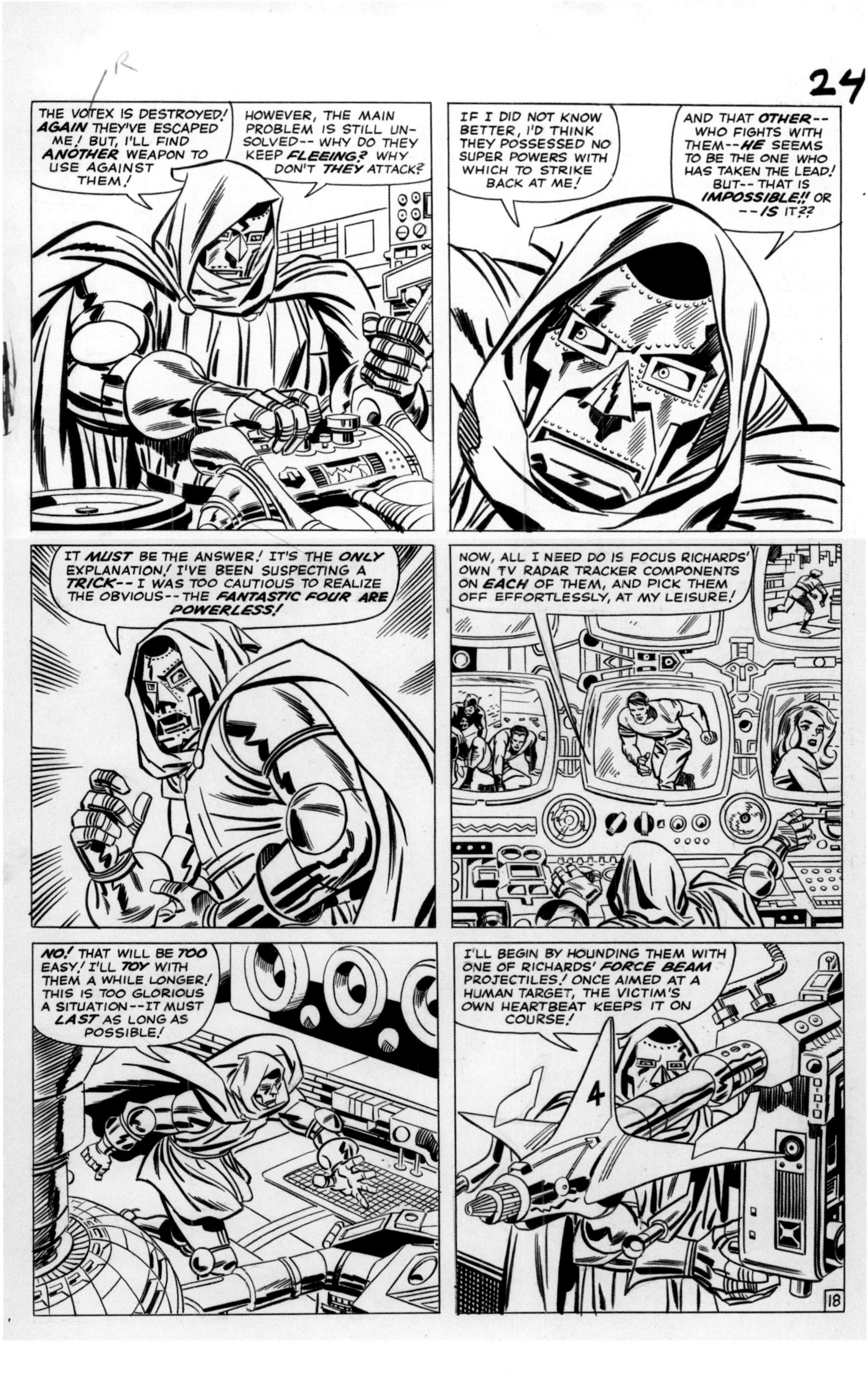

24
THE VOTEX IS DESTROYED! AGAIN THEY'VE ESCAPED ME! BUT, I'LL FIND ANOTHER WEAPON TO USE AGAINST THEM!
HOWEVER, THE MAIN PROBLEM IS STILL UNSOLVED-- WHY DO THEY KEEP FLEEING? WHY DON'T THEY ATTACK?
IF I DID NOT KNOW BETTER, I'D THINK THEY POSSESSED NO SUPER POWERS WITH WHICH TO STRIKE BACK AT ME!
AND THAT OTHER-- WHO FIGHTS WITH THEM--HE SEEMS TO BE THE ONE WHO HAS TAKEN THE LEAD! BUT-- THAT IS IMPOSSIBLE!! OR --IS IT??
IT MUST BE THE ANSWER! IT'S THE ONLY EXPLANATION! I'VE BEEN SUSPECTING A TRICK-- I WAS TOO CAUTIOUS TO REALIZE THE OBVIOUS--THE FANTASTIC FOUR ARE POWERLESS!
NOW, ALL I NEED DO IS FOCUS RICHARDS' OWN TV RADAR TRACKER COMPONENTS ON EACH OF THEM, AND PICK THEM OFF EFFORTLESSLY, AT MY LEISURE!
NO! THAT WILL BE TOO EASY! I'LL TOY WITH THEM A WHILE LONGER! THIS IS TOO GLORIOUS A SITUATION--IT MUST LAST AS LONG AS POSSIBLE!
I'LL BEGIN BY HOUNDING THEM WITH ONE OF RICHARDS' FORCE BEAM PROJECTILES! ONCE AIMED AT A HUMAN TARGET, THE VICTIM'S OWN HEARTBEAT KEEPS IT ON COURSE!
4
18

Jack Kirby, pencils, Joe Sinnott, inks, original interior page artwork, *The Fantastic Four 4th Annual*, November, 1966, ©1966 Marvel Characters, Inc.

Top: Jack Kirby, pencils, Joe SInnott, inks, cover, *The Fantastic Four* #49, April, 1966. Bottom: Jack Kirby, pencils, Joe Sinnott, inks, cover, *The Fantastic Four* #57, December, 1966, ©1966 Marvel Characters, Inc.

stands in the way of what they want. Standard comic book stuff, but amplified by Kirby's in-your-face action and Lee's mocking, pretentious, quasi-hip dialogue.

The series came to a head with the introduction of a character named Galactus, who was announced in issue #48 and appears only in the last page of the story. Galactus, who sucks the energy out of planets for his dinner, sends his herald, the Silver Surfer, out into the cosmos to serve as an advance scout to survey worlds to be annihilated. The Surfer is a quintessential 1960s creation, an almost neuter, all smooth, silver being who flies around on top of a silver surfboard. Once he reaches earth, he is confronted by Ben Grimm's girlfriend, the blind sculptress, Alicia Masters, who through her humanity convinces the herald to turn on his master. There are more forces at work in the story, which weaves together a number of other plot lines from the developing continuity.

With *FF*, Kirby and Lee created a comic book which was an amalgam of everything that had gone before in funny books and which surpassed the sum of its many parts. These stories were created in 1965 and typified some of the best work to be produced by both Kirby and Lee. The page from *The Fantastic Four 4th Annual* on the opposite page, was drawn by Kirby during this period and is illustrative of the frenetic energy he was cramming into his work at the time. This page recounts the re-emergence of the Golden Age Human Torch, who battles Johnny Storm, *FF*'s Torch. The page is inked by Joe Sinnott, who, even though providing a great deal of gloss and slickness to Kirby's work which was not entirely intended, gives the page a satisfying completeness other inkers were unable to capture.

The *FF* was the just the beginning of the Marvel universe. Energized by the positive reception received by the strip, Kirby and Lee went on to create *The Incredible Hulk*, release dated May, 1962; *Thor* in *Journey into Mystery* #83 (plotted by Lee, scripted by Larry Lieber), release dated August, 1962; *Ant Man* in *Tales to Astonish* #35, released dated March,

1963*; Sgt.Fury and his Howling Commandos*, released dated May, 1963; *The Avengers*, release dated September, 1963; and *The X-Men*, release dated September, 1963.[5]

Kirby was now churning out as many as fifty pages in a month. He was drawing most of the lines' covers and defining the look of the entire universe. He also had a hand in designing characters as well as drawing the covers for strips where he was not involved on a regular basis.

In creating their new universe, Kirby and Lee also resurrected other heroes from Marvel's past. In *FF* #4, release dated May, 1962, the Sub-Mariner was given a new lease on life. In *Avengers* #4, release dated March, 1964, the original Captain America was defrosted from imprisonment in an iceberg. Kirby and Lee simply ignored the 1950s version of the hero. In revisiting his co-creation, Kirby lavished enormous attention on the character in stories which appeared in the *Tales of Suspense* title, starting in issue #58, release dated October, 1964. The original Captain was a weakling, who got his strength from an injection of a secret serum. When the superstuff's creator is killed by the Nazis, the good Captain becomes the first and last recipient of the serum and goes off to fight for America as a private in the army. Along the way he picks up a sidekick, Bucky Barnes, who is the mascot of his regiment. In the updated version we learn that Bucky was killed when Cap was frozen. The series was considerably more interesting without him. Bucky's death provided Captain America with angst and self-doubt, which was becoming a fashionable malady for all Marvel's heroes. While the strip was con-

siderably less interesting than *FF*, when Kirby worked on the feature, he created action-packed adventures that were unequaled.

Kirby also lavished significant attention on *Thor*. The strip's premise was that Thor's hammer, disguised as a wooden staff laying around in a secret chamber of a cave, is discovered by a lame, rather meek doctor named Don Blake. When Blake picks up the staff, he is transformed into the Thunder God. The strip got off to a slow start in *Journey into Mystery*, with pedestrian stories and sometimes clumsy artwork by lesser hands. Finally by 1965, Kirby and Lee decided to take the strip on a mythical journey with an extended story arc. Lee's dialogue, again mockingly pretentious, fits the strip perfectly and gave it a larger-than-comics quality. Kirby took full advantage of the fantasy and science fiction angles of the strip and created monumental images to amplify the plot and action required of such an adventure. The inkers, as with *FF*, changed until Vinnie Colletta started inking *Thor* in issue #109. Soon, Colletta would ink all of the Thunder God's adventures with varying degrees of competence and success. Colletta, who had worked primarily in romance comics, had the tendency to work quickly and erase details. Lots of details. He inked primarily with a pen, and many times he lost the line of the drawing by not giving it adequate depth and thickness. Kirby's pencils were so complete that even Colletta could not significantly dampen their spirit and panache. An example of a Colletta-inked *Thor* splash page from issue #142 is on the opposite page. An example of uninked Kirby pencils, demonstrating the energy of his drawing, is on display on page

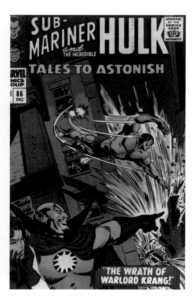

A small sample of mid and late-1960s Marvel covers. Clockwise: Gene Colan, pencils, *Tales of Suspense* #83, November, 1966; Jack Kirby, pencils, *Tales of Suspense* #94, October, 1967; Gene Colan, pencils, *Tales To Astonish* #86, December, 1966; Marie Severin, pencils, *The Incredible Hulk* #103, May, 1968; Gene Colan, pencils, *Daredevil* #37, February, 1968; John Romita, pencils, *Daredevil* #17, June, 1966; John Buscema, pencils, *The Avengers* #43, August, 1967; and Jack Kirby, pencils, *The Avengers* #22, November, 1965, ©1966, 1967, 1968 and 1965, Marvel Characters, Inc.

155. Note that on the *Thor* splash, the margin notes directing that the page be enlarged are in Stan Lee's handwriting; the comments at the top of the page are Kirby's instructions to Lee, so he can write the dialogue for the page. All of the margin notes on Kirby's uninked page are in his handwriting, a clear example of how he structured and crafted the plots of his comic book tales. After Kirby turned in a complete story, Stan might request a correction, but the story's specific details and structure came directly from Kirby. Stan's personality came through with the dialogue he crafted and with his general involvement in the planning of strips.

Kirby was not the only artist at Marvel adding to the mythos of the company's new universe. Steve Ditko also made a major contribution by creating, with Lee, Marvel's best known and most famous character, Spider-Man. Ditko was born in 1927 in Johnstown, Pennsylvania. He grew up reading the funnies and had a special affection for Eisner's *Spirit* and Foster's *Prince Valiant*. Ditko poured over comic books as well and was so enamored of Batman that his mother handmade him a Bat-costume, from scratch.

After serving his hitch in the Army, at the age of 23, Ditko moved to New York to study at the Cartoonists and Illustrators School. While at the School he studied with Jerry Robinson, who had quite an impact on him, heightening his sense of design and composition. By 1953 he had found work in the business, providing artwork for various publishers.[6] Late in that year, Ditko got the opportunity to work in Simon and Kirby's shop. There, he had an opportunity to work directly with Kirby and rub elbows with some of his idols, including Mort Meskin. By 1955, Ditko was making a steady living as an artist for comic books. Late in that year he began an association with Atlas and Stan Lee, producing suspense material. Ditko provided work for Lee for almost a year when work at the company almost completely dried up.

Ditko drew his influences from a variety of sources and boiled them down rather quickly into a highly individual, quirky style

Opposite page: Jack Kirby, pencils, Joe Sinnott, inks, interior page, *Tales of Suspense* #94, October, 1967, ©1967 Marvel Characters, Inc.

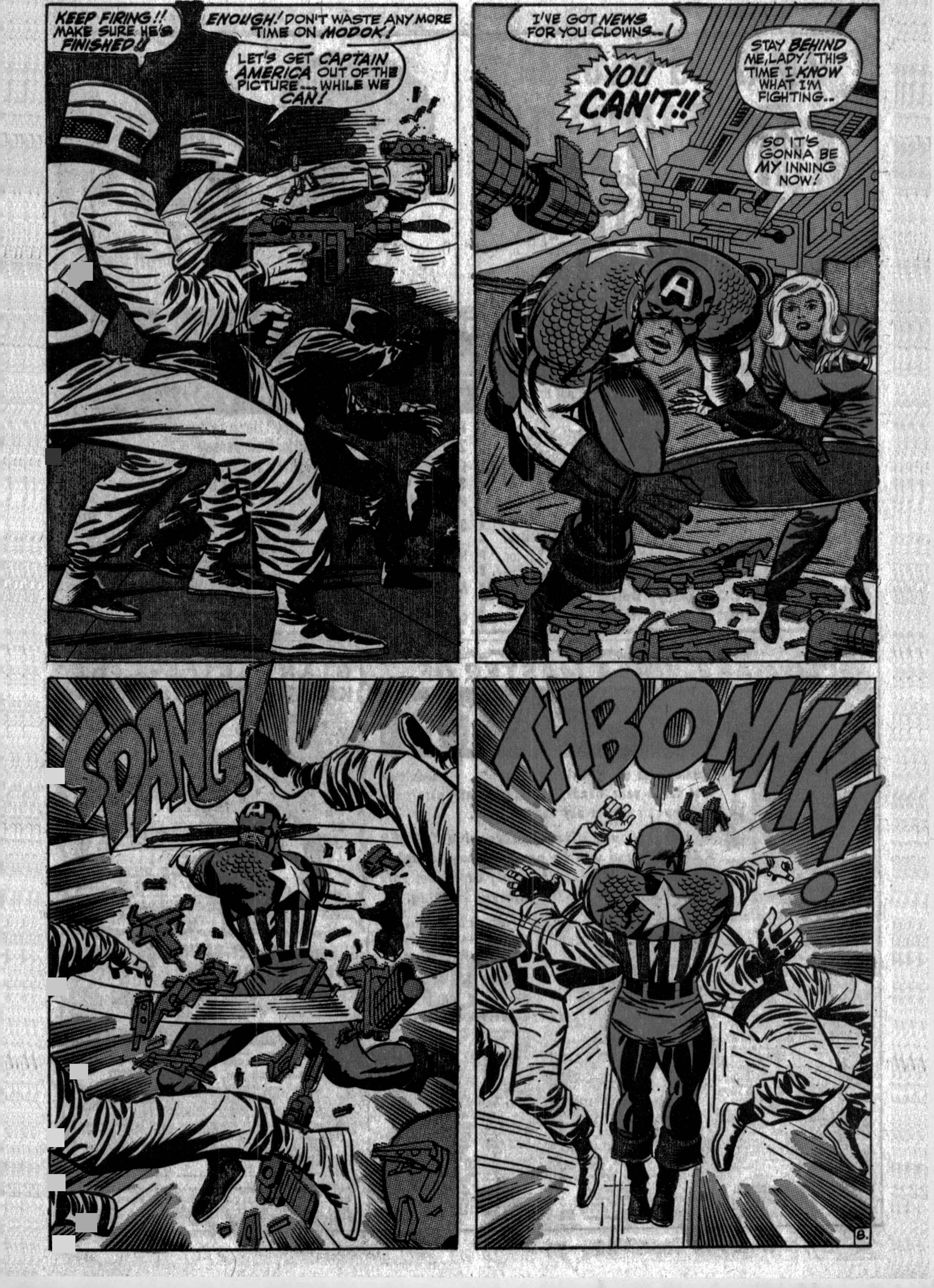
KEEP FIRING!! MAKE SURE HE'S FINISHED!!
ENOUGH! DON'T WASTE ANY MORE TIME ON MODOK!
LET'S GET CAPTAIN AMERICA OUT OF THE PICTURE... WHILE WE CAN!
I'VE GOT NEWS FOR YOU CLOWNS...!
YOU CAN'T!!
STAY BEHIND ME, LADY! THIS TIME I KNOW WHAT I'M FIGHTING..
SO IT'S GONNA BE MY INNING NOW!
SPANG!
THBONNK!
8.

published mostly horror, crime, and science fiction material, had been using Ditko's talents since 1954. Their relationship would be a long-term one, even though Charlton was notorious for paying low rates. The advantage to working for the company was that it gave more freedom to its artists than other publishers. Charlton's attitude was not motivated by altruism; the company just wanted to crank out its products on schedule. Ditko's Captain Atom was not a musclebound hero with perfect anatomy drawn in a slick house style but a character who looked like a regular guy, just with super powers. Indeed, much like Kubert, Ditko excelled at drawing regular looking people thrust into extraordinary situations.

Ditko was also spending time collaborating with Lee on five-page sci-fi stories with

of drawing and inking. By the late 1950s his style had crystallized. Ditko was not afraid to fill in large areas of his panels with black, not as a time saving device, but for effect. He also mastered the art of impeccable pacing and utilized a variety of angles to shoot his stories. He worked pencilling and inking primarily monster and horror fare. By 1958, Lee asked Ditko to come back to Marvel, where he created dozens of science fiction and fantasy stories.[7]

In 1960, Ditko entered the superhero fray by providing artwork for a feature called *Captain Atom*. The good Captain appeared in a comic book called *Space Adventures* #33, release dated March, 1960, published by Charlton Comics, a small family-owned company based in Connecticut. Charlton, which

cute endings. The comic books containing these little gems were so well received that in June, 1961, another title was added to Marvel's line, *Amazing Adventures*. By issue #7, the magazine's title had been changed to *Amazing Adult Fantasy*. Eight issues and one name change later, the title would be discontinued, but first, a little comic book history would be made, and the face of the comics would forever be changed by Mr. Ditko.

The comic book in question was now called *Amazing Fantasy*, and the character was the amazing Spider-Man. As with *FF*, the genesis and creation of Spider-Man has been the topic of dispute since the ole webhead became popular.[8] The facts are clear: Ditko pencilled the origin story of the character from Lee's plot synopsis. Ditko designed the character and his costume. Ditko's style and personality permeated and defined the feature. Kirby did pencil the cover for *Amazing Fantasy* #15, the first appearance of the character, release dated August, 1962, but only after Lee rejected Ditko's version. Spider-Man was the second superhero of the new, improved, Marvel and received his own feature in *The Amazing Spider-Man* #1, release dated March, 1963.

For those of you who do not already know, Spider-Man's alter-ego, Peter Parker, gains his powers after being bitten by a radioactive spider. Parker is a geeky teenager, with the usual problems: girls and school. After he acquires his spider-powers, unlike previous heroes, he still has the same problems. This was one of the ongoing themes of the series: super abilities do not solve your problems, sometimes they make them worse. Parker also works as a freelance newspaper photographer for *The Daily Bugle*, which allows him to get a jump on bad guys and to explain why he is so often at crime scenes. Ditko's world for Spidey, while still a cartoon, had a uniquely different feel from other comics. Ditko's characters were not sleek and heroic but were vulnerably down-to-earth. These qualities, coupled with his mature abilities as a storyteller, distinguished the feature during its early years. With *Spider-Man*, Ditko created a strip that was a reflection of his personal, unconventional sen-

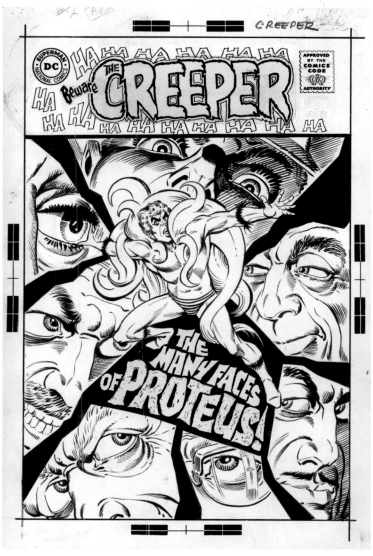

Don Heck, pencils and inks, original cover artwork, *Captain Savage* #14, May, 1969, ©1969 Marvel Characters, Inc.

sibilities, realized in a manner that was the antithesis of the established superhero style of the era.

Ditko was now on a roll. Within four months his next new strip, *Dr. Strange*, premiered in *Strange Tales* #110, release dated July, 1963. Scripted by Lee and drawn and inked by Ditko, *Dr. Strange* was the occult's answer to a superhero. *Dr. Strange* had once been an arrogant surgeon whose hands were injured in a car accident. In an effort to restore himself, he seeks out the "ancient one" and after having a revelation, becomes his apprentice, ultimately evolving into a master of black magic. The strip combined the darkness and moodiness of horror movies with the fight-against-evil mindset of the accelerating super-craze. More than with any strip involving the artist, *Dr. Strange* utilized all of Ditko's sensibilities. *Dr. Strange* was a reflection of the conceptual, B-movie universe Ditko had been spinning tales about since the mid-1950s. The art created the perfect tone for the strip. Ditko's effective brushwork, surreal vistas of the mystic realm, coupled with Lee's mumbojumbo dialogue, created a strip that could be read on several levels and was entertaining on all of them.

The key ingredient with Ditko's work was his conceptualization of his universe, which for a short time became part of the world of Marvel comics. Ditko's artwork became even more effective and assured between 1963 and 1966. He also wrested more control of his strips from Lee to the point where he was almost scripting the features entirely himself. The story goes that after issue #25 of *The Amazing Spider-Man*, Ditko plotted all the stories, and the finished art boards were delivered to Lee just so he could write the dialogue.[9] Ditko worked on other superhero fare at Marvel, but only with *Spider-Man* and *Dr. Strange* did his efforts gel. Finally when a dispute arose over how to conclude an episode of the *Spider-Man* strip, Ditko left Marvel for good.

Ditko would continue his work in comics, only rarely equaling his work at Marvel. For the remainder of the 1960s, he worked for a number of other publishers. His last main-

stream efforts were for DC, where he tried to pick up where he had left off at Marvel. At DC he created two strips, first, *Beware the Creeper*, which premiered in *Showcase* #73, release dated April, 1968 and then *The Hawk and the Dove*, which premiered in *Showcase* #75, release dated June, 1968. Of the two features, *Beware the Creeper* came closest to his work for Marvel. Again, Ditko created his own world in the context of the strip. The origin of the feature is standard fare, the hero receives his powers from a scientist he saves. The interesting angle is the bizarre outfit the character wears. He picks up his hero-duds at a costume store, so he can blend in at a costume party. The Creeper picks up his moniker from his creepy laugh and costume.

Ditko, who could charitably be called eccentric, left the strip due to artistic difficulties. Part of his attitude toward his editors stemmed from his embracing the "objectivist" philosophy of Ayn Rand, author of *Atlas Shrugged* and *The Fountainhead*. Ditko wanted to be appreciated for his art only and maintained that "I never talk about myself…my work is me."[10] Unfortunately in the work environment of the late 1960s, comic book storytellers were not yet considered artists. Ultimately, the times and attitudes would catch up to Mr. Ditko's. After his break with DC, Ditko never produced work on the level of his previous efforts.

In addition to Kirby and Ditko, Lee availed himself of the talents of dependable Don Heck for mountains of artwork on a variety of features. Heck, who was born in Jamaica, New York in 1929, got his art education reading

Terry and the Pirates, taking correspondence courses, and at vocational school. He was in the first class to graduate from what is now known as New York State Tech. By 1949, Heck got his first work in the business in the production department at Harvey. By 1954, he was working for Atlas. It seems that when Heck's friend, artist Pete Morisi, went for a job interview at Atlas with Lee, Morisi took along a sample of one of the comic books he had provided art for, which also contained work pencilled by Heck. As the interview progressed, Lee kept pointing to Heck's work as an example of what he was looking for. Morisi promptly told Lee that Heck was looking for work, which resulted in an interview and a job.[11] Heck's forte was in pencilling and inking action stories involving real, rather than super, people. On occasion, his tales of soldiers in combat had a realistic feel and tone supported by impeccable inking.

In 1963, Heck was assigned the job of pencilling and inking the first *Iron Man* strip in *Tales of Suspense* #39, release dated March, 1963. The strip was conceived by Lee and Kirby, and the script was written by Larry Lieber. Iron Man's outfit, which was just plain clunky looking, was designed by Kirby. Heck handled the origin episode with ease, and the artwork is an example of restrained simplicity. The plot involves an industrialist named Ray Stark, who receives an injury to his heart, which is remedied by a special iron suit and chest plate which give him extraordinary power.

Heck's work was best served by his own inking. His Caniff-inspired brushwork was, for many, an acquired taste, but there was no denying his expert pacing and solid use of lighting in his stories. The cover for *Captain Savage* #14, release dated May, 1969, on page 160, displays Heck's bold brush work and fluid composition. Heck's reputation during the 1960s comes primarily from his association with *The Avengers* and *Iron Man* strips.

By 1964 the Marvel super-universe was complete with the addition of Daredevil, the man without fear. Daredevil, the blind attorney, had lost his sight when he was a boy. He had been hit by a truck and doused with radioactive chemicals. With his vision gone, his other senses become super-acute, giving him his powers. By 1964, Lee's device of giving all of Marvel's characters problems, with loads of angst to boot, was beginning to wear thin. All of the company's characters' self-doubt was becoming a bit, well, predictable and boring. *DD* was not one of the company's more distinguished offerings. For artwork, veteran Bill Everett was brought back into the Marvel fold. He had been out of the business for almost a decade. As with most artists from his generation, he had left the comics to serve in World War II. After his discharge in 1946, Everett went back to work for Timely, drawing among other things, Namora, a female version of Sub-Mariner. With the near collapse of Atlas after the company's loss of its distributor, Everett found work in the greeting card business.[12] Now, he was back and his first effort was shaky. The story was finished late, and other hands may have helped Everett finish the job. Everett, who had been plagued by personal problems, including bouts of alcoholism, did find more work with Marvel, and the results were much more satisfying. Everett, for a short time, succeeded Ditko on the *Dr. Strange* strip and turned in a stylish, beautifully inked version of the feature. Everett worked on several strips and provided finishes for Jack Kirby's pencils as well. His major efforts were on his own creation, Sub-Mariner, and his work was the definitive version of the character.

Lee, who was still editing all of Marvel's titles, depended on a small bullpen of artists in addition to Kirby and Ditko. Also producing artwork for mighty Marvel were Dick Ayers, Larry Lieber (Lee's brother), and Joe Sinnott. The inkers routinely used included veteran production man Sol Brodsky, Chic Stone, Paul Reinman, George Roussos (sometimes credited as "John Bell"), and inker extraordinaire Frank Giacoia (sometimes credited as "Frank Ray"). As Marvel's business picked up and the line expanded, new artists were brought into the company. The *Daredevil* strip was being tossed around like a hot

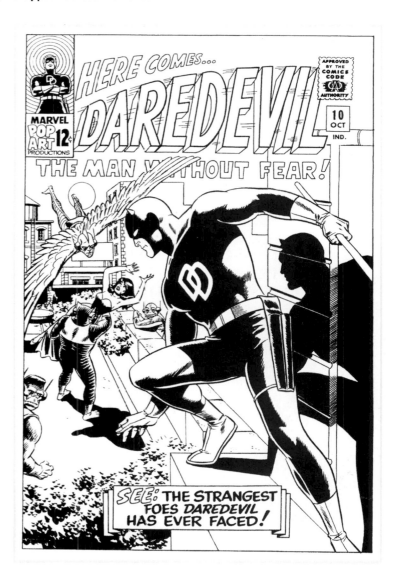

potato, switching artists constantly. After Everett, Joe Orlando took over pencilling chores for three unimpressive issues and was gone. With issue #5, Wally Wood entered the fray.

Woody had been busy since EC had gone out-of-business, occupying himself with work for *Mad*. He also had turned in gorgeous finishes for Kirby on *Sky Masters*, as well as on a never-sold Kirby strip project, *Surf Hunter*. By the end of the 1950s he was also producing handsome illustrations and book covers. Woody's habit of working twenty-four hours straight was catching up with him. He was now experiencing non-stop headaches and turning to alcohol for help. His work was suffering to the point that when he turned in a

John Romita, pencils, Frank Giacoia, inks, original interior page artwork,
Daredevil #15, April, 1966, ©1966 Marvel Characters, Inc.

John Romita, pencils, Mike Esposito, inks, original interior page artwork, *The Amazing Spider-Man* #52, September, 1967, ©1967 Marvel Characters, Inc.

CONTINUED AFTER NEXT PAGE

Mad story featuring Little Orphan Annie, it was rejected, ending his tenure with the company in 1964.[13] His next job was for Marvel on the hornhead. Woody redesigned Daredevil's costume, turning it from yellow to red; devils are supposed to be red. Daredevil was now sleek and athletic. The strip was, despite lackluster story lines, looking a whole lot better. This was not the Woody who had created atmosphere with shadow and detail, but someone less ambitious. Competent and flashy, yes, quirky and inspired, no. By issue #12, Woody was gone from the Marvel universe.[14] He had never been fond of superheroes, but now he would undertake to create a line of hero comic books, as we shall see in Chapter Six.

Re-enter John Romita. Stan had been trying to attract talent back to Marvel and Jazzy Johnny was on his list.[15] Romita was born in Brooklyn in 1930 and attended the School of Industrial Arts. He had spent the last fifteen years, seven of them at Atlas, working in the business and felt burned out.[16] After his separation from Atlas, Romita had started a long tenure pencilling romance stories for DC. Romance work was not a prestige assignment at DC, but it paid the bills. Romita was acutely aware of his second class citizen status at the company and noted that he felt like an "outsider." He remembers, "…it was almost like they were cliquish. They were very cold to their artists and writers. The editors had a terrible reputation where they would play the artists off against each other."[17] Romita, nevertheless, turned in very attractive work depicting the trials and tribulations of young women in love. His style changed during his employment at DC, maturing into a smooth, elegant variant of the slick "DC" style. A close look at his stories reveals a strong Sickles-Caniff influence to his work, which he freely acknowledges. There were other influences which further defined his art, but the dominant feature of Romita's work became his simple, strong, clean line.

By 1965, Romita was at a career and artistic crossroads. He had pencilled and inked hundreds of romance stories and scores of covers, and he could not do another piece of work. "I had the worst artist's block…I absolutely sat there and could not produce a page of art for weeks and weeks," he recalls.[18] Help was on the way from Stan the man. "Why not come back to Marvel?," Stan kept insisting. But Romita had a dilemma; his DC editor, Phyllis Reed, was leaving, and she had recommended Jazzy Johnny as her replacement.[19] Romita decided against becoming a wordsmith and editor, and the rest is Marvel history.

Romita had another problem; he had not worked on superheroes since his stint on the *Captain America* strip in 1953-54. Now he was thrust back into the action/adventure genre, but he would quickly adapt, turning out work worthy of any DC superhero. After flexing his muscles inking a Don Heck *Avengers* job, Stan assigned Jazzy John to take over chores on *DD*. Then, Romita received a call from George Kashdan at DC inquiring if he wanted to take over on the *Metamorpho* strip.

Romita. Kirby's influence was always present, though, especially when Lee was brainstorming with his other artists on how a story should be composed. Romita recalls, "Stan told us to try to absorb the dynamics of Kirby. In other words he never told me to draw like Kirby, just capture his approach."[20] The artists at Marvel were not the only artists taking note of Kirby. Gil Kane was paying attention to Kirby's storytelling and trying to absorb some of Jack's dynamics as well. The result further energized Kane's art as it matured during the mid-1960s.[21] Artists and editors were also beginning to wonder what was going on over at Marvel. They were beginning to take note of the changes that Jack and Stan were making, which was transforming comic book storytelling from anecdotal plot-driven stories to the lengthy character-driven tomes best typified by *FF*.

With Ditko gone, Lee and Romita could now tamper with Spider-Man. Spidey had

Romita gave the offer thumbs down and stayed with mighty Marvel.

Romita's first Marvel strip was *Daredevil*, and as the interior page from issue #15, on page 164, demonstrates, he comfortably re-entered the superhero art world without missing a beat. But just as he was getting comfortable with the ole hornhead, Lee gave him a new assignment: replace Ditko on *Spider-Man*.

Romita's transformation of the character redefined the character's look and took the strip in a different direction. It also made him a star artist in the comic book world. The trouble was, Romita took Spidey away from his roots and firmly replanted him in the mainstream.

In an effort to further define Marvel, Lee had tried to lure Carmine Infantino to transplant DC's slickness into the company's new universe. Infantino demurred and stayed put, but Lee infused some of DC's sheen using

Gene Colan, pencils, John Tartaglione, inks, original splash page artwork, *Daredevil* #34, November,1967, ©1967 Marvel Characters, Inc.

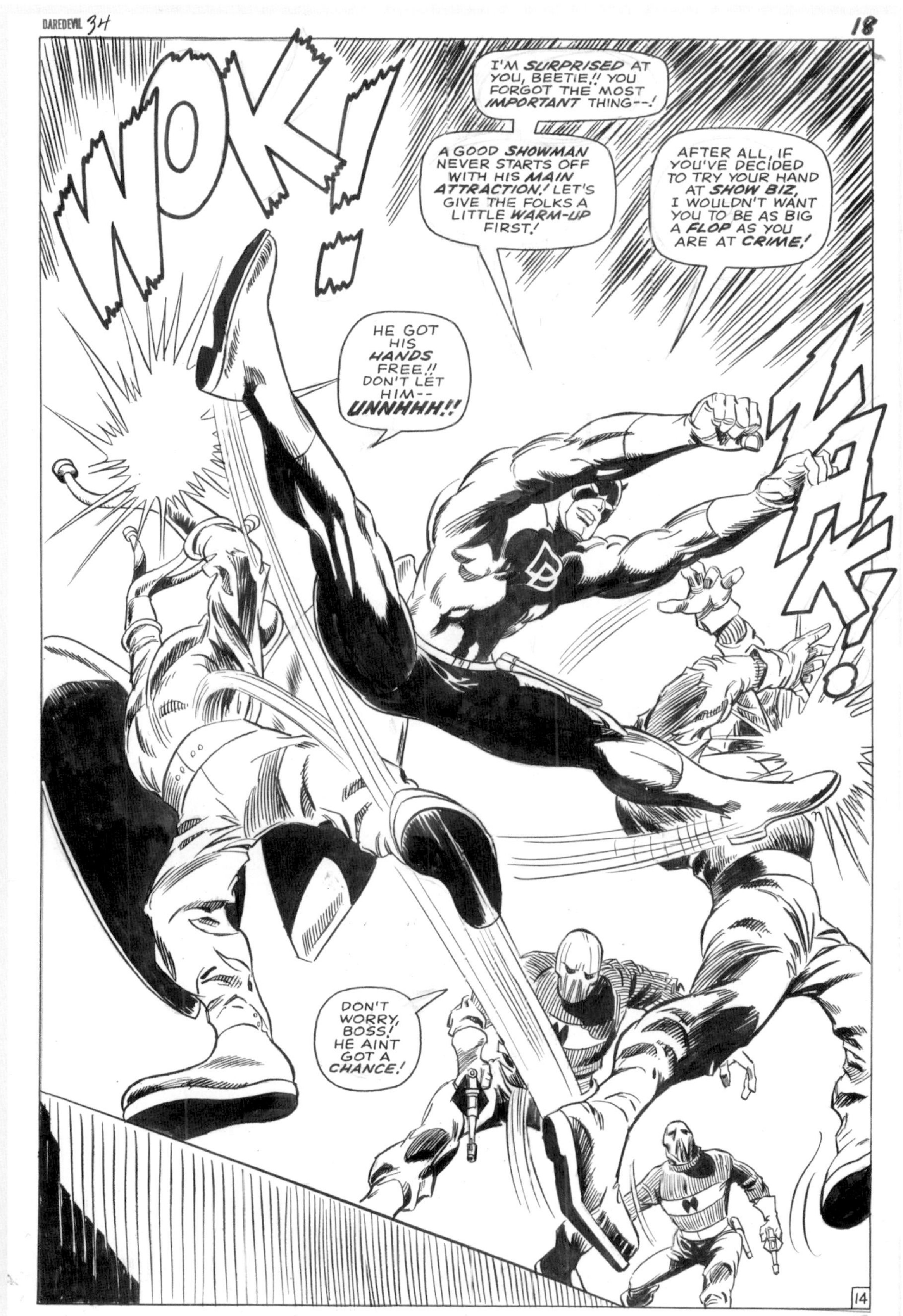
DAREDEVIL 34
18
WOK!
I'M SURPRISED AT YOU, BEETIE!! YOU FORGOT THE MOST IMPORTANT THING--!
A GOOD SHOWMAN NEVER STARTS OFF WITH HIS MAIN ATTRACTION! LET'S GIVE THE FOLKS A LITTLE WARM-UP FIRST!
AFTER ALL, IF YOU'VE DECIDED TO TRY YOUR HAND AT SHOW BIZ, I WOULDN'T WANT YOU TO BE AS BIG A FLOP AS YOU ARE AT CRIME!
HE GOT HIS HANDS FREE!! DON'T LET HIM-- UNNHHH!!
ZAK!
DON'T WORRY, BOSS! HE AINT GOT A CHANCE!
14

Bill Everett, pencils and inks, original interior page artwork, *Sub-Mariner* #50, June, 1972, ©1972 Marvel Characters, Inc. Even though this page was created after the end of the Silver Age, it is still representative of Everett's work on his signature creation.

Lee's Atlas artists who had gone on to greener pastures when the company had lost its distribution. Colan was born in the Bronx in 1926. He had been in the business since 1944 and had worked for Stan in the 1950s turning in work on a diverse selection of titles. His tenure at Atlas ended at the same time Romita and other regulars at the company received the ax. Colan went off to work in advertising and later on educational filmstrips, which proved unsatisfying. At the insistence of his wife, he went back to his first love, the comics.[23]

By the early 1960s, Colan was back, turning in work for Dell, Marvel, and DC. He was working on adventure, western stories, romance, and television show adaptations including *Burkes's Law* and *Ben Casey*. At Marvel, he was pencilling stories under the pseudonym, Adam Austin, out of concern he might jeopardize his DC assignments. Stan kept bugging Colan to come back, full time,

been a troubled kid from NYC. His was an ethnic world of real looking women and populated by characters you might see at the deli. Romita meddled with the quirkiness of the strip: now the women were beautiful movie stars, after all, he had drawn attractive women for DC for the better part of a decade. Marvel staffers would joke that Romita "took Spider-Man uptown."[22] Romita reinvented the character and made it possible for the strip to appeal to a wider audience even if he removed the qualities that had made the strip a surreal standout. Romita worked closely with Lee and listened to his ideas and concerns, unlike Ditko. Romita worked on other Marvel strips, but it was with his work on *The Amazing Spider-Man* that he carved out a niche for himself.

Lee also was now after Gene Colan to come back to Marvel; he needed someone to replace Romita on *Daredevil*. Colan was another of

Gil Kane, pencils and inks, original interior page artwork, *Tales to Astonish* #90, April, 1967, ©1967 Marvel Characters, Inc.

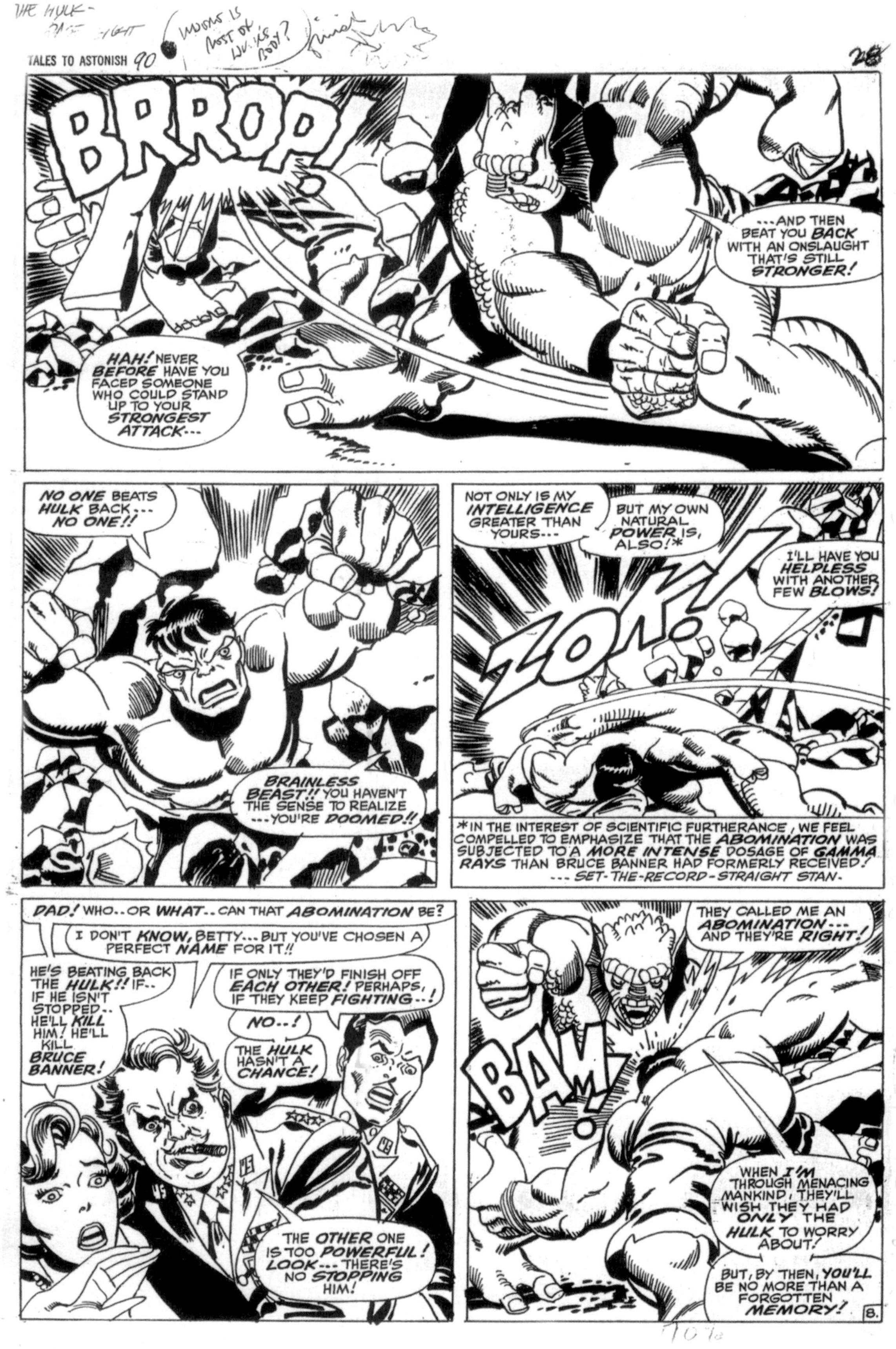
TALES TO ASTONISH 90
BRROP!
HAH! NEVER BEFORE HAVE YOU FACED SOMEONE WHO COULD STAND UP TO YOUR STRONGEST ATTACK---
---AND THEN BEAT YOU BACK WITH AN ONSLAUGHT THAT'S STILL STRONGER!
NO ONE BEATS HULK BACK--- NO ONE!!
BRAINLESS BEAST!! YOU HAVEN'T THE SENSE TO REALIZE ---YOU'RE DOOMED!!
NOT ONLY IS MY INTELLIGENCE GREATER THAN YOURS---
BUT MY OWN NATURAL POWER IS, ALSO!*
ZOK!
I'LL HAVE YOU HELPLESS WITH ANOTHER FEW BLOWS!
*IN THE INTEREST OF SCIENTIFIC FURTHERANCE, WE FEEL COMPELLED TO EMPHASIZE THAT THE ABOMINATION WAS SUBJECTED TO A MORE INTENSE DOSAGE OF GAMMA RAYS THAN BRUCE BANNER HAD FORMERLY RECEIVED! ---SET-THE-RECORD-STRAIGHT STAN-
DAD! WHO--OR WHAT--CAN THAT ABOMINATION BE?
I DON'T KNOW, BETTY--- BUT YOU'VE CHOSEN A PERFECT NAME FOR IT!!
HE'S BEATING BACK THE HULK!! IF-- IF HE ISN'T STOPPED-- HE'LL KILL HIM! HE'LL KILL BRUCE BANNER!
IF ONLY THEY'D FINISH OFF EACH OTHER! PERHAPS, IF THEY KEEP FIGHTING--!
NO--!
THE HULK HASN'T A CHANCE!
THE OTHER ONE IS TOO POWERFUL! LOOK--- THERE'S NO STOPPING HIM!
THEY CALLED ME AN ABOMINATION--- AND THEY'RE RIGHT!
BAM!
WHEN I'M THROUGH MENACING MANKIND, THEY'LL WISH THEY HAD ONLY THE HULK TO WORRY ABOUT!
BUT, BY THEN, YOU'LL BE NO MORE THAN A FORGOTTEN MEMORY!
8.

and after some arm twisting and financial guarantees, he was back and took over *Daredevil*, with issue #20, release dated September, 1966. By 1966, the ole hornhead had been tossed around to at least six artists and was in need of some energized consistency. Romita would have served the strip perfectly but had been drafted on the *Spider-Man* strip. Indeed, one of Romita's regrets was never returning to work on *DD*. Colan's involvement with the strip brought a breath of fresh air to a feature that was in need of a spirited infusion of enthusiasm.

Colan would stay with *Daredevil* for the long term. The strip developed a consistent personality, merging artwork and storyline. As Colan dug in for the duration on the strip, his handling of the storytelling began to use a more cinematic approach influenced by his love of late 1960s films. In one story, Colan used the famous car chase from *Bullitt* as a starting point for an extended sequence. During the late 1960s, Colan also turned in spirited and exceptionally well crafted work on other Marvel titles including extended runs on *Sub-Mariner* and *Iron Man*. The distinguishing features with Colan's work were his fluid, exaggerated line and an ability to easily translate frenetic energy onto the comic book page. Colan's storytelling was not limited only to Marvel, as we will see in the next chapter.

As the Marvel line was growing, Lee was bringing in other artists to fill the demand for artwork. The company's expanded bullpen of pencilers now included Dan Adkins, John Buscema, Jim Steranko, George Tuska, Werner Roth, and Marie Severin. Jack Abel, Frank Giacoia, George Klein, John Severin, Syd Shores, Joe Sinnott and a host of journeymen were also now supplying inks.

John Buscema had come back to Marvel in 1966 to work on several features, but his art was still maturing. His work would not have a real impact until the 1970s. As Buscema came into his own, he would help to further refine the Marvel look and style.

Marie Severin, who had been on the staff back at EC, was now doing production chores. Stan had given her a job at Atlas after EC had

gone under. When everyone was laid off at Atlas, she found work in the art department of the Federal Reserve Bank. In 1964, she went back to Marvel. Lee hired her without even looking at her portfolio, telling her, "Oh Marie, it's really good to see you, we need someone in production."[24] She had been occupied with behind the scenes work until 1966 when someone was needed to prepare an illustration of mighty Marvel characters for an *Esquire* story. Severin got the assignment because Kirby could not be spared. When the artwork came to Martin Goodman's attention, he told Stan to use her as an artist. Severin quickly got to work with well crafted efforts on *The Hulk* in

Top: Jack Kirby, pencils, unpublished, *Thor* page. Below: Jack Kirby, pencils, unpublished cover for *The Fantastic Four*, both circa late-1960s, ©2004 Marvel Characters, Inc.

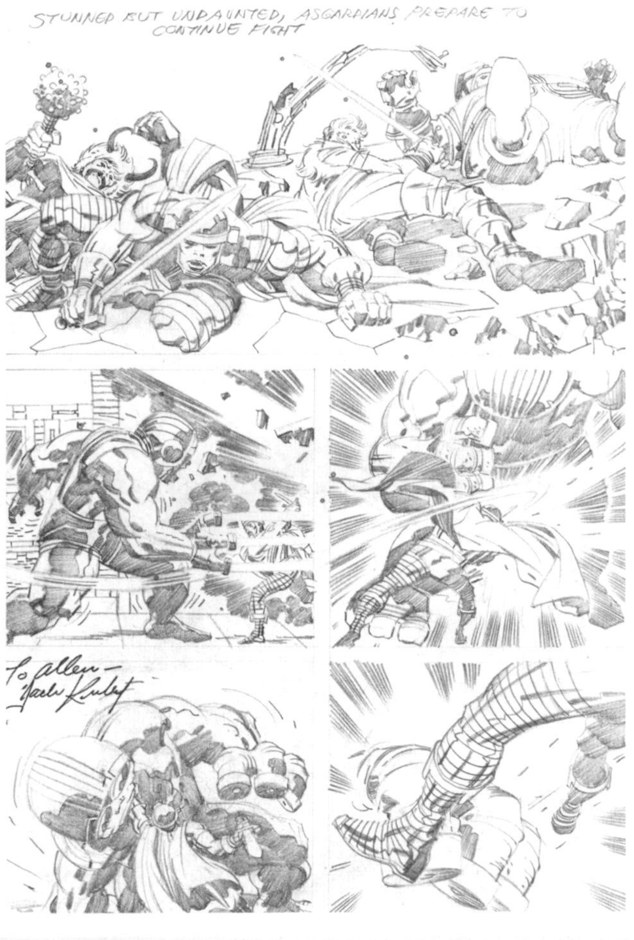
STUNNED BUT UNDAUNTED, ASGARDIANS PREPARE TO CONTINUE FIGHT
To Allen—
Jack Kirby

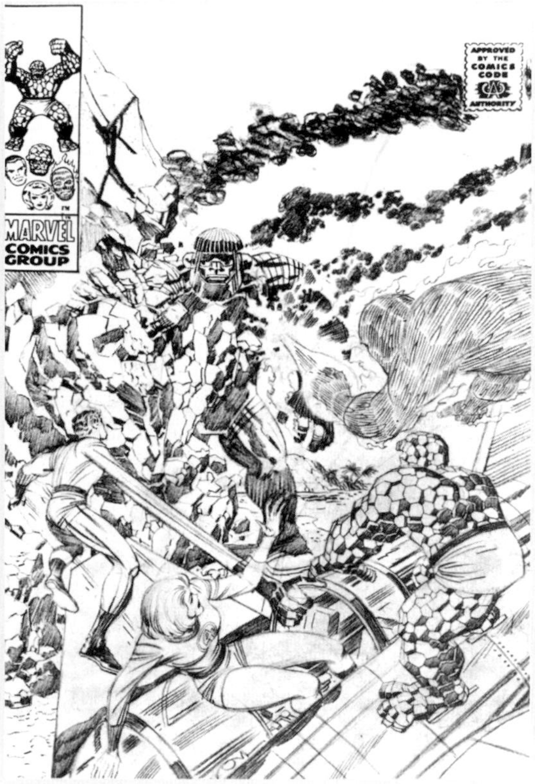
MARVEL
COMICS
GROUP
APPROVED BY THE COMICS CODE AUTHORITY

Tales to Astonish and succeeding Bill Everett on *Dr. Strange* in *Strange Tales*. Severin had a good sense of dynamics and was a solid storyteller. She also contributed some handsome cover artwork on *The Hulk* when the character finally got his own title. She additionally got an opportunity to show some humor with her work on Marvel's parody of its universe in the short-lived title *Not Brand Echh*.

Severin's brother, John, occupied himself inking the work of others. He was an accomplished finisher who could turn even the most lackluster pencils into polished work. His efforts were primarily on Marvel's war features. He did turn in pencils and inks on the *Nick Fury, Agent of Shield* strip in *Strange Tales*, but his more characteristic material saw print in other venues.

Gil Kane also started turning in work on a few titles for Marvel starting in 1966. During the mid-1960s, he had become increasingly restless. Kane was looking to break free from the restrictions imposed on him at DC. Marvel provided another avenue for him to let loose with nonstop action. Kane did just that by pencilling action-packed episodes of *Captain America* in *Tales of Suspense* and *The Hulk* in *Tales to Astonish*. In the 1970's, Kane would define the look of Marvel's covers by pencilling over 800 of them.

By 1967, Stan was beginning to run out of steam. He had been Marvel's only story editor and art director since the company's near collapse. Two years before, he had hired Roy Thomas. Thomas had written letters to Julie Schwartz responding to DC's new heroes back in the early 1960s and had decided to turn his love of the comics into a full-time job. After winning a writing contest for Charlton, Thomas had written some scripts for the company, but that only whetted his appetite to work in the comic book big leagues. He had abandoned his home state of Missouri to come to New York in 1965, leaving his job as a high school teacher to take a position with DC, writing for Mort Weisinger, who had never been known for his charms. After a grand total of two weeks, Thomas had taken an offer from Stan the man. Thomas started out writing

Jack Kirby, pencils, Joe Sinnott, inks (Kirby's pencils were lightboxed and not directly inked), Silver Surfer illustration, ©2004 Marvel Characters, Inc.

Jack Kirby, pencils, Frank Giacoia, inks, original cover artwork, *Marvel Double Feature* #18, October, 1976, ©1976 Marvel characters, Inc. Kirby's retake on his cover from *Tales of Suspense* #94.

scripts for non-hero fare, the *Modeling with Mille* strip to be precise, but soon he was where he was meant to be, writing effective scripts for *The Avengers*. Stan would rely more and more on Thomas until he became editor-in-chief in 1972. But Lee's need to delegate responsibilities he alone had previously overseen was clear evidence that things were changing.[25]

With the departure of Ditko from Marvel in 1966, the company had lost part of its soul. Now, Kirby was becoming increasingly dissatisfied with his perceived role in the Marvel universe. He was still billed as Jack "King" Kirby on the splash pages of the comics he was producing, but by all accounts he clearly did not feel like royalty. Stan was hogging all the limelight and publicity, which was beginning to eat away at Kirby. Stan was, after all, animated and outgoing, the perfect pitchman. Kirby was the antithesis of the persona exuded by Lee, the consummate salesman and boardwalk barker. By 1968, *FF* and *Thor* were losing their sheen and lapsing into predictability. Kirby's art was still rock solid, but the magic was gone.

Lest we not forget, 1968 also witnessed Stan's attempt to put his own handprints on one of Kirby's great creations: the Silver Surfer. When Kirby learned that Stan was giving the Surfer his own book and using artist John Buscema on the strip, he was, to put it mildly, unhappy. Stan would ruin the character by changing Kirby's concept and making the Surfer, well, more like Marvel's other characters. Kirby's concept of the character, of pure energy given corporeal form, a consciousness that only understands cause and effect and is beyond the concepts of good and evil, was changed by Lee. Now the Surfer was merely a man, who, to save his world from Galactus, sacrifices himself by becoming the big guy's herald. Now, Jack became even more resolute to take his creations elsewhere. Kirby was looking to find a new home, and soon Carmine Infantino would give him his opportunity to jump ship to DC. By 1970 Kirby was gone, but the spirit he had put into his work had left several years before.

During this period of transition, Marvel had still been attracting new, young talent. Jim Steranko had come on board by the end of 1966 and attempted to inject something new into the Marvel universe. Steranko, who was born in 1938 and had done a little bit of everything, including work as an escape artist, was an astute student of the comics and their history. The problem was, this was obvious by looking at his work. Steranko cribbed Krigstein in his panel breakdowns, he imitated Kirby in his dynamics, and he affected a pop sensibility in his design devices. It looked fresh and exciting to those who did not know better, but experienced eyes knew where he was coming from. By 1969, he was gone.

By 1968 Marvel was finally getting a new distributor and was able to further expand its line of books. Martin Goodman also made a deal to sell the company which he had created thirty-five years before for a tidy sum. The deal left Goodman in charge and also required that Stan sign a contract to stay on with the purchaser. The new owners, Perfect Film and Chemical Corporation, were not concerned about the artists, just the "man." Jack, John, Gene, Don, Marie, Jim, and the others did not even register on the corporate radar.

Since the mid-1960s, DC had taken notice of what Stan and Jack had been doing. Romita recalls that it was talked about, "quite a bit. They used to discuss why Stan was starting to sell books and why his reputation was growing…" By the late 1960s, with the ascendance of Carmine Infantino, DC was trying to catch up with mighty Marvel, but with few exceptions, they failed.[26]

The house that Stan and Jack had built would endure. What Kirby, Ditko, and Lee all created, in the short span of five years, was, to borrow from Stan, simply incredible! But, for Marvel and the creators of its new universe of characters and sensibilities, the Silver Age had ended by 1968.

NOTES

[1] Interview with John Romita.

[2] Stan Lee and George Mair, *Excelsior! The Amazing Life of Stan Lee*, Fireside, 2002. Stan is excellent at spinning stories and creating and recreating events. He frequently cites his "bad memory," making it difficult to ascertain what really happened with regards to the history of Marvel in the 1960s. Lee has related this story consistently over the years.

[3] Ibid. Julie Schwartz also related the story regarding Goodman and Liebowitz many times over the years and made reference to it in his autobiography, *Man of Two Worlds*.

[4] Disputes by Kirby and Lee over who did what have festered for the last thirty years. Comic book fans who have researched the topic point to various sources to support their theories. Frequently, several sources are referred to which include a Sunday, January 9, 1966, *Herald Tribune Magazine* piece written by Nat Freedland entitled "Super Heroes With Super Problems," which describes an editorial conference between Lee and Kirby; an interview by Ted White with Lee in the fanzine *Castle of Frankenstein* #12, 1968; and various interviews with Kirby including Gary Groth's frank interview with Jack and his wife Roz, which appeared in *The Comics Journal* #134, February, 1990. Documentary evidence of several pages from the original plot synopsis to *FF* #1, surfaced in *Comics Interview* #5, July, 1983, containing Lee's outline, which was again reprinted with numerous observations by Roy Thomas in *Alter Ego* #2, Vol. 2, Summer, 1999.

[5] The Avengers was another superhero team using several of Marvel's newly created characters. The first members were Thor, Iron Man, the Hulk, Ant Man and the Wasp. The team constantly changed as members came, left, and were replaced. The X-Men were a kid superhero team lead by a wheelchair-bound genius. The concept bears a striking resemblance to Arnold Drake and Bruno Premiani's *Doom Patrol* strip which premiered in issue #80 of *My Greatest Adventure*, release dated June, 1963. *The X-Men* premiered three months later. Both strips had similar leaders and main characters who were outcasts. Comic book fans have discussed these similarities for years and the mystery of why Kirby and Lee's strip was so close in concept to *DP*. This conundrum will never be solved.

[6] Bill Hall, editor, *Ditkomania*, various issues, 1984-1994, Bill Hall, Cromwell, Connecticut.

[7] Ibid.

[8] Joe Simon has written he originally conceived of a Spider character, although very different in concept. Simon's character was initially realized, at least as a concept, by C.C. Beck, see: Joe Simon with Jim Simon, *The Comic Book Makers*. Jack Kirby has claimed credit for the character, as well.

[9] See Steve Ditko's letter published in *Comic Book Marketplace* #63, October, 1998. By issue #26, Ditko was being credited as co-plotter which was the great exception in the Marvel universe. Ditko, however, plotted the strip well before that. Kirby, who also turned in finished artwork for Lee to dialogue as well, was, for some reason, never given official credit.

[10] Steve Ditko, "Meet the Men Behind the Creeper," *Showcase* #73, April, 1968.

[11] Lou Mougin interview with Don Heck, *Comics Interview* #100, 1991.

[12] Roy Thomas interview with Bill Everett, *Alter Ego* #11, April, 1978, Mike's Star Reach Productions.

[13] Jim Steranko, "Steranko on Wallace Wood," *Wally Wood Sketchbook*, Vanguard, 2000.

[14] Veteran Bob Powell worked with Woody on *Daredevil* #9-11. In 1965, Wood also provided inks for an *Avengers* story and an *Iron Man* story in *Tales of Suspense*.

[15] Stan Lee liked to come up with nicknames for his staff. Jazzy Johnny Romita was another one of his inspired creations.

[16] Interview with John Romita.

[17] Tom Spurgeon interview with John Romita, *The Comics Journal* #252, May, 2003.

[18] Ibid.

[19] Interview with John Romita.

[20] Interview with John Romita.

[21] Interview with Gil Kane. Also see: John Benson interview with Gil Kane, *Alter Ego* #10, 1969, Alter Ego Enterprises.

[22] Interview with Marie Severin.

[23] Kevin Hall interview with Gene Colan, *Comic Book Profiles* #6, Spring, 1999.

[24] Interview with Marie Severin.

[25] Lou Mougin interview with Roy and Dann Thomas*, Comics Interview* #66 and #67, 1989.

[26] Tom Spurgeon interview with John Romita, *The Comics Journal* #252, June, 2003.

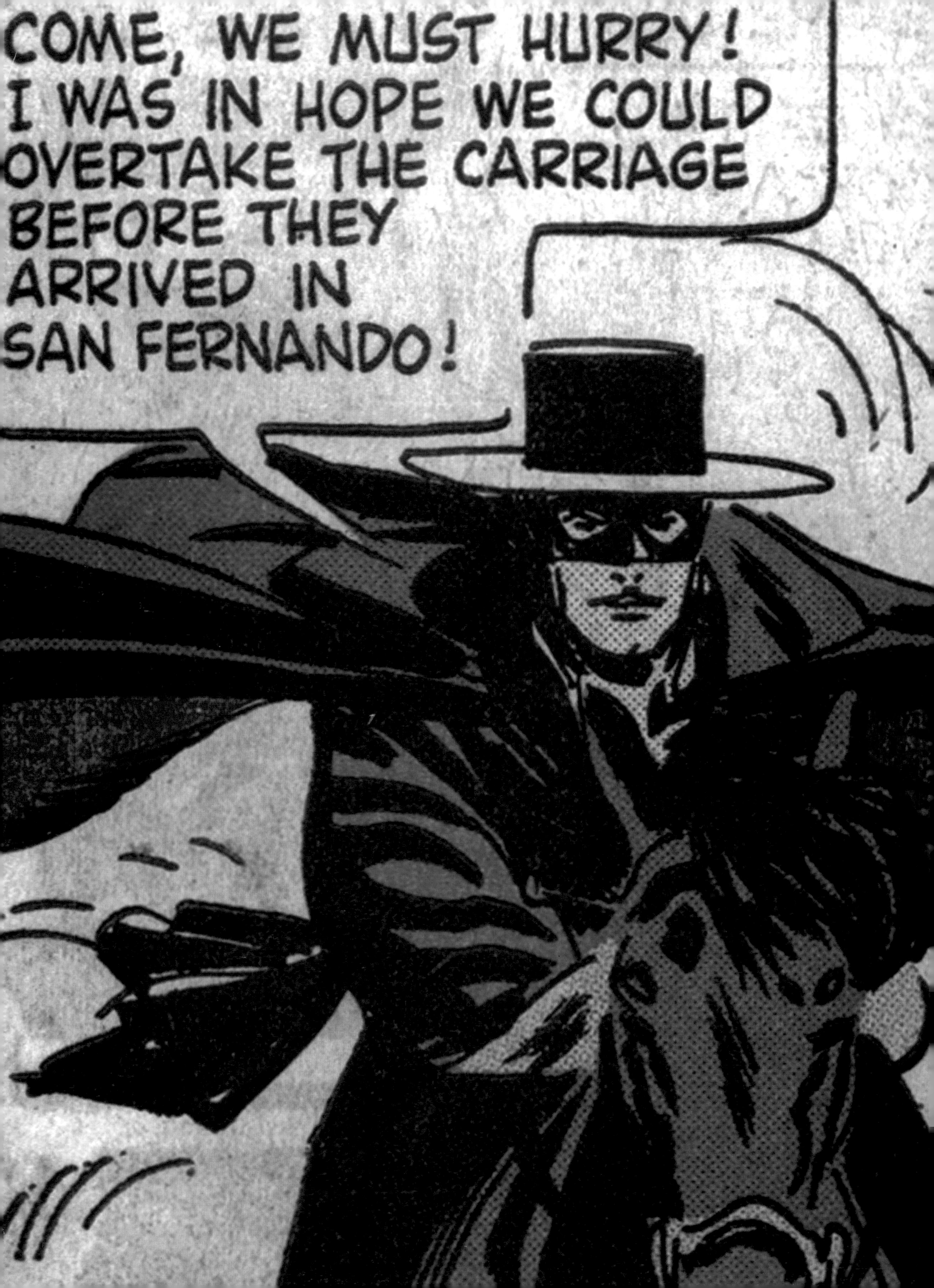
COME, WE MUST HURRY! I WAS IN HOPE WE COULD OVERTAKE THE CARRIAGE BEFORE THEY ARRIVED IN SAN FERNANDO!

6 EVERYBODY ELSE; DELL AND GOLD KEY; THE OTHER PUBLISHERS TAKE A BACK SEAT; WARREN AND GOODWIN GIVE IT A TRY; WALLY WOOD AND MORE SUPERHEROES; WITZEND

When the dust cleared from the changes wrought by the Subcommittee hearings of 1954, not only was Dell still standing, it was the undisputed powerhouse of the industry. Dell was so strong that it never agreed to submit its comic books for approval by the Comics Code Authority, preferring to use its own standards. Dell's power came from its numerous licenses for cartoon characters, movies, and television shows.

Dell's number one properties were its licenses with Walt Disney, which provided it with unstoppable, kid-attractive products. Kids were drawn, like a magnet, to the Walt Disney titles; it was merely an extra bonus that the artwork and storytelling of Carl Barks, in such titles as *Walt Disney's Comics and Stories*, elevated these duck-tales well above kid-fare. Barks' humor, pacing, and overall storytelling was an example for everybody to look at, even the guys doing superheroes.

Dell also published comic books offering *Bugs Bunny* and other Warner Brothers characters, *The Flintstones* and other Hanna-Barbera characters, *The Phantom*, *The Lone Ranger*, *Tarzan*, and *Korak, Son of Tarzan*. The company's line further included numerous television tie-ins such as *77 Sunset Strip*, *Sea Hunt*, and *Zorro*, which were also extremely popular. To add a little originally to their line, Dell published a title created in-house by uncredited talents, as was the practice of the company at that time, called *Turok, Son of Stone*. Dell might have been the name in the little rectangle on the comic books, but

Western Publishing and Lithography were really the folks who actually packaged and prepared the company's wares.[1] Western had been involved since 1938, when George Delacorte hired them to create and print his books.

By the late 1950s, Dell put out solid, professional, and mostly bland comic books. The pool of artistic talent used by the company were, generally, generic, competent journeymen. There were several noteworthy exceptions, which included Alex Toth, Russ Manning, and Dan Spiegle. Jesse Marsh also provided efficient, and, on occasion, striking artwork, as well. To produce its wares, Western called on the services of a legion of artists, who usually pencilled and inked their own work, rather than having these chores split, as was the custom. Artwork was also produced on a regular basis for the company by Phil De Lara, Harvey Eisenberg, Mike Arens, Alberto Becattini, Bob Fujitani, Tom Gill, Al McWilliams, and Frank Thorne.

Unlike most comic book companies, which only had one centralized operation, Western directed its artists and story assignments from two offices, one in New York City and the other in Beverly Hills. As Western provided so many tie-ins associated with Hollywood, their west coast branch not only made logistical sense, it also provided work for artists in the area who wanted to make the crossover to comic book-land. Thus, Western was able to develop talent on both coasts and assembled two distinct groups of competent illustrators

ZORRO'S WHIP SNAPS OUT...

BLAM!

CRACK!

Y!!!!!!!!

AFTER THEM, MEN! TO YOUR HORSES! GET YOUR HORSES!

AH! BERNARDO DID A GOOD JOB OF CUTTING THEIR REINS

COME BACK HORSES! STOP!

CRACK!

BACK INSIDE THE MISSION, TORRES! THE INDIANS HAVE ESCAPED! THERE'S NO REASON FOR YOU TO GIVE YOURSELF UP!

YOU MAY FRIGHTEN MY SOLDIERS, SEÑOR ZORRO, BUT YOU WON'T FIND ME SO EASY TO HANDLE!

THAT REMAINS TO BE SEEN, CAPITAN!

WH-WHAT...?

and writers. Pizzazz was not the strong suit of the company; predictable and dependable comic books were their objective, as the company's slogan proclaimed "Dell Comics are Good Comics."

A majority of the scripts churned out for Western were written by one man: Paul S. Newman. Newman has the distinction of being credited with writing over 4000 scripts, including a stint on *The Long Ranger* strip that lasted for twenty-four years and a run on the *Turok* feature which spanned twenty-six years. Newman's writing may have been a bit stodgy and predictable, but he was a solid, professional craftsman. Another productive workhorse, who churned out scripts on what must have seemed a never-ending basis, was Gaylord DuBois, who is reputed to have penned over 3000 tales for the company.

The most noteworthy artist to work for Dell was Alex Toth. Toth's work in comic books had been interrupted by the Korean War. After he was drafted, Toth spent seventeen months stationed in Tokyo. Serving as the editor of the post's newspaper, he wrote and

drew a strip called *The Adventures of Jon Fury in Japan*, which he found extremely satisfying. After his discharge in 1956, Toth moved to the Los Angeles area finding work with Western. He had briefly visited New York and found that business was terrible. Stan Lee told him, "Alex, get out of the business because it's dead or dying."[2] Lee's advice obviously failed to impress Toth, who took several assignments from Stan the man, even if they were at a reduced page rate. Then, it was back to California and to Western.

At Western, Toth was quickly put to work on a number of different assignments including work on the comic book version of the popular *Zorro* television series. Toth was unhappy having to work from adaptations of the television shows' scripts, which he felt had too much dialogue and not enough action. In order to tighten up the storytelling, he deleted unnecessary dialogue and cut redundant cap-

Richard Powers, painted cover, *Dr. Solar* #2, December, 1962. Painted cover, *Dr. Solar* #4, June, 1963. Painted cover, Dr. Solar #7, March, 1964, ©1962, 1963, and 1964 K.K. Publications, Inc.

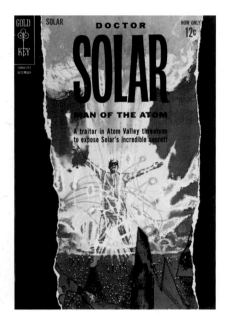

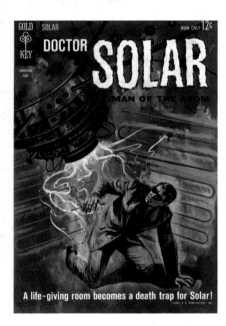

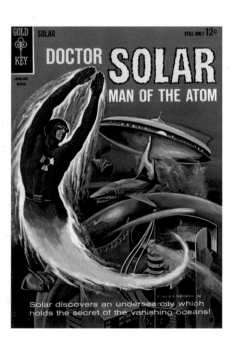

tions wherever possible, which did not go over well with the editor. When he was called on the carpet, in classic Toth-esque indignation, he informed his boss, "Since you won't control your writers' use of superfluous copy and static dialogue, don't expect anything outstanding from me anymore, because I won't give it to you, not with these scripts and your bloody incompetence."[3]

Despite his concerns and protestations about *Zorro*, his advice was not heeded. Nevertheless, Toth's work on the strip is a textbook example of how to tell an action/adventure tale. It is also a great deal of fun, something rarely seen in late 1950s comic books. Kids were not the only ones to look at these stories; Toth's work on *Zorro* impressed many in the business, including a number of his colleagues. By the late 1950s, Toth considered his role in creating comic book stories as akin to being a film director shooting a movie. His stories were carefully paced, shot, and structured, making the most out of every image. *Zorro* and Toth's other work for Dell never used unnecessary effects or linework in the art; there was complete economy in the shading and lighting of these stories, just what was needed, no more, no less. In analyzing his style Toth explained, "It's a picture medium; let the pictures tell the story. Too much verbal exposition demonstrates a distrust of the viewer's intelligence… the kids…respond to visual images far more than they do to words."[4] Toth's comments were not contemptuous of his audience. For Toth, comic books were just like a silent movie; the pictures were primary, only augmented by a necessary, not superfluous, use of text. Such a thoughtful approach to storytelling was not appreciated by his editors and in many quarters was viewed as a "pain."

Toth, who is color-blind, made prominent use of black in his stories, using broad areas of ink impressionistically to simulate backgrounds. He did not skimp on the figures either, giving his characters an energized, animated line. Toth continued to turn in beautiful work for Dell, but by 1961 he had moved on. For the remainder of his career, Toth would

Bob Fujitani, pencils and inks, original interior page artwork, *Dr. Solar* #3. March, 1963, ©1963 K.K. Publications, Inc.

Russ Manning, pencils and inks, original interior page artwork, *Magnus Robot Fighter* #8, November, 1964, ©1964 K.K. Publications, Inc.

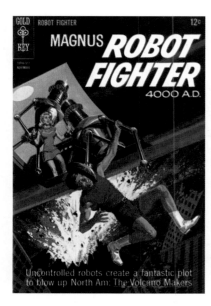  

spend a majority of his time working in television cartoon production, designing characters, storyboards, and preparing concept presentations. Toth brought a comic book sensibility to action cartoons such as Cambria Productions' *Space Angel*. *Space Angel* takes place in the future and stars an eye-patched astronaut hero, who together with his girlfriend, Crystal, and his engineer, Taurus, work for the Earth Bureau of Investigation. There are lots of bad guys, space ships, and exotic locations. The cartoon used very limited animation and, to save money, superimposed real moving lips over the cartoons – odd indeed. There is no denying the stand-out design of *Space Angel*, though. Toth went on to do more design work in the 1960s, including a number of concepts for Hanna-Barbera.

At HB, Toth designed the *Space Ghost* cartoon and a host of other projects. He was also, ironically, brought in to design HB's cartoonization of Kirby and Lee's *FF*. Toth had come full circle; he was now doing concept designs for cartoon television adaptations of comic book characters. During the 1960s, Toth occasionally returned to work for the big guys, DC and Marvel, but his energies were primarily used to conceptualize and design characters and their worlds for cartoons and, on a few occasions, the movies.

One of Toth's more interesting efforts, which was a clear indication of his becoming a California-guy, was his involvement with publisher Pete Millar. Millar, who was a drag racing aficionado, was producing a line of comic books which took a humorous take on the very California universe of hot rods, surfing, and the endless summer. Starting in 1964, Toth began creating a series of short, mostly five-and-six pagers, in magazines called *Big Daddy Roth*, *Drag Cartoons*, *Hot Rod Cartoons*, and *CARtoons*. These strips took a humorous look at drag racing. These features have a sweet 1960s flavor, good humored and naively optimistic. The "big foot" or exaggerated cartoon style used in the strips showcased Toth's diversity and provided him an opportunity to be lightheartedly silly and to "open up" with material where he had few editorial controls. If only his editors in the mainstream had provided him with such freedom.

Dell's titles had been some of the best selling properties in the comic book world. In 1960, their *Walt Disney's Comics and Stories* title sold almost two million copies. In late 1962, comic books were getting a price increase, from ten cents to twelve cents. Dell, however, decided to increase the price of their magazines to fifteen cents, after all they were selling Walt Disney and company! The kids did not see it their way and sales plummeted. Dell's management also decided to try to produce their own products, which did not sit well with Western. The result: the companies split, their long term relationship was over. Western took all the good licenses, and Dell was left with the likes of Mighty Mouse, Felix the

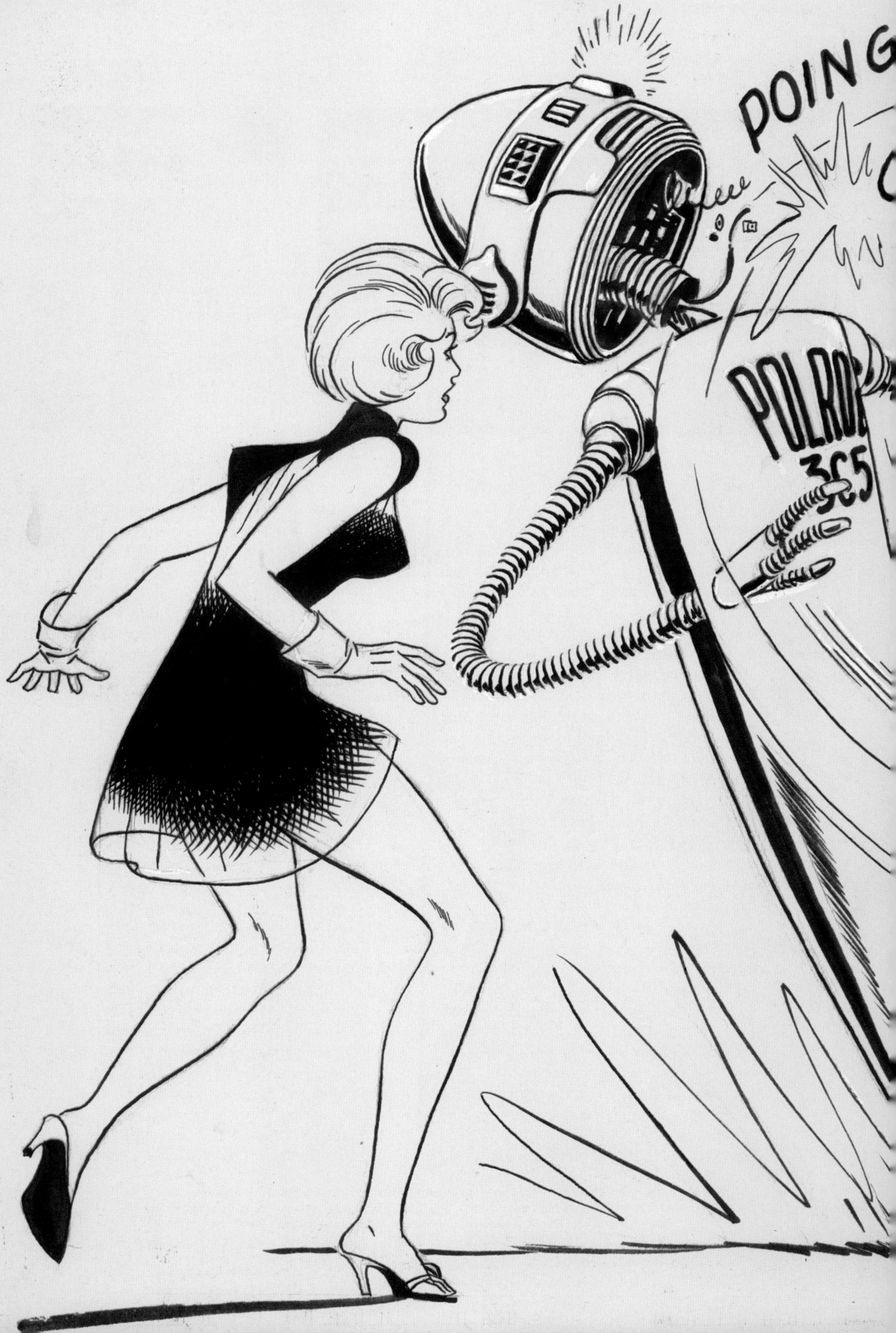
POING

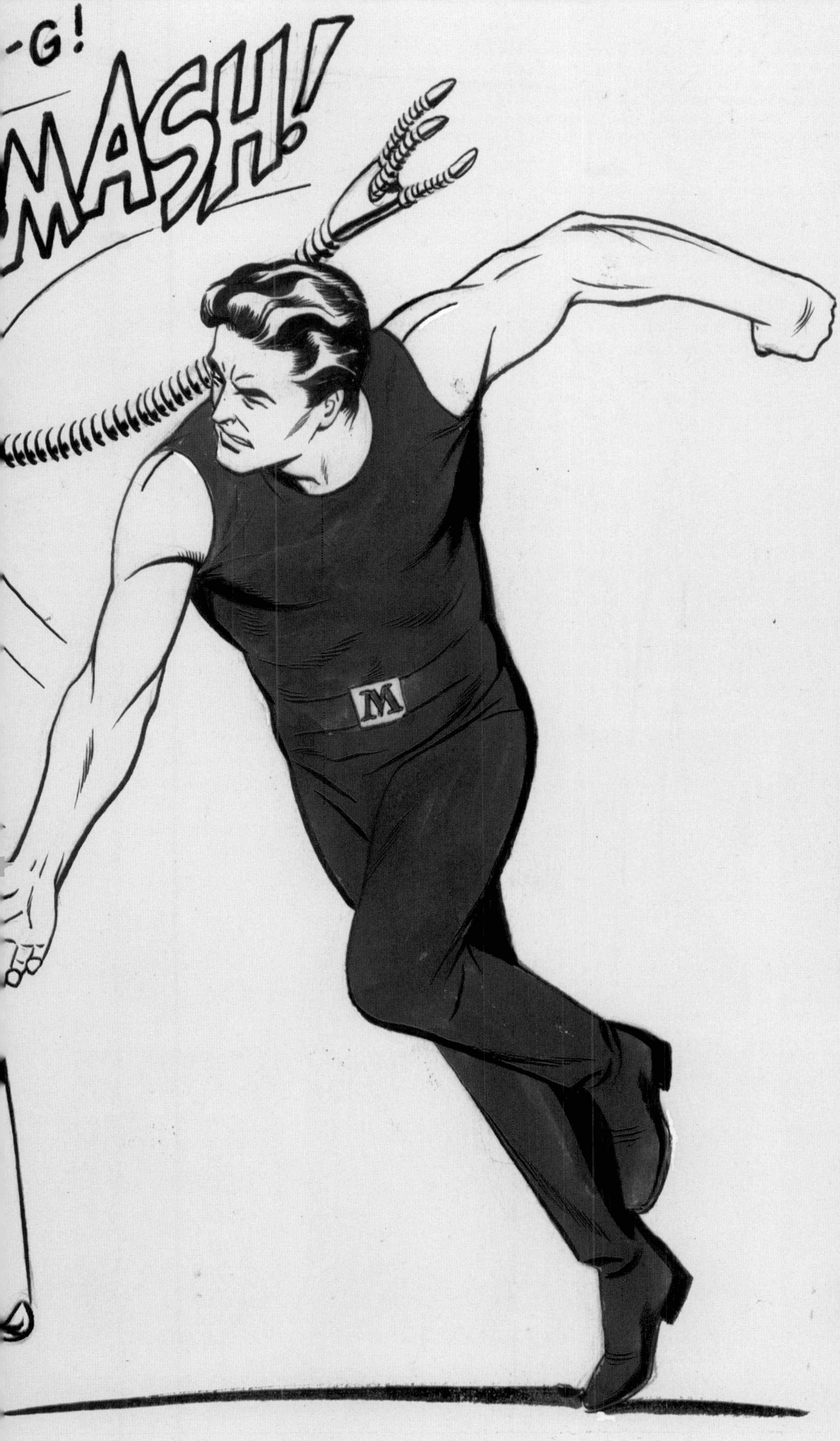
-G!
MASH!
M

Cat, and Mr. Magoo. The kids buying comic books were not impressed.

Over at Western, which now had a new name, Gold Key, they retained their stables of artists and writers and began to develop new concepts to battle the new superhero titles beginning to populate the newsstand and drugstore comics sections. Thus Gold Key's premiere original title was born, *Dr. Solar*, drawn by the dependable, if not too exciting, Bob Fujitani. Dr. Solar, who was billed as "Man of the Atom," was actually a scientist who, as a result of an accident during an atomic experiment, is converted into energy but retains his consciousness and can convert himself back into matter. The title premiered with a release date of October, 1962. Fujitani had been in the business since the early 1940s. By the mid-1940s, he had developed a distinctive style, exaggerating the look of his alluring women and heroic men in tales of action and horror. By the late 1940s, he was working for Charles Biro in a less distinctive style. When he started work for Dell in the late 1950s, his work had become more tasteful, meaning predictable, toned down, and mainstream. Fujitani only provided artwork for the first five issues of *Dr. Solar* and then he was gone. After his work on *Dr. Solar*, Fujitani began a long association working on the *Flash Gordon* newspaper strip.

When *Dr. Solar* premiered, he had no uniform, just green skin, sunglasses, and a lab coat. By issue #5, it was decided to give him a spiffy, formfitting, red outfit with a visor and the logo for atomic radiation on his chest. The costume, like the strip, was routine and not particularly awe-inspiring.

Artist Frank Bolle came in as Fujitani's replacement, providing competent work for fourteen issues. The strip continued under other hands until its demise with issue #27. *Dr. Solar*, as with almost all of Gold Key's titles, used painted cover art, which prominently distinguished their products from the rest of the comic books on the rack. For *Dr. Solar*, the first two covers were painted by Richard Powers, who was succeeded by J.P. Sternberg and then by omnipresent Gold Key cover illustrator, George Wilson. Wilson provided hundreds of cover illustrations for the line's titles which give many of them the feel and look of the pulp covers of the 1930s and 1940s.

With the successful launch of *Dr. Solar*, Gold Key's star artist, Russ Manning, was picked to collaborate on the creation of another original feature, which became the company's most interesting and distinguished original strip, *Magnus Robot Fighter*. Man-

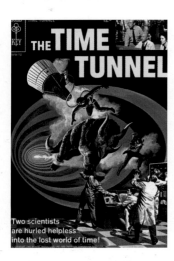

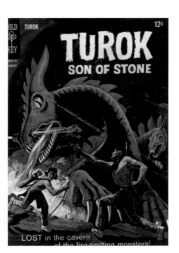

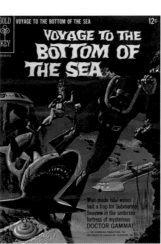

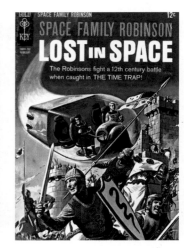

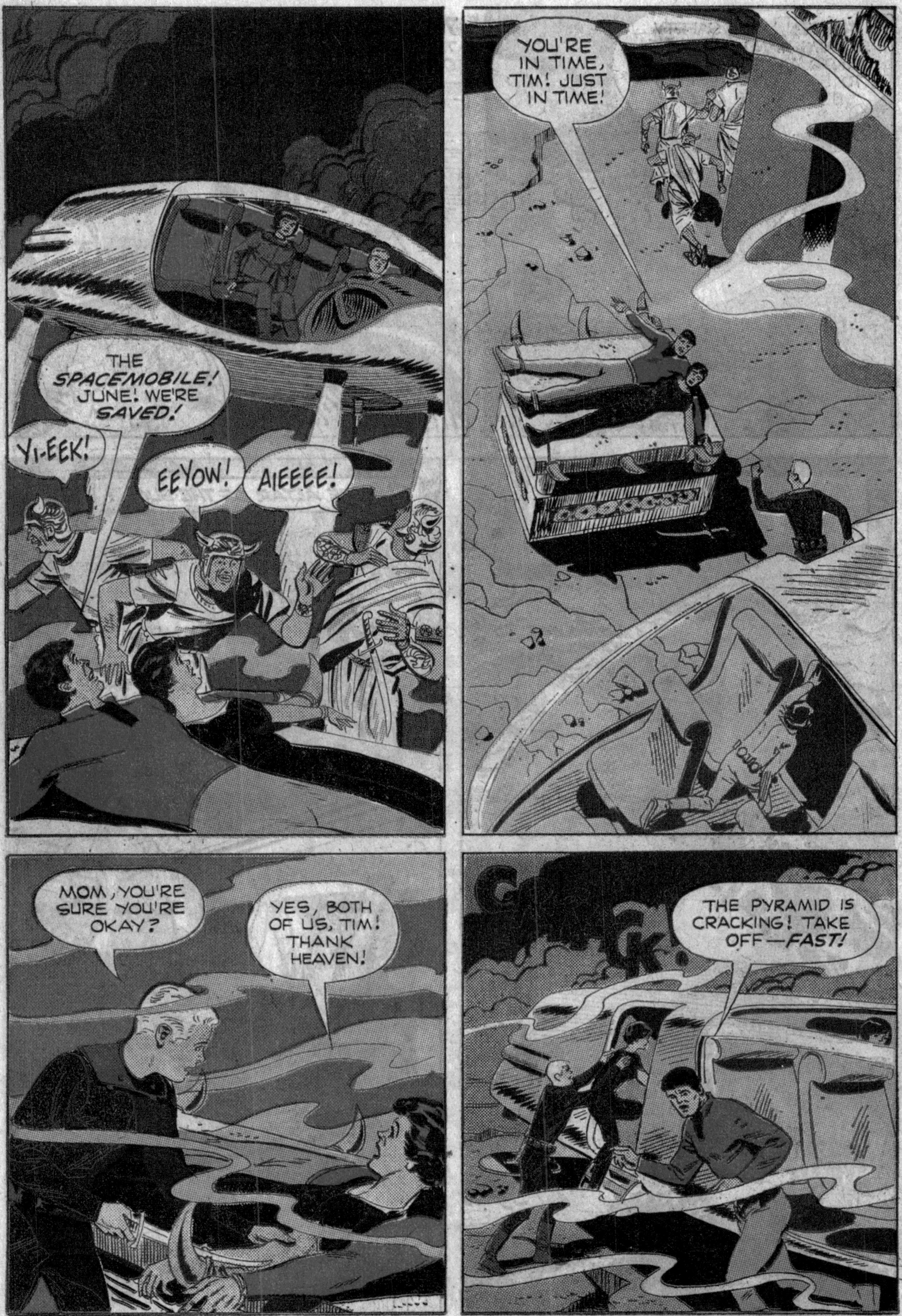
THE SPACEMOBILE! JUNE! WE'RE SAVED!
YI-EEK!
EEYOW!
AIEEEE!
YOU'RE IN TIME, TIM! JUST IN TIME!
MOM, YOU'RE SURE YOU'RE OKAY?
YES, BOTH OF US, TIM! THANK HEAVEN!
THE PYRAMID IS CRACKING! TAKE OFF—FAST!

contacted Marsh, and shortly, he was working for Western.[5]

Manning had professed an admiration for Marsh's Caniff-inspired style, but any influence the older artist had over him was purely internal and intellectual. Manning was aiming for a more complex style based on the illustration-inspired storytelling used by Foster. Manning simplified his approach to storytelling, distilling the anatomy of his figures by the use of a concise pencilling and inking. He developed an elegant, crisp style, a distinguishing factor in his work, making it easy to spot.

By 1962, Manning was an established artist at Western. He had worked on a number of strips and was held in high regard by his editors. Editor Chase Craig had just convinced the top brass at Western to let him try a sci-fi superhero, but the concept was only a pitch; he did not yet have anything specific in mind. When Manning heard from other members of the Western staff about Craig's project, he convinced the editor to let him give it a try

ning was born in Van Nuys, California in 1929. He studied for a-year-and-a-half at the Los Angeles County Art Institute, quitting to go to work as a cartoonist. Manning, who had a lifelong admiration for Edgar Rice Burroughs and his creation, Tarzan, began to hone his skill as a cartoonist, studying Hal Foster's work. Manning also started reading Tarzan fanzines and began corresponding with the publisher of one of them, Vern Coriell, who recommended that he contact *Tarzan* comic book artist Jesse Marsh. Manning took this suggestion and contacted Marsh, and the two started a lifelong friendship. Marsh also served as a mentor to the younger artist and offered to take Manning to Western and "introduce" him. Unfortunately, Manning's luck did not also extend to his continued work as a cartoonist; within six months his employer went out of business, leaving him looking for work. The Korean War interrupted his search for new employment, but by 1952, he was back stateside looking for work as an artist. Manning

Wally Wood, pencils and inks, unpublished original cover artwork, *Warfront*,
©1966 Harvey Publications. The cover was prepared for issue #37, which
has a release date of September, 1966.

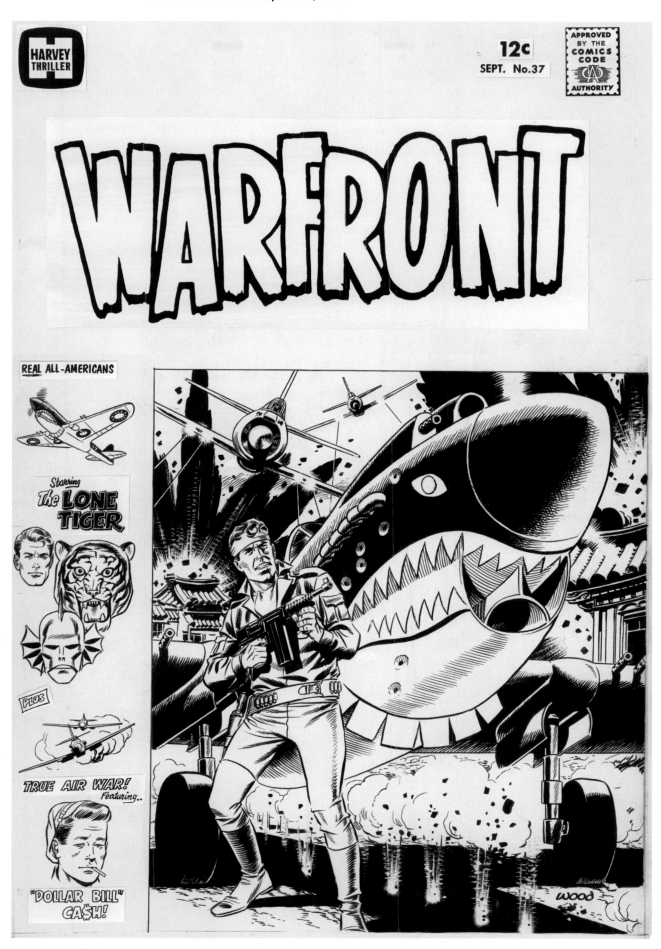

and was given the green light to "Go home and do a couple of pages – writing – on what you think the story should be, draw some sketches, and bring 'em back."[6] Thus, Magnus was born. The strip was a collaboration between Craig, his staff, and Manning. Craig wanted robots; Manning wanted to do a variation on Tarzan in the future. Manning's wife, Dodie, even made the suggestion that Magnus use karate chops to vanquish the robots he fights. The concept drawing on pages 186-187, was prepared while Magnus' costume was undergoing revisions and was the second in a series of proposals.

The final version of the strip takes place in 4000 A.D.; the North American continent is now a megalopolis called North Am, where humans have become too reliant and dependent on robots. Magnus, who was found as an orphan baby by the sentient, gold-plated

robot, 1A, is raised to "lead man's revolt against the tyrant robots!"[7] As part of his education, Magnus is taught to think for himself, and his body is conditioned to smash steel and robots with his bare hands. He takes up residence in North Am and fights "evil" robots. It should also be mentioned he has a very attractive girl friend, Leeja Clane, who adds a romantic interest to the strip.

Manning's concept of the future as sleek and austere is pure fantasy, and his artwork conceptualizes this world with style and verve. The strip is played as action/adventure material with only minor emphasis on it being a cautionary tale. With *Magnus*, Manning had a vehicle to show his diverse talents as a storyteller, and within the confines imposed on comic books in the 1960s, he did remarkably well, creating good, solid tales with handsome art. Magnus premiered in *Magnus Robot Fighter* #1, release dated February, 1963.

During his tenure as artist on *Magnus*, Manning also provided art for the *Korak, Son of Tarzan* feature. When Jesse Marsh retired from the *Tarzan* comic book strip in 1965, Manning replaced him, bringing a vigorous, assured elegance to the world of the ape-man not seen since the feature had been handled by Burne Hogarth. Manning continued to provide artwork for *Magnus* through issue #21, release dated February, 1968. His work on *Tarzan* was so striking that by 1967 he had taken over chores on the daily newspaper strip, and within a year, Manning helmed the Sunday strip as well.

Magnus was not the only original sci-fi strip produced by Gold Key. Another long running feature created under editor Del Connell was a futuristic update of *The Swiss Family Robinson* called *Space Family Robinson*. The strip premiered with a release date of December, 1962 with art by Dan Spiegle. Spiegle was born in 1920 in Cosmopolis, Washington. By the time he entered high school, his family had moved from California to Hawaii, and then back to California. He was never particularly interested in comic books as a kid; his eye had always gone to Roy Crane's *Buz Sawyer* strip. He joined the Navy after the

outbreak of the Second World War and did his hitch in Maui. In 1946, he returned to California and enrolled at the Chouinard Art Institute in Los Angeles on the G.I. Bill. Although his ambition was to work as an illustrator, when his benefits were about to run out, he went to Hollywood and took an interview to provide art and writing chores for a strip featuring Bozo the Clown. At the interview, Spiegle displayed his western genre samples and confessed that he was an illustrator and not a cartoonist. Spiegle remembers, "The fellow looked at my work – the cowboy strip samples – and said his brother was the office manager for the Hopalong Cassidy organization…just around the corner." Spiegle was directed to "show your stuff to them."[8] He did, which started a long-term assignment drawing the strip. The star of Hopalong Cassidy, William Boyd, had bought the rights to his old B-movies with the intent of running them on the newfangled medium of television. The show, which premiered on June 24, 1949, was a national hit, and the strip tie-in became extremely popular, running in two hundred newspapers.

For the next six years, Spiegle was able to experiment with different techniques, increasing his storytelling facility in the process. By 1954, the popularity of the television series had waned, and the strip was cancelled a year later. Spiegle, who considered himself a permanent resident of California, decided to say put, rather than move to New York and began looking for work as a cartoonist. Within less than a year he found steady work at Western. Spiegle's art did not develop significantly during his tenure at Western. He drew mostly television tie-in fare until his assignment on *Space Family Robinson*. In 1965 the CBS network premiered Irwin Allen's *Lost in Space*, which was clearly inspired by the comic book even though a license had not been acquired from Western. Western decided rather than file suit against CBS or Allen, they would settle the matter in exchange for the use of the television show's title, *Lost in Space*. *Space Family Robinson* now became *Lost in Space*. This solved the problem of possibly alienat-

RACE BANNON

HEAD MODELS
#3

DOUG
WILDEY

#4 MOUTH

NO 4 MOUTH

NO 6 MOUTH

ing CBS and Allen, who both licensed shows to Western, and allowed a profitable tie-in with a hit show. Spiegle's work on the strip, which he pencilled and inked, was an example of excellent craftsmanship. He was a talented storyteller, who drew and inked in a simple, attractive style. During his run on *Space Family Robinson,* there were hints that he might break out with efforts that were more inspired, but that would come well after the end of the Silver Age. During his tenure at Western, he was a steady, solid storyteller.

Alex Toth was not the only artist working at Western who would cross over between comic books and animation. Doug Wildey, who is primarily remembered for his design and conceptualization of the *Jonny Quest* cartoon for Hanna-Barbera, worked for Western in the mid-1960s. When Russ Manning took over chores on the *Tarzan* daily strip, Wildey had the task of replacing him on the comic book feature. He also turned in work on the company's television tie-ins.

Wildey had started in the business in the late 1940s, working for pulp publisher Street and Smith. He then spent the 1950s turning in comic book fare for a number of publishers including Atlas. He worked in many of the genres of the time, but his forte was westerns. After work with Atlas all but dried up, he found work in animation doing design work for Alex Toth on *Space Angel.* After his gig on *Space Angel* ended, he decided to stay in California and look for work, which led to his employment with Hanna-Barbera.[9] Wildey's designs on *Jonny Quest* gave the cartoon a distinctive look, with its heavy blacks and its Caniff-inspired characters. *Jonny Quest* premiered on the ABC television network on September 18, 1964, in prime time. The show was an action/adventure story involving the feature's namesake, an 11-year-old boy. The cast of characters included Jonny's kid sidekick, named Hadji, Jonny's globetrotting scientist dad, the comic relief – Bandit the dog, and the group's handsome body guard, secret agent Race Bannon, who looks as if he stepped out of the pages of *Steve Canyon.* The feature had its cast traveling around the world, confronting evil-

Doug Wildey, pencils, original model sheet artwork, Race Bannon from *Jonny Quest*, ©1964 Hanna-Barbera Productions, Inc.

detailing a world war started by an unknown force, first called *Total War* and then renamed *M.A.R.S. Patrol Total War*. The feature was not one of the studio's more inspired efforts. Woody and company also provided artwork for an adaptation of the sci-fi movie *Fantastic Voyage*.

During the 1960s, after its breakup with Western, Dell limped along, using an assortment of journeymen to produce their stories and artwork. On occasion they used first rate talent such as Gil Kane and Steve Ditko on uninspired projects. Dell's line stumbled along during the Silver Age, with products which were lackluster at their best.

What were the other big publishers doing? During the 1960s, Harvey and Archie, it seems, did very little in the way of moving the art of comic book storytelling forward. Their kid's titles were doing very well without an injection of excitement, action, and suspense, so they just sailed along. Harvey kept serving up titles starring Little Dot, Richie Rich, Hot Stuff, Sad Sack, and Casper. Harvey did reprint some Will Eisner *Spirit* material in 1966 and 1967 (with some additional new content added), but, by and large, the company was uninterested in trying something new. Harvey did run with a Jim Steranko concept, *Spyman*, about a secret agent with a cybernetic hand, with artwork by the dependable George Tuska, but the strip fell flat and was gone in three issues. The company also used work by Wally Wood's studio in their *Warfront* title, but, curiously, failed to use the striking cover created by Woody for the issue, which is pictured on page 191.

Archie was equally out-of-sync with the 1960s and produced little other than its hot *Archie* line of titles. The company did try to resurrect Simon and Kirby's *The Fly*, renamed *Fly Man*, *The Shield*, and several of their other old MLJ characters teamed up as *The Mighty Crusaders*. The artwork was by Paul Reinman and then Mike Sekowsky. The only thing that can be said about these features is that they were kitschy.

Over at Charlton, Steve Ditko's home-away-from-Marvel, they were also attempting

doers at every turn and using sci-fi gadgets and technology. The plots were nothing groundbreaking, and today many of them are conspicuously politically incorrect. The look of *Jonny Quest* was unlike any other cartoon television show of the time, with its colorful backgrounds, and its focus on the characters and their jet packs, hydrofoils, and lasers. Wildey would work on other animation projects, but it was with his work on *Jonny Quest* that he reached his widest audience, bringing a comic book sense of design and style to television cartoons.[10]

Western also drew upon the talents of the seasoned hands of Don Heck, George Tuska, Jack Sparling, Mike Sekowsky, Mike Roy, Werner Roth, and Bill Lignante for artwork for its various television and movie tie-ins. Wally Wood and his studio provided artwork for the first three issues of an original feature

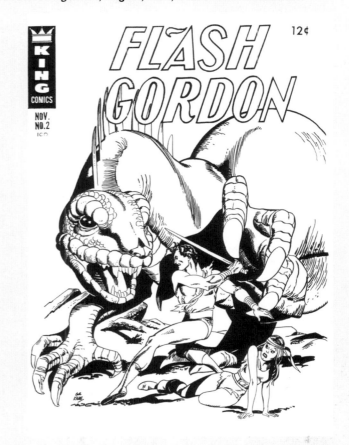

to come up with something to keep in step with the changing times. Charlton was known for paying the lowest rates in the business, and their products clearly reflected this fact. The company was founded by John Santangelo, Sr., who literally built the business from the ground up. He even helped lay the bricks for the company's plant in Derby, Connecticut. Charlton cranked out innocuous products during the 1950s. To attract big city talent, the company had an office in New York to snare interesting and not-so-interesting prospective artists. Apart from the artwork occasionally provided by Al Williamson, John Severin, and Steve Ditko, there was little to distinguish their comic books. Charlton had a writer on staff, Joe Gill, who, over his tenure with the company, cranked out literally thousands of scripts. Charlton had been at the forefront of the Silver Age heroes with Ditko's work on the *Captain Atom* strip in *Space Adventures* in 1960. By the mid-1960s, Charlton was attempting to establish an even more aggressive presence with more superhero titles. Wally Wood even contributed some material for their *D-Day* and *War and Attack* titles in the fall of 1964.

Throughout the 1960s, Charlton relied on a stable of dependable journeymen who churned out thousands of pages of artwork. Their regulars included Bill Fraccio, Frank McLaughlin, Pete Morisi, and Sam Glanzman. Dick Giordano turned in attractive work on many of Charlton's covers. Giordano, who was managing editor of Charlton from 1966 to 1968, would distinguish himself as an editor at the company and later at DC, where he went to work in 1968. Giordano was a good judge of talent and was able to bring out the best in many artists and writers he worked with. When he took up shop at DC, he took a number of Charlton's regulars with him. Giordano remembers, when he was negotiating his job with DC's management, he asked, "I hope you don't mind if I bring some talent with me," to which Irwin Donenfeld replied, "Oh, we rather expected you would."[11] Giordano helped reenergize DC's talent pool with writers Denny O'Neil and Steve Skeates and artist Jim Aparo. Giordano would mature

Steve Ditko, pencil, ink, and wash, interior page, *Eerie* #8, March, 1967, ©1967 Warren Publishing Co.

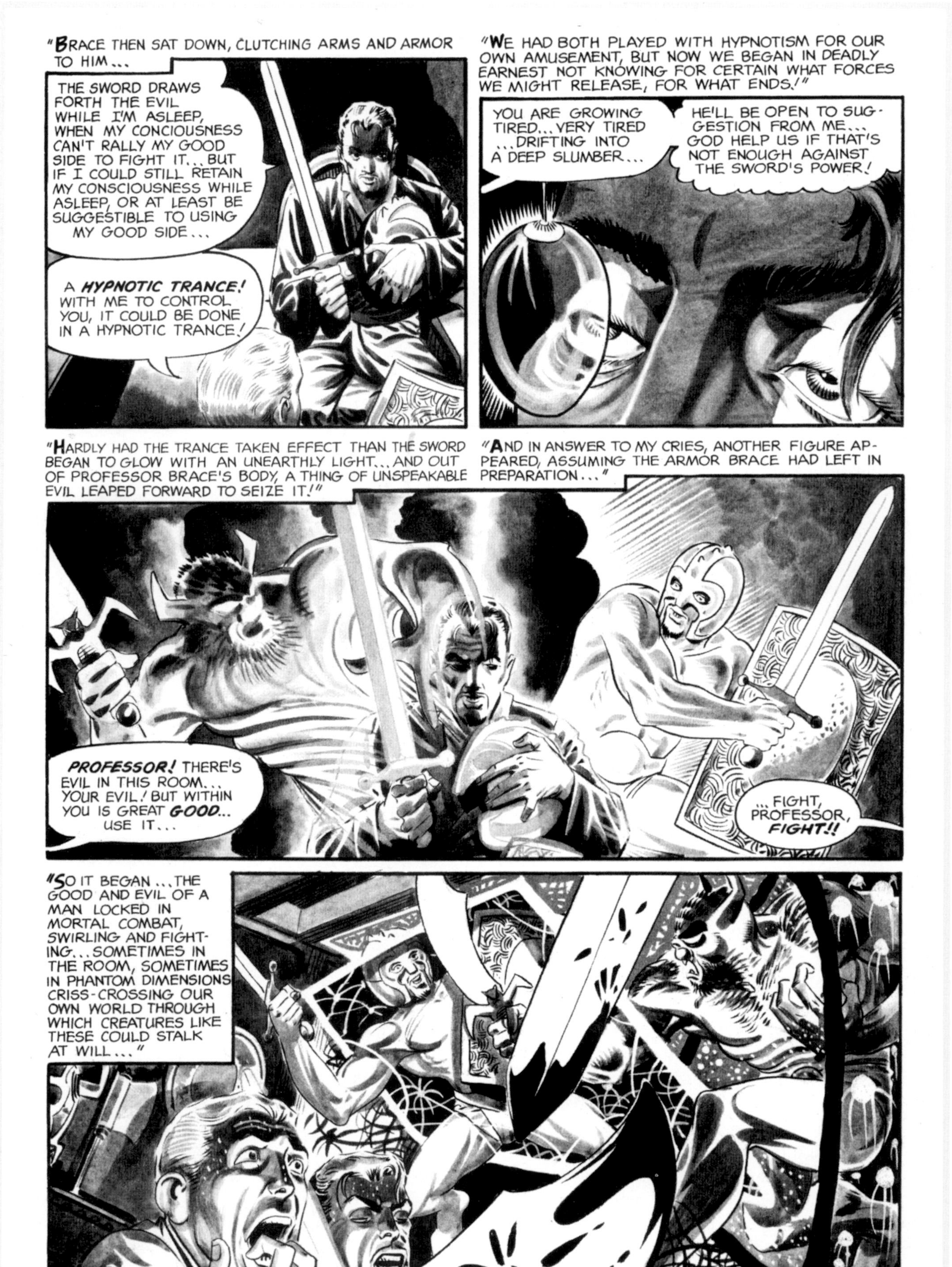
"BRACE THEN SAT DOWN, CLUTCHING ARMS AND ARMOR TO HIM...
THE SWORD DRAWS FORTH THE EVIL WHILE I'M ASLEEP, WHEN MY CONCIOUSNESS CAN'T RALLY MY GOOD SIDE TO FIGHT IT... BUT IF I COULD STILL RETAIN MY CONSCIOUSNESS WHILE ASLEEP, OR AT LEAST BE SUGGESTIBLE TO USING MY GOOD SIDE...
A HYPNOTIC TRANCE! WITH ME TO CONTROL YOU, IT COULD BE DONE IN A HYPNOTIC TRANCE!
"WE HAD BOTH PLAYED WITH HYPNOTISM FOR OUR OWN AMUSEMENT, BUT NOW WE BEGAN IN DEADLY EARNEST NOT KNOWING FOR CERTAIN WHAT FORCES WE MIGHT RELEASE, FOR WHAT ENDS!"
YOU ARE GROWING TIRED... VERY TIRED ...DRIFTING INTO A DEEP SLUMBER...
HE'LL BE OPEN TO SUG-GESTION FROM ME... GOD HELP US IF THAT'S NOT ENOUGH AGAINST THE SWORD'S POWER!
"HARDLY HAD THE TRANCE TAKEN EFFECT THAN THE SWORD BEGAN TO GLOW WITH AN UNEARTHLY LIGHT... AND OUT OF PROFESSOR BRACE'S BODY, A THING OF UNSPEAKABLE EVIL LEAPED FORWARD TO SEIZE IT!"
"AND IN ANSWER TO MY CRIES, ANOTHER FIGURE AP-PEARED, ASSUMING THE ARMOR BRACE HAD LEFT IN PREPARATION..."
PROFESSOR! THERE'S EVIL IN THIS ROOM... YOUR EVIL! BUT WITHIN YOU IS GREAT GOOD... USE IT...
...FIGHT, PROFESSOR, FIGHT!!
"SO IT BEGAN... THE GOOD AND EVIL OF A MAN LOCKED IN MORTAL COMBAT, SWIRLING AND FIGHT-ING... SOMETIMES IN THE ROOM, SOMETIMES IN PHANTOM DIMENSIONS CRISS-CROSSING OUR OWN WORLD THROUGH WHICH CREATURES LIKE THESE COULD STALK AT WILL..."
58

as an artist in the 1970s and provide inking assists on a regular basis for Neal Adams as well as on a host of other artists. Generally, though, Charlton's output was undistinguished.

During the mid-1960s, other publishers also attempted to enter the market with the accelerating popularity of superheroes. The King Features Syndicate, the folks who owned *Flash Gordon, The Phantom,* and *Mandrake the Magician,* among other famous newspaper strips, tried to market comic book versions of these features with little success. King enlisted the talents of Al Williamson and Gil Kane for their *Flash Gordon* comic book, but due to poor distribution these titles never attracted a significant audience.

By 1964, James Warren was ready to make his move into the world of comic books, kind of. The end result was an oversized comic book called *Creepy. Creepy* was really a black-and-white magazine with self-contained parables, which had clever, or so they thought, surprise endings. Who conceived the idea for the magazine is still the subject of debate, as with so many other events in comic book history, but James Warren was the publisher, and Russ Jones was the editor of the first issue of the title.

Creepy featured a master of ceremonies, Uncle Creepy, who introduced the stories, very much in the tradition of the Crypt-Keeper, the Vault-Keeper, and the Old Witch from EC Comics. Warren insisted that *Creepy* was not trying to imitate the EC comics line, and remembers, "I thought many of the EC stories were not suitable for Warren. The EC taste level was not my own...I didn't want to be the 'new generation of EC.'"[12] Nevertheless, the first issue of *Creepy* had stories by avowed EC fans Larry Ivie and Archie Goodwin and used story ideas by EC veteran Joe Orlando. The artwork was provided by EC veterans Joe Orlando, Al Williamson, Reed Crandall, Frank Frazetta, and Angelo Torres as well as by Gray Morrow. The cover was by EC veteran Jack Davis. *Creepy* #1 hit the newsstand racks sometime in late 1964 and by issue #3, which came out in mid-1965, Archie Goodwin had

become editor. *Creepy* and its companion publications *Blazing Combat,* issue #1, released dated October, 1965, and *Eerie,* issue #1, release dated September, 1965, were all firmly and unabashedly in the tradition of the EC line. Warren was correct in insisting that his magazines were not entirely like EC's; his products never pushed the envelope of acceptable taste as Gaines and Feldstein had. The Warren books also lacked the bite, humor, and off-the-wall quality found in the great EC stories.

Warren may have called upon many of the same artists used by Feldstein and Kurtzman, but the end product was vastly different – blander and less inclined to go all out for that 'got'ya' ending. Editor Archie Goodwin was one of the most intelligent and likeable talents in the business and did an admirable job scripting most of the stories for the line's three titles. More importantly, the freedom given by Warren and Goodwin to the artists working for the company coaxed many of the best in the business to turn in sterling work, free

from the restraints of the big funny book publishers. The environment at Warren lured John Severin, Gene Colan, Alex Toth, Wally Wood, Steve Ditko, Russ Heath, George Evans, Joe Orlando, Angelo Torres, Jerry Grandenetti, Gray Morrow, Neal Adams, and Gil Kane, among others, to provide artwork for the company.

As the artwork was reproduced in black-and-white, many of the artists were free to use shade and tone, which gave their work qualities not seen in their colorized comic book counterparts. Several artists turned in work that was moody and nuanced with depth and character absent in their mainstream efforts. One particular stand-out were the stories of Steve Ditko, who used ink washes to give his work dimensions never explored in his work for other publishers.

One of the key factors in Warren's successful attempt to revitalize non-superhero comic books was his editor, Archie Goodwin. Goodwin was born in 1937, in Kansas City,

Missouri and grew up reading EC comic books right off the rack. He remembered reading the biographies of the artists who supplied artwork for EC, which were run in the comic books as features, and thinking "why couldn't I work in comics?"[13] Intent on becoming a comic book artist, Goodwin went to New York and studied at the Cartoonists and Illustrators School. There he discovered he was more "adept at writing." He discovered that scripting stories "came much easier to me than art did." His interest in EC got him involved with others fans and gained him entrée to many of the artists who had created the company's tales of horror, suspense, and science fiction.[14]

Goodwin was receptive to the comic book medium and able to craft stories which were aimed at the talents of the specific artists he worked with. The stories he created for Warren during the mid-1960s stand apart from mainstream comics of the time; they were a distinguished attempt to create short story-oriented comics that were driven by a plot rather

than the characters. Unlike the short five-pagers put out by Marvel or the sci-fi tales churned out by DC and other companies, Goodwin's parables were clever and sometimes even had a visceral edge. He would leave Warren to work for Marvel as a writer. Over the next twenty-five years, he would wear a number of hats at Marvel, including that of editor-in-chief from 1976-1977. He would also have a hand in crafting what would be the crescendo of the Silver Age.

Wally Wood had kept himself busy since his halcyon days at EC, working for Charlton, Harvey, Marvel, Western, Warren, and at the end of the 1960s at DC, but his major effort during the superhero boom was for Tower Comics. Tower was the brainchild of Harry Shorten and Sam Schwartz. Shorten was a paperback book publisher who had been watching the increasing success of superheroes and wanted to jump on the bandwagon. Shorten's idea was to create a line of hero titles that could compete with the big guys, which

then could be collected together in pocket book form and resold to make even more money. As Shorten and his editor Sam Schwartz had both worked for Archie, they also knew the potential for non-hero books as well, which resulted in an Archie knock-off called *Tippy Teen*, which was released in the fall of 1965. Schwartz, who had gotten his start as an artist, was experienced at handling teenage material from his tenure at Archie, but neither he nor Shorten had experience with superheroes. Enter Wally Wood. Woody was essentially given carte blanche to function as an editor and told to come up with a line of books for Tower. His solution was to tap into the ranks of seasoned artists and give them room to strut their artistic predilections. There was no question who was in control, though. Woody would spend hours with his writers and artists hashing and rehashing the plot lines and stories for his line of books. Wood enlisted the talents of Reed Crandall, Gil Kane, Steve Ditko, Mike Esposito, George Tuska, Mike

commitment of his previous efforts. By 1966, Woody was 39; he had been toiling with comic books for over sixteen years and his practice of habitually working, nonstop, was running him into the ground. Characteristically, the self-destructive Wood was not content to labor solely with mainstream work. He had always fancied himself an outsider and a nonconformist. In an effort to venture outside the commercial arena and to provide himself and other artists with a forum for experimentation and personal expression, Woody created and published a magazine called *Witzend*. The first issues of the magazine were a mixed bag, a hodge-podge of new work created for the magazine, illustrations, and stuff that had been sitting in portfolios, unused for years.

The first issue of *Witzend*, which saw print in the summer of 1966, presented some pretty unremarkable stories with artwork by Al Williamson (with finishes by his old EC buddies Frank Frazetta, Roy Krenkel and Angelo

Sekowsky, Chic Stone, Ogden Whitney, and John Giunta.[15] Woody would enlist others to help out along the way, including his assistant, Dan Adkins.

Woody's efforts resulted in a title called *THUNDER Agents* #1, release dated November, 1965, which saw print at the same time *Tippy Teen* hit the market. The line was expanded to also include *Undersea Agent*, *Dynamo*, *Fight the Enemy*, and *NoMan*. *THUNDER Agents* was an attempt to meld the popularity of television shows like *The Man From UNCLE* with comic book heroes. The scripts, many of which were written by the artists working on the strips, were choppy, glib, and generally forgettable. The main ingredient of the features was to put as much action into each story as possible. What these strips lacked in storyline was made up with nonstop action and some very attractive artwork by some of the best artists working at the time.

Wood's work on the various strips in the line, as with so much of what he produced in the 1960s, failed to recapture the intensity and

Top: Neal Adams, pencils and inks, interior page, *Eerie* #9, May, 1967, ©1967 Warren Publishing Co. Bottom: Steve Ditko, pencils and inks, interior page, *Witzend* #3, 1967, ©1967 Wallace Wood. A page from the first *Mr. A* story.

Ditko's artwork is effective, and the story is well structured and paced. The feature's anti-hero is Mr. A, who metes out justice, allowing the bad guy in the story to die, proclaiming, "I have no mercy or compassion for aggressors…only their victims…" For Mr. A, there are only two colors, black and white. *Mr. A* is preachy, but presents an interesting point of view which would gain more saliency in the 1980s and 1990s as American culture reacted against the 1960s. Realizing that the Comics Code would not permit a character the likes of Mr. A in mainstream fare, Ditko created *The Question*, which ran as a backup feature in Charlton comics in 1967 and 1968. Ditko's was one of the more interesting voices in comics, which by the end of the 1960s never recaptured the promise or quality of his previous efforts.

Witzend also saw the creation of a vehicle for Woody to spin his own personal mythology, which during the last decade of his ca-

Torres), Archie Goodwin, Wood, and Jack Gaughan. There were also illustrations by other hands, poetry, and a short story. Woody's idea for a magazine/comic book which gave writers and artists some elbow room to present their unorthodox and fanciful ideas was a good one. The concept was never fully realized and rarely presented material which kept up with the promise of the magazine. After four issues, Wood sold *Witzend* but continued his involvement. *Witzend* did provide a forum for artists to present differing points of view, and no artist better used that opportunity than Steve Ditko.

Ditko had become increasingly alienated from the world of mainstream comic books during his tenure on *Spider-Man*. He resented Stan Lee's interference with *his* strip and began to see himself as a noble artist fighting for the sanctity of his creations. The problem was, he was working on funny books and living at a time when his efforts were accorded little importance. It was in this atmosphere that Ditko created *Mr. A*, which first appeared in *Witzend* #3, in 1967, as the lead feature.

reer would become his most personal and successful work: *The Wizard King*. Wood had always been fascinated by folklore and after reading J.R.R. Tolkein, around 1963, resolved to create his own world of magic, wizards, and elves. In *Witzend* #4, released in 1968, Wood premiered *The World of the Wizard King*, which was presented as a short, written installment, supplemented by illustrations. Wood spent a considerable amount of time for the rest of his career working on this project. In 1978, the first volume of *The Wizard King* saw publication, followed in 1981 by the second installment, *Odkin, Son of Odkin*. After a long and varied career, in declining health, Wood took his own life in 1981, after being told he would have to start kidney dialysis. Woody's legacy, however, of sci-fi yarns, *Mad* send-ups, heroic tales, and *The Wizard King*, still to this day endure as some of the better examples of what comic book storytelling can offer.

Western, Tower, Warren, Archie, and even Charlton, all provided another venue for the second generation to make a living and, in some cases, try something a little different. With the exception of James Warren and Archie Goodwin's experiment, the other publishers did little to distinguish their products, qualitatively, or to surpass the artwork and sto-

ries produced under the watchful eyes of DC's editors or Stan Lee. By the end of 1968, almost all of the superhero titles that had been created by the other guys, during the boom, were gone. After Alex Toth broke with Western, he spent a majority of his time working in animation, although he would consistently work on a handful of comic book titles each year. Russ Manning would focus the rest of his career on the *Tarzan* strip in various formats and then spend some time working on the strip version of *Star Wars*. Steve Ditko was back at Charlton working mainly on horror and suspense material. Dan Spiegle would continue to mature and in the decade to come became an artist to seriously look at. The other publishers had offered a different take on heroes, adventurers, fighting men, and assorted other genres during the Silver Age, and in the process, provided a handful of talented artists opportunities to distinguish themselves.

The Silver Age had been fun while it lasted; the lessons learned by the second generation, which culminated with the DC heroes and Jack and Stan's new take on characterization and storytelling, had taken funny books in a new direction. The best comic books were now more thoughtful and intricately detailed than they had ever been before. Gil Kane had seen

the writing on the wall and wanted to build on the developments of the 1960s: to come up with something new, more adult, more violent, but still very much within the traditions of comic book storytelling. He admired the stories produced by EC and saw them as a starting point for something bigger and more ambitious. What Kane attempted to do capped the Silver Age and is accordingly our next stop.

NOTES

[1] Western owned Whitman Publishing Company, publisher of "Big Little Books," which were literally, little, 3 1/2 inch by 4 inch books, of reprinted newspaper strips and cartoons. Western also produced the kid's line of Little Golden Books.

[2] Jim Amash interview with Alex Toth, *Comic Book Artist* #11, January, 2001.

[3] Davis, Kyle, and Spicer interview with Alex Toth, *The Comics Journal* #98, May, 1985.

[4] Ibid.

[5] Shel Dorf and Rich Rubenfeld interview with Russ Manning, *Comic Book Artist* #22, October, 2002.

[6] Ibid.

[7] Russ Manning, *Magnus Robot Fighter* #1, February, 1963.

[8] Jon B. Cooke interview with Dan Spiegle, *Comic Book Artist* #22, October, 2002.

[9] David W. Olbrich interview with Doug Wildey, *Amazing Heroes* #95, May, 1986.

[10] For the last episodes of *Jonny Quest*, Wildey brought in Alex Toth to help with design chores.

[11] Jon B. Cooke interview with Dick Giordano, *Comic Book Artist* #9, August, 2000.

[12] Jon B. Cooke interview with Jim Warren, *Comic Book Artist* #4, Spring, 1999.

[13] Steve Riggenberg and Kim Thompson interview with Archie Goodwin, *The Comics Journal* #78, December, 1982.

[14] Ibid.

[15] See generally, Lou Mougin, "Back Seat Superheroes," *The Comic Reader* #197, December, 1981, Street Enterprises.

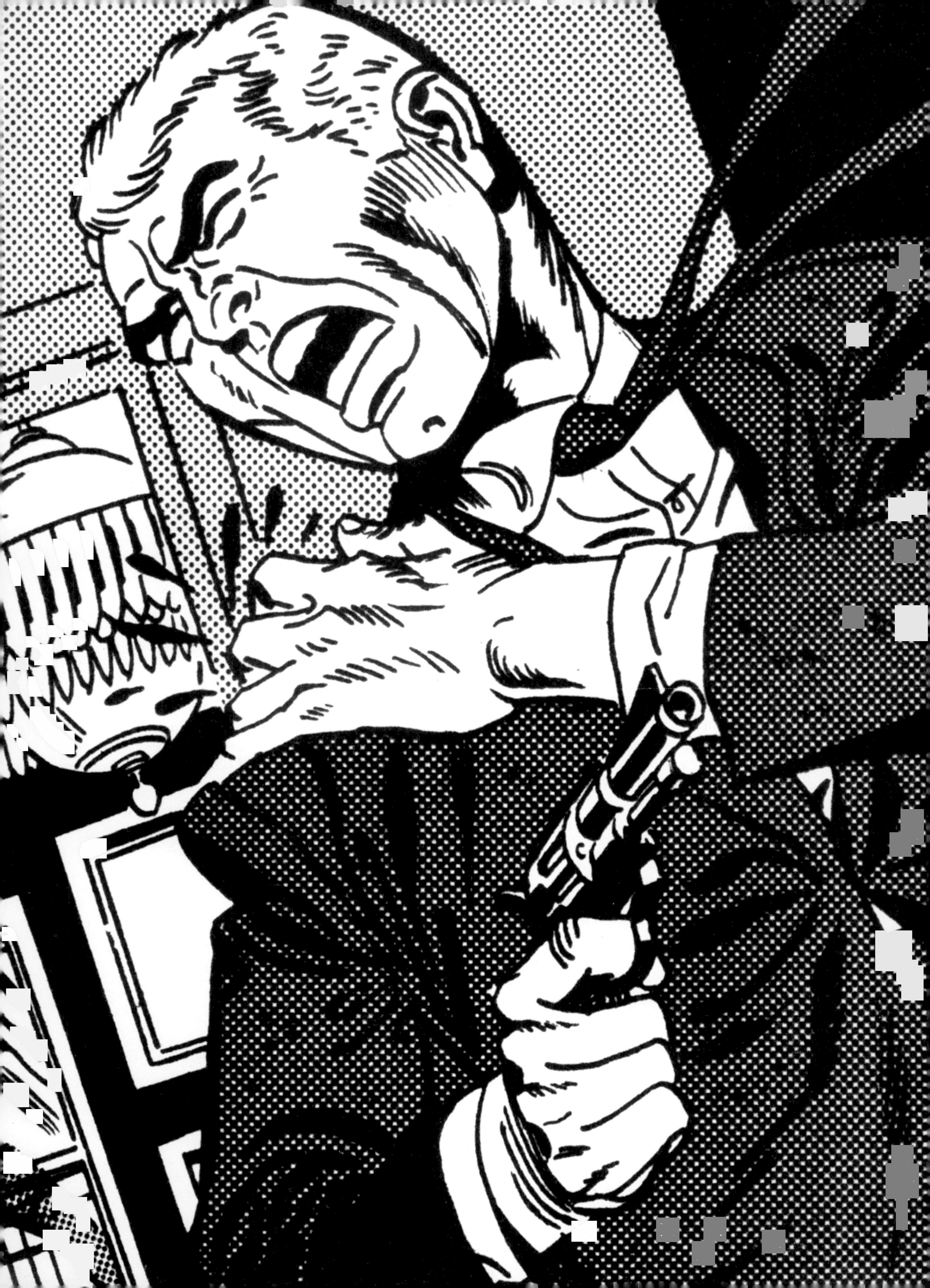

7 GIL KANE TAKES A CHANCE; GOING IT ON HIS OWN; FORCES BEYOND HIS CONTROL; THE END OF THE SILVER AGE; WHAT IT ALL MEANT

The year 1967 bore witness to many events which are nothing more than dim memories today. NASA was gearing up to send astronauts into orbit around the moon within a year. The Vietnam War was beginning to divide the country and make many Americans question their perceptions about themselves and the world. Comic books were hardly high on the agenda of important things to consider.

The *Batman* television show was still on the tube, but its popularity was dropping. In an attempt to bolster the show's ratings, Batgirl was added to attract more boys and girls and maybe even a few more of their dads. The show got worse and the ratings dropped even more.

In 1967, the comic book industry experienced a drop in its sales for the first time since the start of the superhero boom. The popular and dependable *Batman* title saw a circulation decrease of almost one hundred thousand copies.

Throughout the industry, sales figures were down, with decreasing numbers in double-digit percentages. The market was rapidly changing, and, privately, everyone in the business was concerned. Comic book publishers had kept themselves out of politics and the real world, due to the lessons learned from the Subcommittee hearings. Even the most interesting stories produced by Warren were kid stuff compared with the fare that had been produced a decade earlier by Feldstein and Kurtzman at EC. Where would the next trend be?

The movies were reacting to the social upheavals of the 1960s by becoming grittier, more graphic, more antiestablishment, and more violent. Rock Hudson and Doris Day were passé, now. Stars like Dustin Hoffman, Paul Newman, Steve McQueen, Warren Beatty, and Faye Dunaway were coming to the forefront. Arthur Penn's *Bonnie and Clyde* helped set the tone for the movies of 1967: making bank robbers into anti-heroes that everybody would cheer for, only then killing them off in a graphic, gut-wrenching, hail of bullets. Dustin Hoffman, in his first movie role, was playing a 21-year-old, busy being seduced by the 40-something Mrs. Robinson. Paul Newman was showing his very antiestablishment, irreverent attitude in *Cool Hand Luke*. James Bond was back, in the fifth installment of the series with *You Only Live Twice*, which depended more on the fantastic sets of Ken Adam than anything else, even Sean Connery.

Nineteen sixty-seven also saw the release of John Boorman's violent thriller, *Point Blank*. *Point Blank* was virtually ignored by the cognoscenti, who failed to see that it was a stylish essay in single-minded film noir violence and a bellwether of where cinema was going in the next decade. One film buff was watching, Gil Kane, and he ate it up. That Kane loved the movies would be an understatement; he was addicted to them. Kane was quick to admit that the movies influenced his storytelling and inspired him to push his art to keep up with the moving pictures. *Point Blank* would serve as the starting point for Kane's

Gil Kane, pencils and inks, detail from an interior page panel, *His Name is...Savage*, June, 1968, ©2004 The Estate of Gil Kane.

foray into the world of comic book publishing. While working for Warren, Kane had thoughts about something he could do on his own, which had now been simmering for several years. He had seen what Woody was doing with *Witzend*, which was priced at one dollar, and thought even more about doing a comic book of his own. Now, Kane was ready to take a chance with something different.

By 1967, Gil Kane was almost 40-years-old. He was in the top ranks of artists in the business, working for one of the biggest and most successful publishers and doing plenty of work on the side, but he was not happy. In fact, he was downright dissatisfied with his

work for DC and with the comic book industry in general. He knew quality work when he saw it. He was enthusiastic about Jack Kirby's new work for Marvel, but he felt that, by and large, the stories and art being churned out were "banal." He used that description frequently and with pedagogical zeal when talking, or lecturing might be more apt, his colleagues about the state of the art of comic book storytelling. But what was he going do?

He was kicking around the idea of creating a comic book novel. Kane was bored with the simplistic stories he had worked on which were usually no longer than ten or twelve pages. Sometimes he would be handed a "book length" *Green Lantern* story, but this usually amounted to less than twenty full pages. Kane's complaint was not just with the length of the stories; he wanted to use dialogue, text, and artwork combined into a narrative, a novel integrated with pictures. He also wanted to recapture the feel of a movie in comic book form.

Kane had known Archie Goodwin now for several years and they mixed well. He and Goodwin shared an admiration of Kurtzman's work, and EC in general, and the two spent hours talking about expanding the format of comic books into something more substantial. Kane was ready to take the plunge, but where would the money come from? Kane went, samples in hand, to pitch the distributor of Warren's books, Kable Distributing. Things did not start off well, though, and just when Kane thought he would get a thumbs down, the head of the company walked into the meeting. After an intense half-an-hour selling job, Kane got the green light. Kable would take a chance on Kane's project, but he would have to supply a completely finished book. Kable's deal was hardly altruistic; Kane would not receive one cent up-front for his work. Only after Kable recouped its costs of production and printing would Kane receive his back-end cut of forty percent of any net profit; the distributor would keep the rest.

Energized by his deal with Kable, Kane began work on what would be the first comic book novel, *His Name is...Savage*. He also

Gil Kane, pencils and inks, unpublished cover, *His Name is...Savage*, June, 1968. The cover that was used was painted by Robert Foster and bore more resemblance to Lee Marvin than Kane's cover. Not only was the cover changed, the price of the book was also reduced to thirty-five cents.

BEGINNING: A NEW COMICS TRADITION!

HIS NAME IS....

SAVAGE!

50¢

INTRODUCING
SAVAGE...
AGENT-
ASSASSIN
FOR THE
INNER
COUNCIL

started shopping around for a printer and a small band of like-minded souls to help him. After Kane's *Archie* comic book clone ran aground, he was obliged to move out of the studio he had been provided by James Warren as part of his employment. But Kane liked the excitement and atmosphere of being in New York City, so he quickly found another studio in the same building. He then relocated to a studio on 63rd Street, which served as his downtown headquarters for the next five years. Kane's studio also doubled as the corporate office of his fledgling publishing company, Adventure House Press, Inc. *Savage* was the company's first project, but Kane had others in the works, including a comic book novelization of Robert E. Howard's *Conan*. By the beginning of 1968, *Savage* was beginning to take shape. In order to produce a product the size and complexity planned, Kane needed an assistant. Months before, Roger Brand, an aspiring artist, had been up to see him on the recommendation of Wally Wood. Kane liked him but, at the time, did not really need help; nevertheless, the two kept in touch. Now,

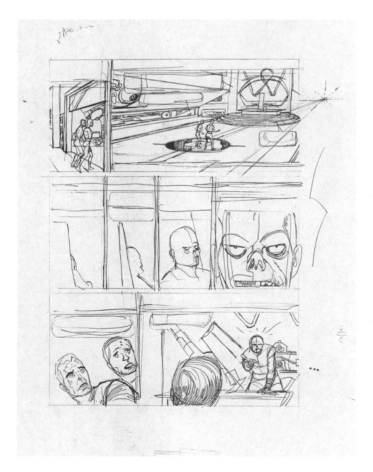

Kane called Brand into the breach. He came, ready to go, bringing his wife in tow to lend a hand.

Kane had made arrangements to print *Savage* with Spartan Printing, one of the big boys in the industry, and everything was moving forward. Then, he received a call from Spartan. Kane was advised, "We can't involve ourselves with something that might be pornographic."[1] Kane desperately tried to convince them that *Savage* was nothing more than an adventure story, even showing them samples, but nothing would change the company's decision. In a corner, Kane went to another printer, who agreed to take the job. The next day, Kane received virtually the same call – the printer could not be involved with anything that might be pornographic.

What Kane was planning with *Savage* was generally known, but the story had not even been fully pencilled at that point, nor had the dialogue been completely written. The story

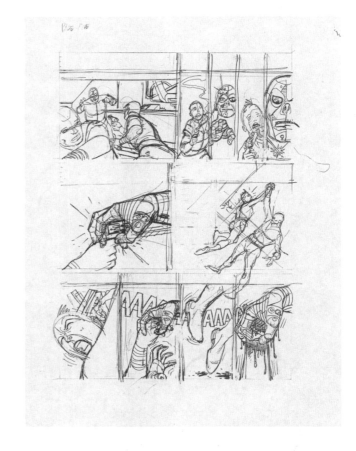

was only in outline form. The problem was, Kane was not interested in having his book approved by the Comics Code Authority, and the powers who ran the business knew it.[2] Kane continued to ask around for recommendations for other printers, and it was suggested he contact the printer for the magazine *Ramparts*. *Ramparts* was a left-wing magazine whose editors did not give a damn about the establishment. They published one of the first articles about a possible conspiracy in the assassination of John F. Kennedy; Che Guevara's diaries – complete with an introduction by Fidel Castro; the prison diaries of Eldridge Cleaver; and even championed the Black Panthers. So, Kane went to their printer who agreed to print *Savage*; after all, they would print just about anything, and they even beat the other printers' bids. Kane breathed a sigh of relief. Now all he had to do was to finish the book on deadline and make it good.

In the clutch, he brought Archie Goodwin on board to write the dialogue and drafted Frank Giacoia to help with the inking.[3] Kane always believed that the Comics Code Authority tried to sabotage *Savage*, but no one will ever know. What was everybody so afraid of?

In designing *Savage*, Kane was restricted only by time constraints and a need for sleep. Archie Goodwin recalled that when he would deliver the scripted story, "it was like going into some emergency center or a camp under siege. Gil, Roger Brand, Michele Brand, Frank Giacoia…were all holed up…grinding day and night to get the material done. And the only good thing about it was I could walk out."[4] Savage was, perhaps, the most ambitious comic book produced for its time. Before the first page was pencilled, Kane had prepared detailed roughs or breakdowns, which laid out each page in a loose, unfinished form. Kane would then use these pages as reference for the finished pencils. The pages that these roughs were drawn on, measuring approximately 16 inches by 20 inches, gave Kane a large area on which to craft his story. When these roughs were finished, Kane placed

PAGE EIGHT

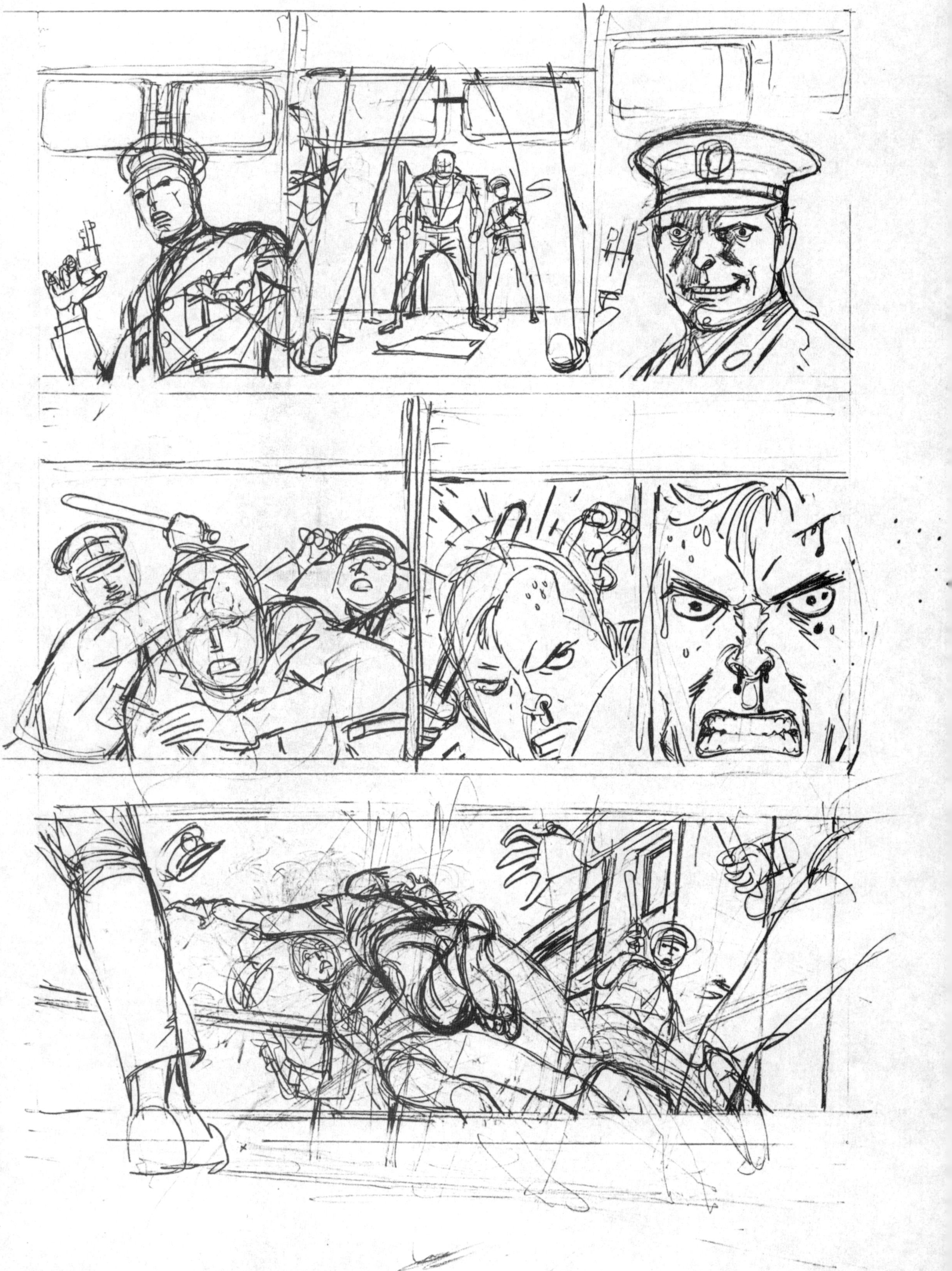

them on a lightbox, an opaque piece of glass with a light source behind it. Placing a fresh piece of paper over the rough, he structured his finished pencils. The page was then inked and the text added, finishing the artwork. The tones seen in these pages come from the application of transparent patterns that are cut from sheets with an adhesive backing that were then placed on the artwork, giving it various shades. This material is called zip-a-tone. The techniques used by Kane in *Savage* were nothing new in comic books, but the story, the main character's driving violence, and the stylized and vividly choreographed action, were.[5]

On pages 210-211, two sequential pages from *Savage*, together with their roughs, are on display. The first, page 9 in the story, introduces the reader to the arch-evil-guy of the story, Simon Mace. Two of his henchmen have performed poorly, and their work is up for review. Simon, it seems, is unhappy with their efforts. The idea, which is right out of *Thunderball* and *You Only Live Twice,* is nicely set up, first with the small vertical panel of the two henchmen walking into Mace's office, followed by a long shot, with the bad guy's chair turned with its back facing the viewer. In the next set of panels, just as with a movie, each successive vertical panel exposes the mangled face of Mace. The dialogue is supplemented by text throughout, although this page hardly needs too much exposition. Note that in the last panel, Kane changed the design of the finished page from that of the rough, pulling back for a long shot. The next sequential page is where *Savage* gave an obvious hint to its readers that it was not standard comic book fare. Kane ratchets up the violence, which set *Savage* apart from everything that was being done at the time. The last set of panels, showing Mace dispatching the two henchmen, is flawlessly broken down, as Mace crushes the hand of his victim whose screams run throughout the four panels.

Two more sequential pages, together with their roughs, on this and the opposite page, and on pages 214-215, further drive home the point that *Savage* was more in tune with the thematic currents of contemporary cinema of

its time, rather than those of funny books. Above, we see Page 13 of the book. Here, Kane expertly choreographs Savage's encounter with a sadistic guard. Notice how the first panel starts with a medium shot, then the next panel reverses the angle, shooting between the guard's legs to show Savage, only to move to a close-up of the guard's face in the next panel. Kane keeps the camera moving in this page and continues to cut back and forth until Savage leaps out at the guard.

The other pages from *Savage* on display in this chapter amply demonstrate the influence of late 1960s movies on Kane's novel in pictures. *Savage* is a rather obvious homage to the movies of its era. Savage's plot, a standard thriller, takes a second seat to its real motivation: to present a moody, taut, relentless action tale driven by violence. The excuse for all the action is the storyline. A mega-

Gil Kane, pencils and inks, page fourteen and the corresponding rough layout page (on the opposite page), *His Name is...Savage*, June, 1968.

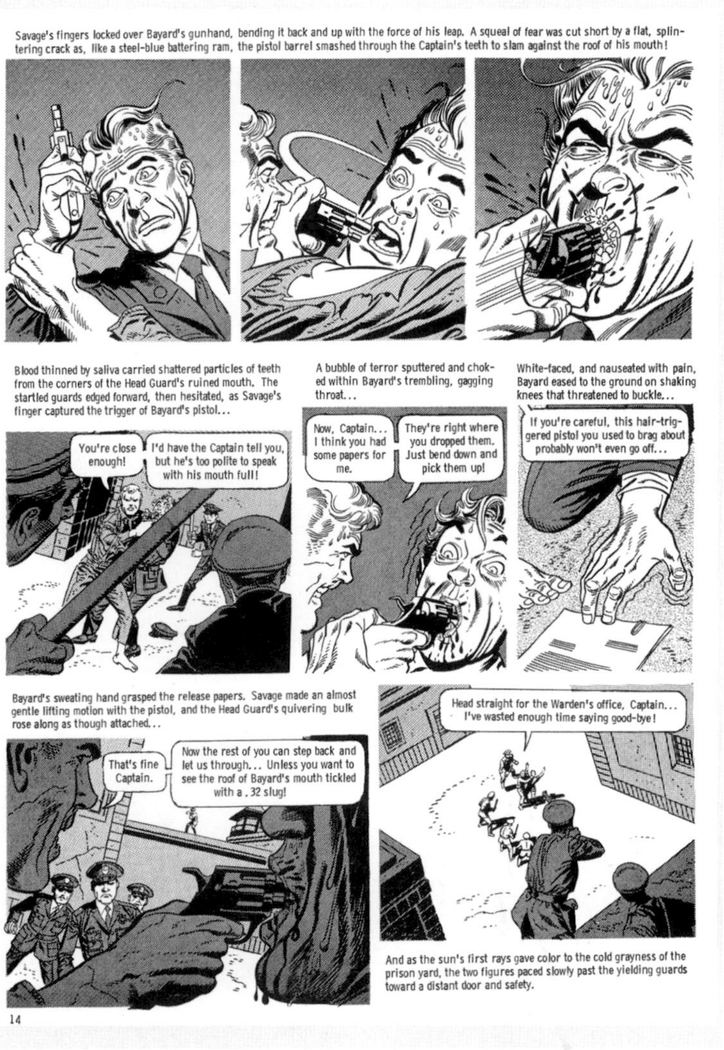

Savage's fingers locked over Bayard's gunhand, bending it back and up with the force of his leap. A squeal of fear was cut short by a flat, splintering crack as, like a steel-blue battering ram, the pistol barrel smashed through the Captain's teeth to slam against the roof of his mouth!
Blood thinned by saliva carried shattered particles of teeth from the corners of the Head Guard's ruined mouth. The startled guards edged forward, then hesitated, as Savage's finger captured the trigger of Bayard's pistol...
You're close enough!
I'd have the Captain tell you, but he's too polite to speak with his mouth full!
A bubble of terror sputtered and choked within Bayard's trembling, gagging throat...
Now, Captain... I think you had some papers for me.
They're right where you dropped them. Just bend down and pick them up!
White-faced, and nauseated with pain, Bayard eased to the ground on shaking knees that threatened to buckle...
If you're careful, this hair-triggered pistol you used to brag about probably won't even go off...
Bayard's sweating hand grasped the release papers. Savage made an almost gentle lifting motion with the pistol, and the Head Guard's quivering bulk rose along as though attached...
That's fine Captain.
Now the rest of you can step back and let us through... Unless you want to see the roof of Bayard's mouth tickled with a .32 slug!
Head straight for the Warden's office, Captain... I've wasted enough time saying good-bye!
And as the sun's first rays gave color to the cold grayness of the prison yard, the two figures paced slowly past the yielding guards toward a distant door and safety.
14

lomaniac ex-general attempts to start a third world war, and only Savage can stop him. The movie that clearly helped set the stage for *Savage* was *Point Blank. Point Blank* arrived in New York theatres on September 18, 1967 and starred Lee Marvin, Angie Dickinson, Carroll O'Connor, John Vernon, and Keenan Wynn. The plot of *Point Blank* involves Lee Marvin's character's attempt to get his share of a heist from his partner who double-crossed him and left him for dead. The movie, however, is really about style, mood, and violence as the propelling force for the story. In his review in *The New York Times*, Bosley Crowther characterized the film as being "...candid and calculatedly sadistic..." Not only did Kane borrow Lee Marvin's face from the film, he also appropriated the actor's portrayal of relentless, amoral violence. This was something new to comic books. Sure, the funny books of the late 1940s and 1950s had violence, which was grotesque and even chilling, but it was not the propelling element of those stories. Even the most nasty EC's stories used violence as a one-line joke, even when the joke was not too funny.

Savage represents a beginning and an end of a period in the history of comic books. *Savage* gave artists and writers in the business an example of how comic books could be used to speak to an adult audience with more mature material. *Savage* also represented a break with the past in attempting to aim the content of a comic book above its traditional audience. Kane felt stifled having to draw endless fights where no one was really hurt and where the violence was only sugarcoated action. With *Savage,* he was able to go all the way and in the process thumb his nose at the comic book establishment, something he clearly intended. *Savage* was obviously not a mainstream effort, and Archie Goodwin was so concerned that its content was offensive he insisted his name not be used in the credits, which instead acknowledge "Robert Franklin" along with Gil Kane as the authors of the story. In 1982, looking back fourteen years after his involvement, Goodwin remembered that when he scripted *Savage*, he was working for Marvel comics, and that since, "*Savage* was going to be violent atypical comic book material," he was concerned that it might reflect badly on his employer. He was worried that someone offended might ask, "Why did you hire this sick, violent depraved guy?"[6]

Kane delivered *Savage* to the printer right on the heels of his deadline. In fact, he inked the last page of the story at the printer. After the book was ready to hit the newsstands, the same problems that had plagued Kane earlier – the campaign of anonymous telephone calls whispering the word, "pornographic" – surfaced yet again. Almost no one would take the book for distribution other than Kable. Of the 200,000 copies printed, only 20,000 made it to newsstands. *Savage* was the first and last production of Kane's fledgling company. *Savage* may have failed to make money and gain a wide audience, but it succeeded in getting the interest and attention of artists and writers in the business. Carmine Infantino was horrified by *Savage*; others thought it was a portent of things to come.[7]

Savage was not without its faults. The dialogue and captions are sometimes overly repetitive and unnecessary. The prose used by Goodwin run on, and on, and on. Goodwin was forced to admit that the script needed to be edited. The crunch of churning out forty-one pages in thirty days, coupled with the tasks of production and the shoestring budget of the project, made any serious attempt to edit the script impossible.

Even though *Savage* failed, it succeeded in letting the genie out of the bottle. The young Turks in the business all saw what Kane had tried, and over the next decade the tone of comics changed, in part, due to the influence of *Savage*. Kane's attempt to publish his own comic book also signaled that storytelling, as a form of self-expression, was back. Not since the heady days of EC had anything as radical been tried. The clear message that was telegraphed by the not-so-anonymous forces in-

Gil Kane, pencils with ink finishes, unfinished contents page for another anticipated, but never realized *Savage* story.

volved with scuttling *Savage* was: go outside the Comics Code and the same thing will happen to you. Upon hearing what had happened to Kane with *Savage*, Jack Kirby is reported to have said, "If they can do that to Gil Kane, they can do it to anybody."[8]

The question of who did what to stop *Savage* from succeeding is one of those dark little secrets no one will ever really get to the bottom of. Historically, the powers in the business had always enforced unwritten rules of discipline, with differing degrees of severity, upon those who challenged the established way of things. In 1947, Siegel and Shuster had challenged DC over the ownership rights of Superman. A settlement was arranged, and the two were then blackballed from work in the business. Siegel was able to find work as a writer and even later went back to DC; Shuster was not as lucky and spent the rest of his life in poverty until he and his ex-partner received a public-pressured retirement pension

from the company. Kane emerged from *Savage* down, but not out. In creating *Savage*, Kane established a reputation for himself as an artists' artist. After *Savage*, Kane did not miss a beat and continued to turn out hundreds of pages of work a year, first for DC and then for Marvel.

Comic book fans and historians will argue forever about when the Silver Age ended, but with *Savage*, the art of comic book storytelling took a new direction. Kane would go on to try his hand at another comic book novel, published in 1971, in a pocket book format, called *Blackmark*. *Blackmark* was Kane's personal take on the sword and sorcery genre and had been conceived at the same time as *Savage*. *Blackmark* sold over sixty percent of its print run, but its publisher, Bantam, did not know how to promote it, and the title saw but one installment. In the 1980s, everybody was talking about the creation of a new expanded comic book form, the graphic novel, but what they had forgotten was, Gil Kane had been there with *Savage* and *Blackmark* twenty years earlier. Just another example of comic book history revisionism.

What had it all been for, anyway? Why had Kane spent so much time and effort with *Savage*? Certainly not for the money, even Kane knew he would never get rich from his work for Adventure House Press. Indeed, what had it been that drew all the young kids who became the second generation to join the ranks of storytellers who oversaw the creation of the Silver Age? Most had been lured, as youngsters still in grade school, to comic books by Superman, Batman, Captain America and the rest of the masked and caped heroes. Most, after some youthful exuberance and promise, lapsed into the drudgery of churning out their wares as journeymen. A few saw their calling not primarily as artists, but as storytellers, bringers of dreams. Comic books had, after all, been the dream factories for the masses, the immigrants, and even the kids of the high and the mighty. Comic books cut across class lines; they were for everybody.

A few saw their calling as a craft, to be practiced, refined, and nurtured. Alex Toth had

Gil Kane, pencils and inks, unpublished splash page from
another unrealized *Savage* story. This page is clearly an
homage to a Will Eisner *Spirit* splash.

been the pied piper of depicting characters who were not posed, using natural movement as a guide. He rendered his artwork with a simple assured line. Toth brought a new sense of elegance and cinematic panache to funny books that influenced everyone. Infantino and Kane followed in his footsteps and went in their own different directions, leading many in the pack of the second generation. The artists of the Golden Age had visited the issues of design, page breakdown, and simplification of form before, but the best storytellers of the second generation rigorously honed and sharpened these ideas, creating a coherent vernacular that is still the reference for artists working in comic books today.

Lest we not forget Jack Kirby, who was there through it all. Jack was there from the

There were no skills, no devices left Reynard against the killing machine Blackmark had become. The screaming silver sword battered through every defense, every feint or parry until it tore the Commonlander's blade from his grasp, then, in a murderous backstroke, slammed flatly into Reynard himself. The Warlord was lifted into the air and driven crashing into a huge oaken table, screaming as beneath his chain mail muscle and ligament tore and ripped.

Every fibre of Blackmark's being seemed to throb with the sword's lashing sonic power as he advanced. Yet even as the ancient science gripped him, drawing him to the kill, he sensed a terrible quiet in the hall. The awesome silence of men gripped by fear beyond understanding.

All science appeared as sorcery to these Lords of New Earth, and the sword's wild power must seem like the blackest, most hell-spawned of all. This was not the way Blackmark had meant for it to be. For Reynard, to be destroyed by its pulsing steel, would only divide them further, make them fear him as a witch-warrior, and cost him the very unity for which he strived.

With all his might, Blackmark fought the sword's throbbing force, struggling to move the power stud back to its off position, wondering what would happen if the day ever came when he used it at more than half its potential. And was suddenly touched by the cold hand of fear.

But one look at the murderous glow flaring in Blackmark's eyes as he advanced, tightly gripping the crackling whining blade, told everyone that Reynard's pain would be short lived.

beginning, and he set the standard for superhero storytelling. His stories and artwork, done in collaboration with Stan the man, bristle with rigor and energy that radiated off its pages. Just as Toth had defined how to tell a story with mortals, Kirby defined how to dispense myths populated by archetypes. Today, retrospectively, several of the high muckety-mucks of comic books as art have been dismissive of Jack's talents; after all, his stories did not deal with real people and important issues. Ah, but great myths have always served a different purpose, and sometimes in a roundabout way, espouse high ideals despite being cloaked in capes and masks.

By the end of the Silver Age, the art and conventions of comic books were beginning to spill out in other unanticipated directions as well, which witnessed the birth and growth of underground comix. The art of comic book storytelling would continue to grow, and new influences would come which shifted the styles and tones of the funny books away from the paths espoused by Toth, Kirby, and Kane. By the 1970s, the influence of Neal Adams was being felt, together with a new group of artists who would build on what had come in the Silver Age, but that, is another story.

NOTES

[1] Interview with Gil Kane.
[2] James Warren also avoided the restrictions of the Comics Code.
[3] Steve Ringgenenberg interview with Archie Goodwin, *The Comics Journal* #78, December, 1982.
[4] Ibid.
[5] As we have already seen from many of the examples in this book, zip-a-tone was used by a number of comic artists. Many artists used zip-a-tone and craftint paper in combination, as well, to achieve various tonal effects.
[6] Ibid.
[7] Interview with Gil Kane.
[8] Interview with Mark Evanier.

INDEX

E

F

G

H

U

V

W

X

Y